The OXFORD Illustrated Junior Dictionary

Compiled by
Rosemary Sansome, Dee Reid, Alan Spooner

Illustrated by
Barry Rowe

OXFORD
UNIVERSITY PRESS

OXFORD

UNIVERSITY PRESS

Great Clarendon Street, Oxford OX2 6DP

Oxford University Press is a department of the University of Oxford.
It furthers the University's objective of excellence in research, scholarship,
and education by publishing worldwide in

Oxford New York

Auckland Bangkok Buenos Aires Cape Town Chennai
Dar es Salaam Delhi Hong Kong Istanbul Karachi Kolkata
Kuala Lumpur Madrid Melbourne Mexico City Mumbai Nairobi
São Paulo Shanghai Taipei Tokyo Toronto

Oxford is a trade mark of Oxford University Press

© Oxford University Press 1989, 1996, 2000

First published 1989
Second edition 1996
Third edition 2000

British Library cataloguing in Publication Data available

The Oxford Illustrated Junior Dictionary is based on the text of *The Oxford Junior Dictionary*

ISBN 0-19-9107041 (paperback)
5 7 9 10 8 6 4
ISBN 0-19-9107033 (hardback)
1 3 5 7 9 10 8 6 4 2

Typeset by Pentacor PLC, High Wycombe
Printed and bound in Great Britain by
Butler & Tanner Ltd, Frome and London

Do you have a query about words, their origin, meaning, use, spelling,
pronunciation, or any other aspect of the English language? Then write to
OWLS at Oxford University Press, Great Clarendon Street, Oxford, OX2 6DP.

All queries will be answered using the full resources of the
Oxford Dictionary Department

Contents

Aa

abandon *verb* **abandons, abandoning, abandoned**
1 to leave someone or something somewhere without meaning ever to return to them. *People who abandon pets are cruel.*
2 to stop doing something before it is finished. *We abandoned our game when it started to rain.*

abbreviation *noun* **abbreviations**
a short way of writing something. *Dr is an abbreviation for* doctor.

ability *noun* **abilities**
the power, skill, or opportunity to do something. *Owls have the ability to see in the dark.*

able *adjective* **abler, ablest**
If you are able to do something, you can do it. *Will you be able to go to the party?*

aboard *adverb, preposition*
on or on to a ship, bus, train, or an aeroplane. *Climb aboard!*

abolish *verb* **abolishes, abolishing, abolished**
to put an end to something.

about *adverb, preposition*
THIS WORD HAS SEVERAL USES. HERE ARE SOME OF THE WAYS YOU CAN USE IT: *I got home at about four o'clock. I read a book about animals. She left all her toys lying about.*

above *adverb, preposition*
THIS WORD HAS SEVERAL USES. HERE ARE SOME OF THE WAYS YOU CAN USE IT: *He looked up at the stars in the sky above. She hung the picture above the fireplace. He's in the year above me at school.*

abroad *adverb*
in another country. *a holiday abroad.*

absent *adjective*
away. *She was absent from school yesterday.*

abuse *verb* **abuses, abusing, abused**
1 to be cruel to someone or something.
2 to say rude things to someone.

accelerator *noun* **accelerators**
the pedal which you press with your foot to make a car go faster.

accent *noun* **accents**
the way people say their words. *a Scottish accent.*

accept *verb* **accepts, accepting, accepted**
to take what someone offers you. *He accepted the invitation to the party.*

accident *noun* **accidents**
something bad that happens which you did not plan to happen. *He broke his leg in a road accident.*
accidentally *adverb*

accompany *verb* **accompanies, accompanying, accompanied**
1 to go with someone. *Dad accompanied us to the station.*
2 to play a musical instrument while someone sings or dances. *She accompanied me on the piano.*

account *noun* **accounts**
1 a description or story about something that has happened. *He gave the police an account of the car accident.*
2 a list that tells you how much money you owe or have spent. *a bank account.*

accurate *adjective*
correct, exact. *He gave an accurate description of the thief.*
accurately *adverb*

accuse *verb* **accuses, accusing, accused**
to say that someone has done something wrong. *They accused me of breaking the window.*

ace *noun* **aces**
one of the four cards in a pack of cards marked to show it is number one. *the ace of clubs.*

ache *verb* **aches, aching, ached**
to have a pain that goes on hurting. *My stomach aches because I have eaten too much ice cream.*

achieve *verb* **achieves, achieving, achieved**
to do or finish something after trying hard.

achievement *noun* **achievements**
something difficult or special that you have done. *Winning the competition was a great achievement.*

acid *noun* **acids**
a liquid that can burn your clothes and skin. Lemon juice and vinegar contain weak acids.

acorn *noun* **acorns**
the nut of an oak tree.

acrobat *noun* **acrobats**
someone who does exciting jumping and balancing tricks.

across *adverb, preposition*
1 from one side to the other. *He walked across the road.*
2 on the other side of something. *The park is across the river.*
3 measuring from side to side. *The room is 3 metres across.*

act *verb* **acts, acting, acted**
1 to do something. *She acted quickly to put out the fire.*
2 to take part in a play.

action *noun* **actions**
1 doing something, especially something exciting. *I like films with lots of action.*
2 something that a person has done. *The doctor's quick action saved her life.*

active *adjective*
busy, doing things, working.

activity *noun* **activities**
1 a lot of things happening and people doing things. *On sports day the school is full of activity.*
2 something that you do. *Swimming is one of her favourite activities.*

actor *noun* **actors**
a person who acts in a play.

actress *noun* **actresses**
a woman who acts in a play.

actual *adjective*
real. *What is the actual date of your birthday?*
actually *adverb*

add *verb* **adds, adding, added**
1 to put something with something else. *You can add sugar to your tea.*
2 to put numbers together to make a bigger number. *If you add 2 and 2 you get 4.*

adder *noun* **adders**
a small poisonous snake.

addition *noun*
putting numbers together. *We are doing addition and subtraction in arithmetic.*

address *noun* **addresses**
the details of where a person lives that you put on a letter.

adjective *noun* **adjectives**
a word that tells you what someone or something is like. In *a tall man* and *a fast car*, *tall* and *fast* are adjectives.

admire *verb* **admires, admiring, admired**
1 to think someone or something is very good.
2 to look at something and enjoy it. *We admired the lovely view.*

admit *verb* **admits, admitting, admitted**
1 to let someone come in. *No child under ten years of age can be admitted.*
2 to say you were the person who did something wrong. *He admitted that he broke the window.*

adopt *verb* **adopts, adopting, adopted**
to take someone into your family as your own child.

adore *verb* **adores, adoring, adored**
to love very much.

adult *noun* **adults**
someone who is fully grown.

advance *verb* **advances, advancing, advanced**
to move forward.

advantage *noun* **advantages**
something that helps you to do better than other people. *She has an unfair advantage because she is taller than us.*

adventure *noun* **adventures**
something exciting that happens to you.

adverb *noun* **adverbs**
a word that tells you how, when, or where something happens. In these sentences, *slowly, now,* and *somewhere* are adverbs: *He walks slowly. Do it now. I left my jumper somewhere.*

advertise *verb* **advertises, advertising, advertised**
to tell people about something to make them want to buy or use it.

advertisement *noun* **advertisements**
anything which advertises things.

advice *noun*
something you say to someone to help them decide what to do. *My advice is to do your homework first.*

advise *verb* **advises, advising, advised**
to tell someone what you think it would be best for them to do. *The doctor advised her to take more exercise.*

aerial *noun* **aerials**
wires or metal rods for picking up or sending out radio and television programmes.

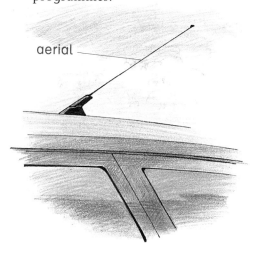
aerial

aeroplane *noun* **aeroplanes**
a machine that can fly, with wings and an engine.

affect *verb* **affects, affecting, affected**
to make someone or something different in some way. *Her handwriting was affected by her sore finger.*

affection *noun*
the feeling you have for someone you like. *The class had a great affection for their teacher.*

afford *verb* **affords, affording, afforded**
to have enough money to pay for something. *I can't afford to buy you any more sweets.*

afraid *adjective*
frightened. *I'm not afraid of dogs.*

after *preposition*
1 later than. *You finished after me.*
2 following. *I went swimming after school.*

afternoon *noun* **afternoons**
the time from the middle of the day until about six o'clock.

afterwards *adverb*
later. *We had lunch and afterwards we played in the garden.*

again *adverb*
once more. *Try again!*

against *preposition*
1 on the opposite side to. *We played against your team and won.*
2 on or next to. *He leant against the wall.*

age *noun*
how old someone or something is. *She is tall for her age.*

agent *noun* **agents**
   someone whose job it is to arrange
   things for people. *a travel agent.*

aggressive *adjective*
   rough, violent, likely to attack people.
   The dog looks rather aggressive.
   aggressively *adverb*

agree *verb* **agrees, agreeing, agreed**
   to think the same as someone else. *My
   brother thinks he's really clever but I
   don't agree.*

agriculture *noun*
   the work that farmers do, growing
   food.

aground *adverb*
   touching the bottom in shallow water.
   The ship ran aground.

ahead *adverb*
   in front. *I went on ahead to open the
   gate. She's ahead of me in arithmetic.*

aid *noun* **aids**
   something that helps. *My granny wears
   a hearing aid.*

aid *verb* **aids, aiding, aided**
   to help. *We sent blankets to aid the
   victims of the earthquake.*

aim *verb* **aims, aiming, aimed**
   1 to point a gun at something. *She
   aimed the gun at the target.*
   2 to throw, kick, or shoot at
   something you are trying to hit. *He
   aimed the ball into the far corner of the
   net.*
   3 to try to do something. *They aimed to
   finish in time for tea.*

air *noun*
   what everyone breathes. *Let's go out for
   some fresh air.*

aircraft *noun* **(the plural is the same)**
   any aeroplane or helicopter.

airport *noun* **airports**
   a place where people can get on or off
   aeroplanes.

alarm *noun* **alarms**
   a warning sound or sign.

album *noun* **albums**
   1 a book to put things like
   photographs or stamps in.
   2 a record with several pieces of music
   on it.

alcohol *noun*
   a liquid which is part of drinks like
   beer and wine.

alcoholic *adjective*
   containing alcohol.

alert *adjective*
   lively and ready for anything.

alien *noun* **aliens**
   1 a person from another country.
   2 in stories, a person from another
   planet.

alight *adjective*
   on fire. *The whole house was alight.*

alive *adjective*
   living. *Is the hamster still alive?*

all *adjective, pronoun*
   1 everyone or everything. *Not all
   children like ice cream. Are you all
   listening?*
   2 the whole of something. *He's eaten
   all the cake.*

alley *noun* **alleys**
   a very narrow street.

alligator *noun* **alligators**
   a kind of crocodile.

allotment *noun* **allotments**
   a piece of land which you pay to use,
   where you can grow vegetables, fruit,
   or flowers.

allow *verb* **allows, allowing, allowed**
   to let something happen, to permit.
   Mum allowed us to go out.

all right *adjective, interjection*
1 safe and well, not hurt. *Are you all right?*
2 agree. *All right, I'll play.*

ally *noun* **allies**
a person or country fighting on the same side.

almost *adverb*
very nearly. *We're almost home now.*

alone *adverb*
without others. *My granny lives alone.*

along *adverb, preposition*
1 from one end to the other. *He ran along the top of the wall.*
2 forward. *He walked along slowly.*
Come along! hurry up.

aloud *adverb*
in a voice that can be heard. *Do not read to yourself – read aloud.*

alphabet *noun*
all the letters people use in writing, arranged in a particular order.

АБВГДЕЖЗИЙКЛМНОПР
СТУФХЦЧШЩЪЬЬЭЮЯ

ص ض ط ظ ع غ ف ق ك ل م ن ﻫ و ي
ا ب ت ث ج ح خ د ذ ر ز س ش

ΑΒΓΔΕΖΗΘΙΚΛΜΝ
ΞΟΠΡΣΤΥΦΧΨΩ

अ आ इ ई उ ऊ ऋ ए ऐ ओ औ क ख ग घ ङ
च छ ज झ ञ ट ठ ड ढ ण त थ द ध न
प फ ब भ म य र ल व श ष स ह

alphabetical *adjective*
arranged in the order of the letters of the alphabet. The words in a dictionary are arranged in alphabetical order so that you can find them easily.

already *adverb*
1 by this time. *He was already there when we arrived.*
2 before now. *I've already done that.*

also *adverb*
as well. *We had jelly and also ice cream.*

altar *noun* **altars**
a special table used in religious ceremonies.

alter *verb* **alters, altering, altered**
to change. *The sign at the end of the road has been altered.*

alteration *noun* **alterations**
a change in someone or something. *Mum made some alterations to my dress because it was too big.*

although *conjunction*
though. *We kept on running, although we were tired.*

altogether *adverb*
counting everything or everyone. *There are twenty-nine in our class altogether.*

aluminium *noun*
a very light metal, coloured like silver.

always *adverb*
at all times, every time.

amateur *noun* **amateurs**
1 someone who does something as a hobby.
2 someone who takes part in a sport and is not paid.

amaze *verb* **amazes, amazing, amazed**
to surprise greatly. *She amazed everyone by winning the race.*

amazing *adjective*
surprising, wonderful. *He told us an amazing story.*

ambition *noun* **ambitions**
something that you want to do very much. *Her ambition is to be a doctor.*

ambulance *noun* **ambulances**
a van for taking injured or ill people to hospital.

ambush *verb* **ambushes, ambushing, ambushed**
to wait in a hiding-place and attack someone by surprise.

ammunition *noun*
anything that is fired from a gun.

among *preposition*
1 in the middle of. *Your books must be somewhere among these.*
2 between.
Share the sweets among you.

amount *noun* **amounts**
how much or how many there are. *He spent a large amount of money.*

amuse *verb* **amuses, amusing, amused**
1 to make someone laugh or smile. *The clown amused the children.*
2 to keep someone happy or busy. *We played games to amuse ourselves on the long journey.*
amusing *adjective*

amusement *noun* **amusements**
1 something that entertains you. *We went on all the amusements at the fair.*
2 a feeling that you have when you think something is funny. *I watched in amusement as the kittens played.*

anaesthetic *noun* **anaesthetics**
a drug or gas or injection used so that you don't feel pain.

ancestor *noun* **ancestors**
a member of the same family who lived long ago.

anchor *noun* **anchors**
a heavy metal hook joined to a ship by a chain. It is dropped into the sea, where it digs into the bottom to keep the ship still.

ancient *adjective*
very old. *This church is ancient – it was built hundreds of years ago.*

angel *noun* **angels**
a messenger sent by God.

anger *noun*
a strong feeling that you get when you are not pleased.

angle *noun* **angles**
the corner where two lines meet.

angler *noun* **anglers**
a fisherman who uses a rod, hook, and line.

angry *adjective* **angrier, angriest**
feeling anger. *Mum looked angry so I kept quiet.* **angrily** *adverb*

animal *noun* **animals**
anything that lives and can move about. Birds, fish, snakes, wasps, and elephants are all animals.

ankle *noun* **ankles**
the thin part of the leg where it is joined to the foot.

anniversary *noun* **anniversaries**
a day when you remember something special that happened on the same day in another year. *Today is their 25th wedding anniversary.*

announce *verb* **announces, announcing, announced**
1 to tell a lot of people about something important. *They announced the winner of the competition.*
2 to introduce a programme on radio or television.

announcement *noun* **announcements**
a public statement about something people need to know. *I have an important announcement to make.*

annoy *verb* **annoys, annoying, annoyed**
to make someone rather angry.

annual *adjective*
happening every year. *We have an annual school outing in June.*
annually *adverb*

annual *noun* **annuals**
1 a book that comes out once a year.
2 a plant which lives only one year. *Sunflowers are annuals.*

anorak *noun* **anoraks**
a waterproof jacket with a hood.

another *adjective, pronoun*
1 a different one. *Choose another hat – that one is too big.*
2 one more. *You've had one cake – you can't have another.*

answer *noun* **answers**
something you say or write to someone who has said or written something to you. *the answer to a question, an answer to a letter.*

answer *verb* **answers, answering, answered**
to give or send an answer to someone. *Can anyone answer this question? Have you answered Granny's letter?*

ant *noun* **ants**
a tiny insect.

Antarctic *noun*
the very cold sea and land in the south of the world.

antelope *noun* **antelopes**
a wild animal that looks like a deer, found in Africa and parts of Asia.

antique *adjective*
old and worth a lot of money. *My aunt collects antique china.*

anxious *adjective*
worried. *Mum was anxious when I was late home.*
anxiously *adverb*

any *adjective, pronoun*
1 some. *Have you got any sweets? I haven't any.*
2 at all. *Are you any better?*
3 no special one. *Take any book you want.*

anybody, anyone *pronoun*
any person.

anything *pronoun*
any thing.
It's so dark, I can't see anything.

anywhere *adverb*
at, in, or to any place.
I can't find my book anywhere.

apart *adverb*
away from each other. *Those two dogs fight if you don't keep them apart.*

ape *noun* **apes**
an animal like a large monkey with long arms and no tail.

apologize *verb* **apologizes, apologizing, apologized**
to say that you are sorry for doing something wrong.

apostrophe *noun* **apostrophes**
a mark like this ' that you use in writing.

apparatus *noun*
special things that you use for doing something. *This apparatus is used for scientific experiments.*

appeal *verb* **appeals, appealing, appealed**
to ask for something that you need. *He appealed for help.*

appear *verb* **appears, appearing, appeared**
1 to come and be seen. *He suddenly appeared from behind the curtain.*
2 to seem. *It appears to be the wrong size.*

appearance *noun*
1 what someone looks like. *His appearance was very untidy.*
2 coming so that you can be seen. *The appearance of the rabbit surprised everyone.*

appendix *noun* **appendixes**
the small tube inside the body that sometimes causes an illness called **appendicitis**

appetite *noun* **appetites**
the wish for food. *She lost her appetite while she was ill.*

applaud *verb* **applauds, applauding, applauded**
to clap to show that you are pleased. *The audience applauded very loudly.*

applause *noun*
clapping. *The applause lasted for ages.*

apple *noun* **apples**
a round, crisp, juicy fruit.

appointment *noun* **appointments**
a time when you have arranged to go and see someone. *I have got an appointment at the dentist's tomorrow.*

approach *verb* **approaches, approaching, approached**
to come near to. *The train was approaching the station.*

appropriate *adjective*
suitable. **appropriately** *adverb*

approve *verb* **approves, approving, approved**
to say that something is good or suitable.

approximate *adjective*
not exact. *The approximate time of arrival is two o'clock.*
approximately *adverb*

apricot *noun* **apricots**
a round, soft, juicy fruit. It has a large stone in it and a thin, orange skin.

April *noun*
the fourth month of the year.

apron *noun* **aprons**
something worn over the front of the body to keep the clothes underneath clean.

aquarium *noun* **aquariums**
a large, glass container where fish are kept.

arcade *noun* **arcades**
a covered place that you can walk through, with shops on each side or with video games and other amusements. *an amusement arcade.*

arch *noun* **arches**
a curved part of a bridge, building, or wall.

architect *noun* **architects**
a person who draws plans for buildings.

Arctic *noun*
the very cold sea and land in the north of the world.

area *noun* **areas**
1 the size of a flat place. *We measured the area of the playground.*
2 a part of a place, town, country, or the world. *You must not play in this area. Desert areas have very little rain.*

argue *verb* **argues, arguing, argued**
to talk about something with people who do not agree with you. *Stop arguing, you two!*

argument *noun* **arguments**
talking in an angry or excited way to someone who does not agree with you.

arithmetic *noun*
finding out about numbers.

arm *noun* **arms**
the part of the body between the shoulder and the hand.

armchair *noun* **armchairs**
a comfortable chair with parts at the side for you to rest your arms on.

armour *noun*
metal clothes worn in battles long ago. *The knight wore a suit of armour.*

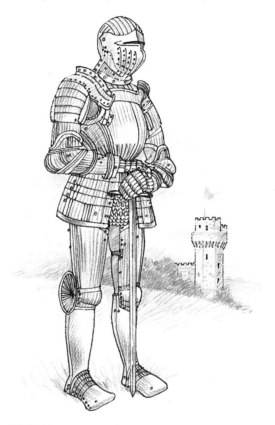

army *noun* **armies**
a large group of people trained to fight on land in a war.

around *adverb, preposition*
1 all round. *Around the castle there was a thick forest.*
2 here and there. *toys lying around.*

arrange *verb* **arranges, arranging, arranged**
to put in a certain order or place. *Arrange the chairs in a circle.*

arrangement *noun* **arrangements**
something that you have decided will happen.
We made an arrangement to meet after school.

arrest *verb* **arrests, arresting, arrested**
to take someone prisoner. *The policeman arrested the thief.*

arrive *verb* **arrives, arriving, arrived**
to come to the end of a journey. *We arrived home at six o'clock.*

arrow *noun* **arrows**
a pointed stick that is shot from a bow.

art *noun*
drawing and painting.

artery *noun* **arteries**
one of the tubes that carry your blood from your heart to other parts of your body.

article *noun* **articles**
1 a particular thing. *an article of clothing.*
2 a piece of writing. *an article in a magazine.*

artificial *adjective*
not natural, made by people or machines.
artificial flowers.

artist *noun* **artists**
someone who draws or paints pictures.

ash *noun* **ashes**
1 the grey powder left when something has been burned.
2 a kind of tree.

ashamed *adjective*
feeling very sorry, unhappy, and guilty about something.

ashore *adverb*
on land. *The sailors went ashore.*

aside *adverb*
to one side. *Stand aside!*

ask *verb* **asks, asking, asked**
to speak in order to find out or get something.
'What's your name?' she asked.

asleep *adjective*
sleeping.

aspirin *noun* **aspirins**
a small white pill. You swallow it when you have a cold or a pain to make you feel better.

ass *noun* **asses**
a donkey.

assembly *noun* **assemblies**
the time when the whole school meets together.

assess *verb* **assesses, assessing, assessed**
1 to say what you think the cost or value of something is.
2 to test pupils to find out what they have learned.

assist *verb* **assists, assisting, assisted**
to help.

assistant *noun* **assistants**
1 someone whose job is to help someone more important. *an assistant to the manager.*
2 someone who serves in a shop.

assorted *adjective*
with different sorts put together.

asthma *noun*
an illness that makes breathing difficult.

astonish *verb* **astonishes, astonishing, astonished**
to surprise someone very much.

astonishment *noun*
great surprise. *We stared in astonishment at the spaceship.*

astronaut *noun* **astronauts**
someone who travels in space.

astronomer *noun* **astronomers**
someone who studies the sun, the stars, and the planets.

astronomy *noun*
finding out about the sun, the stars, and the planets.

ate *verb* see **eat**

athlete *noun* **athletes**
someone who trains to be good at running, jumping, or throwing.

atlas *noun* **atlases**
a book of maps.

atmosphere *noun*
the air around the Earth.

atom *noun* **atoms**
one of the very tiny things that everything is made up of.

attach *verb* **attaches, attaching, attached**
to join or fasten something to another thing.
Attach a label to your suitcase.

attack *verb* **attacks, attacking, attacked**
to do something in order to beat or hurt someone.

attempt *verb* **attempts, attempting, attempted**
to try to do something. *The prisoner attempted to escape.*

attend *verb* **attends, attending, attended**
1 to be present somewhere. *Did he attend school yesterday?*
2 to listen carefully. *Are you attending to me?*

attendance *noun*
being at a place in order to take part in something. *attendance at school.*

attention *noun*
careful listening, reading, or thinking.
pay attention take notice.

attic *noun* **attics**
a room or rooms inside the roof of a house.

attract *verb* **attracts, attracting, attracted**
1 to interest someone. *The toy attracted the baby's attention and he stopped crying.*
2 to make something come nearer. *The magnet attracted the small piece of metal.*

attractive *adjective*
pleasant to look at, beautiful.
attractively *adverb*

auction *noun* **auctions**
a sale when things are sold to the people who offer the most money for them.

audience *noun* **audiences**
people who have come to a place to see or hear something.

August *noun*
the eighth month of the year.

aunt, aunty *noun* **aunts, aunties**
the sister of your mother or father, or your uncle's wife.

author *noun* **authors**
someone who writes books or stories.

authority *noun*
the power to make other people do as you say.
The police have the authority to stop speeding cars.

autograph *noun* **autographs**
your name written by yourself. *I collect autographs of famous people.*

automatic *adjective*
able to work on its own without a person controlling it. *an automatic washing machine.*
automatically *adverb*

autumn *noun*
the part of the year when leaves fall off the trees and it gets colder.

available *adjective*
ready for you to buy or use. *More paper is available if you need it.*

13

a b c d e f g h i j k l m n o p q r s t u v w x y z

avalanche *noun* **avalanches**
a large amount of snow, rock, or ice sliding suddenly down a mountain. *The climbers were buried underneath an avalanche.*

avenue *noun* **avenues**
a road, often with trees along each side.

average *adjective*
ordinary or usual. *She's of average height for her age.*

avoid *verb* **avoids, avoiding, avoided**
to keep out of the way of someone or something.

await *verb* **awaits, awaiting, awaited**
to wait for.

awake *adjective*
not sleeping.

award *noun* **awards**
a prize. *an award for bravery.*

aware *adjective*
knowing about something. *I was aware of somebody watching me.*

away *adverb*
1 not here. *She is away today.*
2 to or in another place. *He ran away. Put your books away now.*

awful *adjective*
(*informal*) very bad. *This tastes awful.*
awfully *adverb*

awkward *adjective*
1 difficult to do or use. *This big box is awkward to carry.*
2 clumsy. *He uses very awkward movements when he dances.*
3 not convenient. *They arrived at an awkward time.*

axe *noun* **axes**
a tool for chopping wood.

axle *noun* **axles**
a rod that goes through the centre of wheels.

Bb

baby *noun* **babies**
a very young child.

back *noun* **backs**
1 the part behind or opposite the front. *The answers are in the back of the book. We sat in the back of the car.*
2 the part of a person or an animal between the neck and the bottom.

backward, backwards *adjective, adverb*
1 towards the back. *She fell backwards and hit her head.*
2 in the opposite way to usual. *You've got your jumper on backwards.*

bacon *noun*
thin slices of dried or salty meat from a pig.

bacteria *plural noun*
tiny living things, some of which cause diseases.

bad *adjective* **worse, worst**
1 of the kind that people do not want, or do not like. *bad manners, a bad smell.*
2 serious. *a bad accident.*
badly *adverb Are you badly hurt?*

badge *noun* **badges**
something that you pin or sew on to your clothes, to show which school or club you belong to or how important you are.
a school badge.

badger *noun* **badgers**
a grey animal that digs holes in the ground. It has a white face with black stripes on it.

bad-tempered *adjective*
cross, angry.

bag *noun* **bags**
a container made of plastic, paper, cloth, or leather that you carry things in.

bait *noun*
food put on a hook or in a trap to catch animals.

bake *verb* **bakes, baking, baked**
1 to cook or to be cooked in an oven. *I baked a cake.*
2 to make something very hot, or to be very hot. *The sun baked the ground hard.*

baker *noun* **bakers**
someone whose job is to make or sell bread and cakes.

balance *noun* **balances**
a pair of scales for weighing things.

balance *verb* **balances, balancing, balanced**
to keep or make something steady, to be steady. *The seal balanced a ball on its nose.*

balcony *noun* **balconies**
1 a platform with a rail round it outside an upstairs window.
2 the seats upstairs in a cinema or theatre.

bald *adjective*
without any hair on the head.

bale *noun* **bales**
a large bundle of something. *a bale of hay.*

ball *noun* **balls**
1 a round object that you hit, kick, or throw in games. *a tennis ball.*
2 a big party with a lot of dancing. *Cinderella had to be back from the ball by twelve o'clock.*

ballerina *noun* **ballerinas**
a woman who dances in ballets.

ballet *noun* **ballets**
a story told on the stage in dancing, mime, and music. *Swan Lake is my favourite ballet.*

balloon *noun* **balloons**
1 a small, coloured, rubber bag that you can blow up.
2 a very big bag filled with hot air or gas so that it floats in the sky.

balloon 2

bamboo *noun*
a tall plant with stiff, hollow stems.

ban *verb* **bans, banning, banned**
to say that someone must never do a certain thing. *They have banned skateboarding in the playground.*

banana *noun* **bananas**
a long fruit with a thick yellow skin.

band *noun* **bands**
1 a group of people who play music together. *a brass band.*
2 a group of people. *a band of robbers.*
3 a thin strip of material. *a rubber band.*

bandage *noun* **bandages**
a strip of material for wrapping round part of the body that has been hurt.

bandit *noun* **bandits**
a person who attacks and robs people.

bang *noun* **bangs**
a sudden very loud noise.

15

bang *verb* **bangs, banging, banged**
to hit or shut with a loud noise. *Don't bang the door!*

bangle *noun* **bangles**
a ring worn round the arm. *a gold bangle.*

banish *verb* **banishes, banishing, banished**
to send someone away from a place as a punishment.

banisters *noun*
the posts and rail at the side of a staircase.

banjo *noun* **banjos**
a musical instrument with strings that you play with your fingers.

bank *noun* **banks**
1 a place that looks after money and valuable things for people.
2 the ground near the edge of a river, canal, or lake.
3 a sloping piece of ground.

banner *noun* **banners**
a flag with words on it. *The banner says 'Stop the war'.*

banquet *noun* **banquets**
a large special meal for a lot of people. *a wedding banquet.*

bar *noun* **bars**
1 a long piece of wood or metal.
2 a block of chocolate, toffee, or soap.
3 a place that serves food and drinks at a counter. *a coffee bar.*

barbecue *noun* **barbecues**
1 a metal frame for cooking meat over a fire.
2 an open-air party where food is cooked over a fire.

barbed wire *noun*
wire with sharp spikes in it, used for making fences.

barber *noun* **barbers**
a man whose job is to cut men's and boys' hair.

bare *adjective* **barer, barest**
1 without any clothes on.
2 without any covering or decoration. *bare walls.*

barely *adverb*
only just, hardly. *I was so tired that I could barely walk.*

bargain *noun* **bargains**
1 a promise to give something in return for something else. *They made a bargain to swap the toys.*
2 something that costs much less than usual. *You can get bargains at jumble sales.*

barge *noun* **barges**
a long boat with a flat bottom. Barges are used on canals.

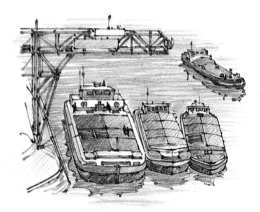

bark *noun*
the hard covering round the trunk and branches of a tree.

bark *verb* **barks, barking, barked**
to make the sharp, loud sound a dog makes.

barley *noun*
a plant grown by farmers. Its seed is used for making food and beer.

barn *noun* **barns**
a large building on a farm, where you keep animals or grain.

barnacle *noun* **barnacles**
a sea creature that sticks to rocks and the bottoms of ships.

barrel *noun* **barrels**
1 a round, wooden container with flat ends. *a barrel of beer.*
2 the tube at the front of a gun.

barren *adjective*
without trees or plants. *barren land.*

barrier *noun* **barriers**
a fence or something that stands in the way.

barrow *noun* **barrows**
a small cart that you push.

base *noun* **bases**
the bottom part of something. *The base of the statue was made of wood.*

basement *noun* **basements**
the rooms in a building that are below the ground.

bash *verb* **bashes, bashing, bashed**
(*informal*) to hit very hard.

bashful *adjective*
shy.
bashfully *adverb*

basic *adjective*
1 most important and necessary. *A person's basic needs are food, clothes, and somewhere to live.*
2 simple. *basic skills in First Aid.*

basin *noun* **basins**
a large bowl.

basket *noun* **baskets**
a container made of straw or thin strips of metal that you carry things in.

basketball *noun*
a game for two teams of five players who try to throw a ball into a high net.

bat *noun* **bats**
1 an animal like a mouse with wings that comes out at night.
2 a piece of wood for hitting a ball in a game.

bat *verb* **bats, batting, batted**
to have a turn at playing with a bat in games like cricket.

bath *noun* **baths** (rhymes with *path*)
a large container which you can fill with water to sit in and wash yourself all over.

bath *verb* **bathes, bathing, bathes**
to put a person or animal in water and wash him or her.

bathe *verb* **bathes, bathing, bathed**
(rhymes with *save*)
1 to swim in the sea or a river. *They bathed in the pool.*
2 to wash part of yourself carefully and gently. *He bathed his cut finger.*

bathroom *noun* **bathrooms**
the room where you can have a bath or wash.

baton *noun* **batons**
1 a stick used by a conductor of an orchestra.
2 a stick that a runner in a relay-race passes to the next person in the team.

batsman *noun* **batsmen**
the person who uses the bat in cricket or rounders.

batter *noun*
a mixture of flour, eggs, and milk used to make pancakes or to cook fish in.

batter *verb* **batters, battering, battered**
to damage something by hitting it again and again.

battery *noun* **batteries**
a closed container that gives electricity. You put batteries inside torches and radios to make them work.

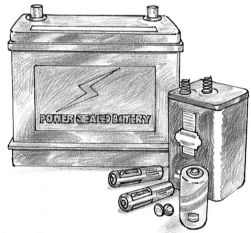

battle *noun* **battles**
fighting between groups of people.

battlements *noun*
the top of a castle wall with gaps through which people could fire at the enemy.

battleship *noun* **battleships**
a very large ship used in war.

bawl *verb* **bawls, bawling, bawled**
to shout or cry loudly. *The hungry baby was bawling.*

bay *noun* **bays**
a place where the land bends inwards and sea fills the space.

bayonet *noun* **bayonets**
a sharp blade that can be fixed to a gun.

bazaar *noun* **bazaars**
1 a group of stalls selling different things to get money for something. *a church bazaar.*
2 a market in Africa or Asia.

beach *noun* **beaches**
land by the edge of the sea, covered with sand or small stones.

bead *noun* **beads**
a small ball of wood, glass, or plastic with a hole through the middle. Beads are threaded on a string to make necklaces.

beak *noun* **beaks**
the hard pointed part of a bird's mouth.

beaker *noun* **beakers**
a kind of tall cup. Some beakers have no handle.

beam *noun* **beams**
1 a long strong piece of wood.
2 a line of light. *the beam of a torch.*

beam *verb* **beams, beaming, beamed**
to smile happily. *She beamed when she heard the good news.*

bean *noun* **beans**
the long thin part of some plants or one of the seeds which grow inside it. *baked beans, runner beans.*

bear *noun* **bears**
a big wild animal with thick fur.

bear *verb* **bears, bearing, bore, borne**
1 to carry. *This ice is too thin to bear your weight.*
2 to put up with. *I couldn't bear the pain any longer.*

bear *verb* **bears, bearing, bore, born**
to give birth to. *I was born in Birmingham.*

beard *noun* **beards**
hair growing on a man's chin.

beast *noun* **beasts**
1 any big animal.
2 a horrible person.

beat *noun*
a regular rhythm. *Jo likes music with a strong beat.*

beat *verb* **beats, beating, beaten**
1 to do better than someone else. *Jo always beats Sam at tennis.*
2 to hit often. *It's cruel to beat animals.*
3 to stir hard. *Dad beat some eggs to make an omelette.*
4 to make a regular rhythm. *After running, my heart beats fast.*

beautiful *adjective*
1 very nice to look at, hear, or smell. *a beautiful picture.*
2 enjoyable, pleasant. *beautiful weather.*
beautifully *adverb*

beauty *noun*
if something has beauty you enjoy looking at it or listening to it. *the beauty of the sunset.*

beaver *noun* **beavers**
a furry animal with a long flat tail that swims and builds dams in the river.

became *verb* see **become**

because *conjunction*
for the reason that. *He was angry because I was late.*

beckon *verb* **beckons, beckoning, beckoned**
to move your hand to show someone that you want them to come nearer.

become *verb* **becomes, becoming, became**
to come to be.
It suddenly became very cold yesterday.

bed *noun* **beds**
1 a piece of furniture you sleep on, a place to sleep.
2 a piece of ground for growing flowers or vegetables. *a flower bed.*
3 the ground at the bottom of a sea or river. *the sea bed.*

bedclothes *noun*
things you put on a bed, such as sheets and blankets.

bedroom *noun* **bedrooms**
the room where you sleep.

bee *noun* **bees**
an insect that can fly, sting, and make honey.

beech *noun* **beeches**
a kind of tree.

beef *noun*
meat from a cow.

beefburger *noun* **beefburgers**
minced beef made into a round flat cake and cooked.

beehive *noun* **beehives**
a box for keeping bees in.

beer *noun* **beers**
a brown alcoholic drink.

beetle *noun* **beetles**
an insect with hard wings and a shiny body.

beetroot *noun* **the plural is the same**
a round, dark red vegetable.

before *adverb, conjunction, preposition*
1 earlier than. *I was here before you.*
2 in front of. *It vanished before my eyes.*

began *verb* see **begin**

beggar *noun* **beggars**
someone who lives by asking other people for money, clothes, or food.

begin *verb* **begins, beginning, began, begun**
to start. *I'm beginning to understand. I have begun to learn the piano. What time does the film begin?*

beginner *noun* **beginners**
someone who has just started learning something.

beginning *noun* **beginnings**
the start of something.

begun *verb* see **begin**

behave *verb* **behaves, behaving, behaved**
to show good or bad manners in front of other people. *He's behaved badly. She's behaving well.*
Behave yourself! Be good!

behaviour *noun*
how you behave.

behind *adverb, preposition*
at the back of. *He hid behind the wall.*

being *noun* **beings**
a creature. *They looked like beings from another planet.*

belief *noun* **beliefs**
what someone believes.

believe *verb* **believes, believing, believed**
to feel sure that something is true. *Do you believe in witches?*

bell *noun* **bells**
a metal thing that rings when it is hit. *The bell rang at the end of the lesson.*

bellow *verb* **bellows, bellowing, bellowed**
to shout and make a lot of noise like an angry bull.

belly *noun* **bellies**
the stomach.

belong *verb* **belongs, belonging, belonged**
1 to be someone's. *That pen belongs to me.*
2 to be part of something. *Sam belongs to a football club.*
3 to be in the proper place. *Your coat belongs on the peg, not on the floor.*

belongings *noun*
things which belong to you. *Make sure you take your belongings when you get off the train.*

below *adverb, preposition*
underneath; less than. *Write your address below your name. The temperature was below zero.*

belt *noun* **belts**
a stiff band of leather or other material that you wear round your waist.

bench *noun* **benches**
a wooden or stone seat for more than one person.

bend *noun* **bends**
a part of a road or river that is not straight. *She drove carefully round the bend.*

bend *verb* **bends, bending, bent**
1 to become or make something curved or not straight. *The branches were bent by the weight of the apples.*
2 to lean over so that your head is nearer to the ground. *He bent down to do up his shoes.*

beneath *adverb, preposition*
underneath. *fish beneath the waves.*

bent *verb* see **bend**

berry *noun* **berries**
a small round fruit with seeds in it. *blackberries, strawberries.*

beside *preposition*
at the side of. *a house beside the sea.*

besides *preposition*
as well as. *Ten people besides me also won prizes.*

best *adjective*
better than any other. *my best friend.*

bet *verb* **bets, betting, bet**
to say what you think will happen. If you are right you win money, but if you are wrong you lose money.

betray *verb* **betrays, betraying, betrayed**
1 to give away a secret.
2 to give information about your friends or country to the enemy.

better *adjective*
1 more useful, that you like more. *My new pen is better than my old one.*
2 more good at. *She's better than me at swimming.*
3 well again after an illness. *I'm better now, thank you.*

between *adverb, preposition*
1 in the middle of two people or things. *I sat between Mum and Dad.*
2 among. *Share the money between you.*

beware *verb*
be careful. *Beware of the dog.*

bewildered *adjective*
very puzzled and worried. *The dog was bewildered by all the noises in the town.*

bewitched *adjective*
under a spell.

beyond *adverb, preposition*
further than. *Don't go beyond the end of the road.*

biased *adjective*
unfairly liking one side more than another. *The referee was biased.*

Bible *noun* **Bibles**
the holy book that is read in all Christian churches.

bicycle *noun* **bicycles**
a machine with two wheels and pedals, that you can ride.

big *adjective* **bigger, biggest**
large, of great size. *London is a big city.*

bike *noun* **bikes**
(*informal*) a bicycle.

bill *noun* **bills**
1 a piece of paper that tells you how much money you owe. *He paid all his bills.*
2 a bird's beak.

billion *noun* **billions**
1,000,000,000; one thousand million.

bin *noun* **bins**
a large container, often with a lid. *a rubbish bin.*

bind *verb* **binds, binding, bound**
to tie together. *The prisoner's hands were bound behind his back.*

bingo *noun*
a game where each person has a card with different numbers on it. When the person who controls the game says all the numbers on the card, you win the game.

binoculars *noun*
a special pair of glasses like two tubes joined together. When you look through them, things far away seem much nearer.

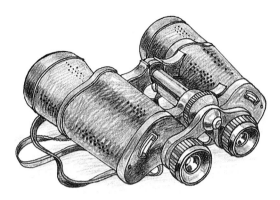

biology *noun*
the study of the life of animals and plants.

bird *noun* **birds**
any animal with feathers, wings, and a beak.

Biro *noun* **Biros**
a pen in which ink comes from a metal ball at the end.

birth *noun*
the beginning of life, when a baby leaves its mother and starts to breathe. **date of birth** the date when you were born.

birthday *noun* **birthdays**
the day each year when you remember the day you were born. *I had a party on my birthday this year.*

biscuit *noun* **biscuits**
a kind of small, thin, dry cake.

bishop *noun* **bishops**
an important priest in the Christian church who is in charge of other priests.

bit *noun* **bits**
1 a very small amount of something. *a bit of cake, bits of paper.*
2 the part of a bridle that goes into a horse's mouth.

bit *verb* see **bite**

bitch *noun* **bitches**
a female dog.

bite *verb* **bites, biting, bit, bitten**
to use the teeth to cut into something. *Your dog's bitten me. Stop biting your nails! She bit into the apple.*

bitter *adjective*
1 having a sharp taste, not sweet.
2 unhappy because you are envious or disappointed.
bitterly *adverb He cried bitterly.*

black *noun, adjective*
1 the colour of the sky on a very dark night.
2 with a dark skin.

blackberry *noun* **blackberries**
a small, soft, black berry that grows on bushes.

blackbird *noun* **blackbirds**
a bird often seen in gardens. The male is black with an orange beak, but the female is brown.

blackboard *noun* **blackboards**
a smooth, hard black or dark green surface that you can write on with chalk.

blacksmith *noun* **blacksmiths**
someone whose job is to make horseshoes and other things out of iron.

blade *noun* **blades**
1 the flat, sharp part of a knife or sword.
2 something shaped like a blade. *a blade of grass.*

21

blame *verb* **blames, blaming, blamed**
to say that some other person or thing is the cause of something bad that has happened.
Don't blame me if we're late!

blank *adjective*
with nothing written or drawn on it. *a blank page.*

blanket *noun* **blankets**
a thick warm cover used on a bed.

blast *noun* **blasts**
1 a sudden, rushing wind, a rush of air.
2 the loud sound that an explosion makes.

blast *verb* **blasts, blasting, blasted**
to blow up with explosives.

blaze *noun* **blazes**
a large, strong fire.

blaze *verb* **blazes, blazing, blazed**
to burn brightly. *The fire was blazing in the grate.*

blazer *noun* **blazers**
a kind of jacket. A blazer usually has a badge on its top pocket.

bleach *noun*
a chemical that you use to kill germs or to make clothes whiter.

bleach *verb* **bleaches, bleaching, bleached**
to make something white.

bleak *adjective* **bleaker, bleakest**
windy, cold, and miserable. *a bleak winter's day.*

bleat *verb* **bleats, bleating, bleated**
to make the sound sheep make.

bleed *verb* **bleeds, bleeding, bled**
to lose blood. *My nose is bleeding.*

bleep *verb* **bleeps, bleeping, bleeped**
to make short, high sounds. *The computer bleeps if you enter a wrong command.*

blend *verb* **blends, blending, blended**
to mix together.

bless *verb* **blesses, blessing, blessed**
to ask God to look after someone and make them happy. *God bless you.*

blew *verb* see **blow**

blind *adjective*
not able to see.
blindly *adverb*

blind *noun* **blinds**
a piece of material that you pull down to cover a window.

blink *verb* **blinks, blinking, blinked**
to close your eyes and open them again very quickly.

blister *noun* **blisters**
a small swelling on the skin. It has liquid inside and hurts when you touch it.

blizzard *noun* **blizzards**
a storm with a lot of snow and wind.

blob *noun* **blobs**
a round drop of liquid, or a round lump of something. *a blob of jelly.*

block *noun* **blocks**
1 a thick piece of something hard and solid. *a block of wood.*
2 a tall building with lots of flats or offices inside. *a block of flats, an office block.*

block *verb* **blocks, blocking, blocked**
to be in the way, or to put something in the way, so that nothing can get through. *A flock of sheep blocked the road.*

blood *noun*
the red liquid that carries oxygen around inside your body.

bloom *verb* **blooms, blooming, bloomed**
to be in flower. *Roses bloom in summer.*

blossom *noun* **blossoms**
flowers on a tree. *apple blossom.*

blot *noun* **blots**
a spot of liquid spilt on something.

blouse *noun* **blouses**
a piece of clothing worn on the top half of the body by women and girls.

blow *verb* **blows, blowing, blew, blown**
1 to make air come out of the mouth. *She blew out the candles and cut the cake.*
2 to move along with the wind. *Tiles were blown off the roof.*

blue *noun, adjective*
the colour of the sky on a fine day.

bluebell *noun* **bluebells**
a wild plant with flowers like tiny blue bells.

blunder *verb* **blunders, blundering, blundered**
1 to make a big mistake.
2 to move about very clumsily.

blunt *adjective* **blunter, bluntest**
not sharp. *a blunt knife.*

blur *verb* **blurs, blurring, blurred**
to make something look not clear. Smudged writing is blurred.

blush *verb* **blushes, blushing, blushed**
to go red in the face because you feel shy or guilty.

boar *noun* **boars**
1 a male pig.
2 a wild pig.

boar 2

board *noun* **boards**
1 a long thin piece of wood.
2 a piece of wood used for a special purpose. *a noticeboard, a chess board.*

board *verb* **boards, boarding, boarded**
to get on an aeroplane, bus, ship, or train.

boast *verb* **boasts, boasting, boasted**
to talk in a way that shows you are much too proud of what you can do. *He boasted about how good he was at football.*

boat *noun* **boats**
something that floats and has room in it for taking people or things over water.

body *noun* **bodies**
1 all of a person or animal that can be seen or touched.
2 all of a person but not the arms, legs, and head.
3 a dead person. *The police found a dead body in the river.*

bodyguard *noun* **bodyguards**
a person or persons whose job is to protect someone.

bog *noun* **bogs**
a piece of ground so wet and soft that your feet sink into it.

boil *noun* **boils**
a big painful spot on the skin.

boil *verb* **boils, boiling, boiled**
1 to bubble and give off steam. *Is the water boiling?*
2 to heat liquid until it boils. *I boiled the water to make tea.*
3 to be cooked or to cook something in boiling water.
We boiled the potatoes.

bold *adjective* **bolder, boldest**
1 brave and not afraid.
2 large and easy to see. *bold handwriting.*
boldly *adverb*

bolt *noun* **bolts**
1 a piece of metal that you slide across to lock a door.
2 a thick metal pin like a screw. *nuts and bolts.*

bolt *verb* **bolts, bolting, bolted**
1 to lock something with a bolt. *Remember to bolt the back door.*
2 to rush off suddenly. *The horse bolted.*
3 to swallow food quickly without chewing it. *He bolted his dinner and went out to play.*

bomb *noun* **bombs**
a thing that explodes and hurts people or damages things.

bone *noun* **bones**
one of the hard white things inside the body of a person or an animal that makes up the skeleton. *an ankle bone.*

bonfire *noun* **bonfires**
a large fire built in the open air.

bonnet *noun* **bonnets**
1 the part of a car that covers the engine.
2 a hat that is tied under the chin.

boo *verb* **boos, booing, booed**
to show that you don't like someone or something by shouting 'boo'.

23

a b c d e f g h i j k l m n o p q r s t u v w x y z

book *noun* **books**
a thing that you read or write in, that has a lot of pieces of paper joined together inside a cover.

book *verb* **books, booking, booked**
1 to arrange for something to be reserved for you. *Mum booked our summer holiday.*
2 to write someone's name in a book when they do wrong. *The police booked her for speeding.*

bookcase *noun* **bookcases**
a piece of furniture made for holding books.

boom *verb* **booms, booming, boomed**
to make a loud, deep sound. *The guns boomed away in the distance.*

boomerang *noun* **boomerangs**
a curved stick that comes back to the person who throws it.

boot *noun* **boots**
1 a kind of shoe that also covers the ankle. *Wellington boots.*
2 the part of a car for carrying luggage.

border *noun* **borders**
1 the narrow part along the edge of something. *a white tablecloth with a blue border.*
2 the line where two countries meet. *You need a passport to cross the border.*

bore *verb* **bores, boring, bored**
1 to make someone tired by being dull.
2 to make a hole with a tool.
3 see **bear** *verb*
bored *adjective* **boring** *adjective*

born, borne *verb* see **bear** *verb*

borrow *verb* **borrows, borrowing, borrowed**
to get the use of something for a short time and agree to give it back. *I've borrowed these library books.*

boss *noun* **bosses**
the person who is in charge.

bossy *adjective*
behaving as if you were the boss.

both *adjective, pronoun*
the two of them.
Hold it in both hands. We both like swimming.

bother *verb* **bothers, bothering, bothered**
1 to worry or annoy someone.
Is the loud music bothering you?
2 to take trouble over doing something.
He never bothers to tidy his room.

bottle *noun* **bottles**
a tall glass or plastic container with a narrow neck that you keep liquids in. *a milk bottle.*

bottom *noun* **bottoms**
1 the lowest part of anything.
2 the part of the body that you sit on.

bough *noun* **boughs**
a large branch of a tree.

bought *verb* see **buy**

boulder *noun* **boulders**
a large rock.

bounce *verb* **bounces, bouncing, bounced**
to spring back after hitting something hard.

bound *verb* **bounds, bounding, bounded**
to leap.
The dog bounded over the gate.
bound to certain to.
It's bound to rain if we go for a picnic.

bound *verb* see **bind**

boundary *noun* **boundaries**
a line marking the edge of some land.

bouquet *noun* **bouquets**
a bunch of flowers.

bow *noun* **bows**
(rhymes with *go*)
1 a strip of bent wood with string joining each end. It is used for shooting arrows.
2 a wooden rod with strong hairs stretched along it and joining each end, for playing the violin.
3 a knot with loops. *a bow in her hair.*

bow *verb* **bows, bowing, bowed**
(rhymes with *cow*)
to bend forwards to show respect. *He bowed to the Queen.*

bowl *noun* **bowls**
a round, open container for liquid or food.

bowl *verb* **bowls, bowling, bowled**
to send a ball for the batsman to hit in cricket or rounders.

box *noun* **boxes**
a container, usually in the shape of a square or a rectangle. *a cardboard box.*

box *verb* **boxes, boxing, boxed**
to fight with your fists.
boxing *noun*

boxer *noun* **boxers**
a person who fights with his fists.

boy *noun* **boys**
a male child or teenager.

brace *noun* **braces**
a piece of wire worn across teeth to straighten them.

bracelet *noun* **bracelets**
beads, a chain, or a ring worn round the arm.

braces *noun*
a set of straps worn over the shoulders to keep trousers up.

bracket *noun* **brackets**
1 one of a pair of marks like these ( ) that you use in writing.
2 a piece of metal fixed to a wall to support something.

brag *verb* **brags, bragging, bragged**
to boast.

Braille *noun*
a pattern of raised dots on paper so that blind people can read by touching them with their fingers.

brain *noun* **brains**
the part inside the head that controls the body of a person or an animal. It also lets you think and remember things.

brake *noun* **brakes**
the part of a car or bicycle that makes it slow down or stop.

bramble *noun* **brambles**
a blackberry bush or a prickly bush like it.

bran *noun*
the outside part of the seeds of corn which you can eat to add fibre to your diet.

branch *noun* **branches**
a part that sticks out from the trunk of a tree.

brand *noun* **brands**
the name of things you buy that show the maker. *a new brand of tea.*

brass *noun*
a yellow metal made by mixing copper with zinc. *brass candlesticks.*
brass band a group of musicians playing instruments that are made of brass, such as trumpets and trombones.

brave *adjective* **braver, bravest**
ready to do dangerous things without fear. **bravely** *adverb*

bravery *noun*
being brave.

bray *verb* **brays, braying, brayed**
to make the harsh sound a donkey makes.

bread *noun*
a food made from flour and baked in the oven. *a loaf of bread.*

breadth *noun*
the measurement or distance from one side of something to the other; the width. *We measured the length and breadth of the garden.*

break *noun* **breaks**
1 a gap, a place where something is broken. *a break in the hedge.*
2 a short rest. *a break from work.*

break *verb* **breaks, breaking, broke, broken**
1 to make something go into smaller pieces. *I broke the window.*
2 to go into smaller pieces. *I dropped the cup and it broke.*
3 to fail to keep a law or promise. *He's broken the rules.*
break down If a car or machine breaks down, it stops working. *We were late because the car broke down.*

breakfast *noun* **breakfasts**
the first meal of the day.

breast *noun* **breasts**
1 one of the two parts on the front of a woman's body that can produce milk to feed a baby.
2 a person's or animal's chest.

breath *noun* **breaths**
the air that a person breathes. *They could see their breath in the frosty morning air.*

breathe *verb* **breathes, breathing, breathed**
to take air into your lungs through your nose or mouth and send it out again.

breed *noun* **breeds**
a particular kind of animal. *What breed of dog is that?*

breed *verb* **breeds, breeding, bred**
1 to produce young ones. *Birds breed in the spring.*
2 to keep animals to get young ones from them. *Jo's friend breeds rabbits.*

breeze *noun* **breezes**
a gentle wind.

bribe *noun* **bribes**
money or a present that you give to someone to tempt them to do something.

bribe *verb* **bribes, bribing, bribed**
to tempt someone to do something by offering them money.

brick *noun* **bricks**
a small block used in building.

bride *noun* **brides**
a woman on the day she gets married.

bridegroom *noun* **bridegrooms**
a man on the day he gets married.

bridesmaid *noun* **bridesmaids**
a girl or woman who walks behind the bride at her wedding.

bridge *noun* **bridges**
something built over a river, railway, or road so that people, cars, or trains can cross it.

bridle *noun* **bridles**
the leather straps that you put over a horse's head to control it.

brief *adjective* **briefer, briefest**
short. *a brief letter.*
briefly *adverb*

26

briefcase *noun* **briefcases**
a flat case for carrying papers in.

briefs *noun*
pants.

bright *adjective* **brighter, brightest**
1 with a lot of light. *a bright sunny day.*
2 with a strong colour. *a bright red jumper.*
3 clever. *a bright boy.*
4 cheerful. *a bright smile.*
brightly *adverb*

brilliant *adjective*
very bright or very good.
brilliantly *adverb*

brim *noun* **brims**
1 the edge round the top of a container. *a cup filled to the brim.*
2 the part of a hat that sticks out round the edge. *a sun hat with a wide brim.*

bring *verb* **brings, bringing, brought**
1 to carry here. *Bring your book.*
2 to lead here. *Yesterday he brought his friend.*

brink *noun*
the edge of a dangerous place. *He trembled on the brink of the precipice.*

brisk *adjective* **brisker, briskest**
quick and lively. *a brisk walk.*
briskly *adverb*

bristle *noun* **bristles**
a short, stiff hair like the hairs on a brush.

brittle *adjective*
likely to break or snap.
brittle twigs.

broad *adjective* **broader, broadest**
measuring a lot from side to side.
a broad river.

broadcast *noun* **broadcasts**
a television or radio programme.

bronchitis *noun*
an illness of part of the lungs that causes a very bad cough.

broke, broken *verb* see **break** *verb*

bronze *noun*
a brown metal made by mixing copper and tin.
a bronze statue.

brooch *noun* **brooches**
a piece of jewellery that you pin to your clothes.

brook *noun* **brooks**
a small stream.

broom *noun* **brooms**
a brush with a long handle that you sweep floors with.

broth *noun*
a thin soup made from meat and vegetables.

brother *noun* **brothers**
a man or boy who has the same parents as another person.

brought *verb* see **bring**

brow *noun* **brows**
1 the forehead. *He wiped the sweat from his brow.*
2 the top of a hill. *When they reached the brow of the hill they rested.*

brown *noun, adjective*
the colour of earth or clay.

bruise *noun* **bruises**
a dark mark on your skin that comes after something hits it.

bruise *verb* **bruises, bruising, bruised**
to give someone a bruise. *Tom fell and bruised his arm.*

brush *noun* **brushes**
a tool with short, stiff hairs. Brushes are used for making hair tidy, cleaning, sweeping, scrubbing, and painting.
a hairbrush, a paintbrush.

brush *verb* **brushes, brushing, brushed**
to use a brush to do something. *I brush my teeth twice a day.*

bubble *noun* **bubbles**
a small ball of air or gas inside a liquid.

bubble *verb* **bubbles, bubbling, bubbled**
to be full of bubbles. *When water boils, it bubbles.*

bubbly *adjective*
full of bubbles.

bucket *noun* **buckets**
a container with a handle but no lid, used for carrying liquid.

buckle *noun* **buckles**
a metal or plastic thing on the end of a belt that you use to join it to the other end.

bud *noun* **buds**
a flower or leaf before it has opened.

Buddhism *noun*
the religion that follows the teachings of Buddha.

Buddhist *noun* **Buddhists**
a person who follows the teachings of Buddha.
Buddhist *adjective a Buddhist temple.*

budge *verb* **budges, budging, budged**
to move slightly.

budgerigar *noun* **budgerigars**
a small, brightly coloured bird kept as a pet.

buffet *noun* **buffets**
a place where you can get drinks and snacks.

bug *noun* **bugs**
1 an insect.
2 (*informal*) a germ, or an infectious illness. *a flu bug.*

bugle *noun* **bugles**
a small, brass musical instrument that you blow into.

build *verb* **builds, building, built**
to make something by putting parts together.
The bridge is built of stone.

building *noun* **buildings**
something that has been built. Houses, schools, theatres, shops, and churches are all buildings.

built *verb* see **build**

bulb *noun* **bulbs**
1 the part of an electric lamp that gives light.
2 something that looks like an onion and is planted in earth. Daffodils, tulips, and some other flowers grow from bulbs.

bulge *verb* **bulges, bulging, bulged**
to swell out. *His pockets were bulging with conkers.*

bulk *noun*
a large amount.

bull *noun* **bulls**
a male cow, elephant, or whale.

bulldozer *noun* **bulldozers**
a heavy machine that moves earth and makes land flat.

bullet *noun* **bullets**
a small piece of metal made to be fired from a gun.

bullock *noun* **bullocks**
a young, male ox.

bull's-eye *noun* **bull's-eyes**
the centre of a target.

bully *noun* **bullies**
someone who hurts or frightens a smaller or weaker person.

bully *verb* **bullies, bullying, bullied**
to hurt or frighten someone who is smaller or weaker than you.

bump *noun* **bumps**
a lump, a swelling.

bump *verb* **bumps, bumping, bumped**
to knock against something. *I bumped my head on the door.*

bumper *noun* **bumpers**
a bar along the front or back of a car. It protects the car if it hits something.

bumpy *adjective* **bumpier, bumpiest**
not flat but full of bumps. *a bumpy road.*

bun *noun* **buns**
a small, round cake.

bunch *noun* **bunches**
a group of things joined or tied together. *a bunch of flowers.*

bundle *noun* **bundles**
a group of things tied together. *a bundle of sticks.*

bungalow *noun* **bungalows**
a house without any upstairs rooms.

bunk *noun* **bunks**
a bed that has another bed above or below it.

buoy *noun* **buoys**
(rhymes with *boy*)
a thing that floats in the sea to warn ships about danger.

burden *noun* **burdens**
something that has to be carried.

burger *noun* **burgers**
minced meat or other things made into a flat cake and cooked.

burglar *noun* **burglars**
someone who gets into a building to steal things.

burial *noun* **burials**
the burying of a dead person.

burn *verb* **burns, burning, burned** or **burnt**
1 to give out heat, light, and flames. *Paper burns easily.*
2 to damage something with heat. *Sam burnt the toast.*

burrow *noun* **burrows**
a hole in the ground that an animal lives in. *Rabbits live in burrows.*

burst *verb* **bursts, bursting, burst**
1 to break open suddenly because there is too much inside. *The balloon burst.*
2 to make something break open. *Sam blew up the paper bag and burst it.*

bury *verb* **buries, burying, buried**
to put something or someone in a hole in the ground and cover it over.

bus *noun* **buses**
a large road vehicle for people to travel in.

bush *noun* **bushes**
a plant that looks like a small tree. *a rose bush.*

business *noun* **businesses**
1 buying and selling things. *the business of selling cars.*
2 a shop or firm or industry. *The record business is doing well.*

bustle *verb* **bustles, bustling, bustled**
to hurry in a busy way. *She bustled about, tidying the house.*

busy *adjective* **busier, busiest**
1 doing things all the time. *I'm very busy today.*
2 full of activity. *a busy street.*
busily *adverb*

butcher *noun* **butchers**
someone whose job is to cut up meat and sell it.

butter *noun*
a yellow food made from milk. You spread it on bread.

buttercup *noun* **buttercups**
a wild flower with shiny yellow petals.

butterfly *noun* **butterflies**
an insect with large white or coloured wings.

butterscotch *noun*
hard toffee made from sugar and butter.

buttocks *noun*
the part of the body you sit on, your bottom.

button *noun* **buttons**
a small round thing that you sew on clothes and push through a hole or loop to hold them together.

buy *verb* **buys, buying, bought**
to get something by giving money for it. *I bought my bike for £30.*

buzz *verb* **buzzes, buzzing, buzzed**
to make the sound a bee makes.

bypass *noun* **bypasses**
a main road which goes round a town, not through it.

Cc

cab *noun* **cabs**
1 the part of a lorry, bus, or train where the driver sits.
2 a taxi.

cabbage *noun* **cabbages**
a large round vegetable with a lot of green leaves.

cabin *noun* **cabins**
1 a room in a ship or aeroplane.
2 a small hut. *a log cabin.*

cabinet *noun* **cabinets**
a cupboard. *a bathroom cabinet.*
the Cabinet *noun*
the most important people in the government.

cable *noun* **cables**
strong, thick wire or rope.

cackle *verb* **cackles, cackling, cackled**
to laugh and make the sound a hen makes.

cactus *noun* **cacti**
a plant with a thick green stem, covered in prickles. Cacti grow in hot, dry places and do not need much water.

café *noun* **cafés**
a place where you can buy a drink or food.

cage *noun* **cages**
a large box with bars across it for keeping animals or birds in.

cake *noun* **cakes**
a food that you make with flour, fat, eggs, and sugar and bake in the oven.

calamity *noun* **calamities**
something very bad that happens suddenly.

calculator *noun* **calculators**
a machine that can do sums.

calendar *noun* **calendars**
a list showing all the days, weeks, and months in a year.

calf *noun* **calves**
1 a young cow, elephant, or whale.
2 the part of your leg between the knee and the ankle.

call *verb* **calls, calling, called**
1 to speak loudly.
2 to give a name to someone or something. *They called the baby Robert.*
3 to tell someone to come to you. *Mum called us in for tea.*

calm *adjective* **calmer, calmest**
1 still. *a calm sea.*
2 not noisy or excited. *Keep calm. You're safe now.*

calorie *noun* **calories**
a unit used to measure the amount of energy produced by food. If your diet has too many calories, you may put on weight.

camcorder *noun* **camcorders**
a camera for taking video pictures.

came *verb* see **come**

camel *noun* **camels**
a big animal with one or two humps on its back. Camels are used instead of horses in deserts, because they can travel for a long time without eating or drinking.

camera *noun* **cameras**
a machine for taking photographs.

camouflage *verb* **camouflages, camouflaging, camouflaged**
to hide something by making it look like its surroundings.

camp *noun* **camps**
a group of tents or huts where people live for a short time.

camp *verb* **camps, camping, camped**
to make a camp, or stay in a camp. *We went camping last summer.*

can *noun* **cans**
a tin. *a can of beans.*

can *verb* **could**
to be able to. *She can swim, but I can't. He could swim if he tried.*

canal *noun* **canals**
a kind of river that people have made for boats to travel on.

canary *noun* **canaries**
a small yellow bird.

cancel *verb* **cancels, cancelling, cancelled**
to say that something which has been arranged will not happen. *My piano lesson was cancelled.*

cancer *noun* **cancers**
a serious disease in which lumps grow in the body.

candle *noun* **candles**
a stick of wax with string through the centre. It gives light as it burns.

cane *noun* **canes**
a long, thin stick, usually a stick of bamboo.

cannibal *noun* **cannibals**
a person who eats humans.

cannon *noun* **cannons**
a big gun that fires heavy metal balls.

canoe *noun* **canoes**
a light, narrow boat that you move by using a paddle.

canteen *noun* **canteens**
a kind of café that sells food to people in a school, factory, or office.

canter *verb* **canters, cantering, cantered**
to go on a horse at a speed between trotting and galloping.

canvas *noun*
1 strong material for making things like tents.
2 material that you paint pictures on. *an artist's canvas.*

cap *noun* **caps**
1 a kind of hat, usually with a stiff brim at the front. *a peaked cap.*
2 a lid. *Put the cap back on the bottle.*

capable *adjective*
able to do something. *You're capable of better work.*

capacity *noun* **capacities**
the largest amount a container can hold. *The capacity of a milk bottle is one pint.*

capital *noun* **capitals**
1 the most important city in a country. *London is the capital of England.*
2 one of the big letters you put at the beginning of names and sentences. A, B, C, D, and so on are **capital letters.**

capsule *noun* **capsules**
1 something that looks like a sweet, but has medicine inside.
2 a separate part at the front of a spaceship. It can move on its own away from the main part.

capsule 2

captain *noun* **captains**
1 a person in charge of a ship or aeroplane.
2 someone in charge of a team. *He's the captain of the school football team.*

captive *noun* **captives**
a person or an animal that is not free.

capture *verb* **captures, capturing, captured**
to catch someone. *The police captured the thieves.*

car *noun* **cars**
a machine with an engine that you drive along the road.

caramel *noun*
soft toffee.

caravan *noun* **caravans**
a house on wheels that can be pulled by a car or truck from place to place.

card *noun* **cards**
1 thick, stiff paper.
2 a piece of card with a picture and a message on it. You send cards to people at special times like Christmas. *a birthday card.*
3 one of a set of small pieces of card with numbers or pictures on them, used in games. *a game of cards.*

cardboard *noun*
very thick, strong paper.

cardigan *noun* **cardigans**
a knitted jacket with buttons.

care *noun* **cares**
worry or trouble. *You should take more care over your schoolwork.*
to take care of something to look after it. *Sam took care of the puppy.*

care *verb* **cares, caring, cared**
to be interested or concerned. *He doesn't care who wins.*
to care for someone to look after them.

careful *adjective*
making sure that you do things safely and well. *Be careful when you cross the road.*
carefully *adverb*

careless *adjective*
not careful, making mistakes.
carelessly *adverb*

caretaker *noun* **caretakers**
someone whose job is to look after a building. *the school caretaker.*

cargo *noun* **cargoes**
things taken by ship or aeroplane from one place to another.

carnation *noun* **carnations**
a garden plant with white, pink, or red flowers that smell very sweet.

carnival *noun* **carnivals**
a colourful procession with people wearing fancy dress.

carol *noun* **carols**
a song that people sing at Christmas.

carpenter *noun* **carpenters**
someone whose job is to make things out of wood.

carpet *noun* **carpets**
a thick cover for the floor.

carriage *noun* **carriages**
1 one of the separate parts of a train where people sit.
2 a vehicle on wheels pulled by horses.

carriage 2

carried *verb* see **carry**

carrot *noun* **carrots**
a long, thin, orange vegetable.

carry *verb* **carries, carrying, carried**
to take people, animals, or things from one place to another. *I carried the books upstairs.*

cart *noun* **carts**
a kind of box on wheels. It is pulled by a horse or pushed by a person.

carton *noun* **cartons**
a box made of cardboard or plastic. *a carton of milk.*

cartoon *noun* **cartoons**
1 a film that has drawings instead of actors.
2 a drawing that tells a joke.

cartridge *noun* **cartridges**
a case or tube that holds film, tape, or ink.

carve *verb* **carves, carving, carved**
1 to cut wood or stone to make a picture or a shape. *carved out of wood.*
2 to cut off slices of meat.

case *noun* **cases**
1 a container. *a pencil case.*
2 a suitcase.

cash *noun*
coins or paper money.

cassette *noun* **cassettes**
a small flat box with a tape inside it for recording or playing sounds or moving pictures. You put it inside a cassette player. *a video cassette.*

cast *noun* **casts**
all the actors in a play.

cast *verb* **casts, casting, cast**
to throw.

castle *noun* **castles**
a large, strong building with thick, stone walls. Castles were built so that people could defend themselves against enemies.

casualty *noun* **casualties**
a person killed or injured in an accident or in a war.

cat *noun* **cats**
a furry animal with a long tail often kept as a pet.

catalogue *noun* **catalogues**
a list of things you can buy or look at. *a catalogue of library books.*

catapult *noun* **catapults**
a piece of elastic joined to a stick shaped like a Y for firing small stones.

catch *verb* **catches, catching, caught**
1 to capture. *The police caught the bank robbers.*
2 to get hold of something. *I'll throw the ball and you try to catch it.*
3 to get an illness. *I caught a cold last week.*

catching *adjective*
If an illness is catching it passes easily from one person to another. *I hope your cold isn't catching.*

caterpillar *noun* **caterpillars**
a long, creeping creature that will turn into a butterfly or moth.

cathedral *noun* **cathedrals**
a big, important church.

catkin *noun* **catkins**
one of the tiny flowers that hang down in groups on some trees.

cattle *noun*
cows and bulls kept by a farmer.

caught *verb* see **catch**

cauldron *noun* **cauldrons**
a large pot used for cooking. *a witch's cauldron.*

cauliflower *noun* **cauliflowers**
a vegetable with a thick white stalk covered in small, hard, white flowers.

cause *verb* **causes, causing, caused**
to make something happen. *The wind caused the door to slam.*

caution *noun*
great care.

cautious *adjective*
taking care, doing what is safe.
cautiously *adverb*

cave *noun* **caves**
a big hole under the ground or inside a mountain.

caveman *noun* **cavemen**
a person who lived in caves long ago.

cavern *noun* **caverns**
a big, deep cave.

CD
short for compact disc.

cease *verb* **ceases, ceasing, ceased**
to stop doing something.

ceiling *noun* **ceilings**
the part of a room above your head.

celebrate *verb* **celebrates, celebrating, celebrated**
to do something special on an important day or when you are happy about something. *What shall we do to celebrate your birthday?*

celebration *noun* **celebrations**
a party for something special.

celery *noun*
a vegetable with white stalks that can be eaten raw.

cell *noun* **cells**
1 one of the small rooms where prisoners are kept in a prison.
2 the tiniest part of a living thing.

cellar *noun* **cellars**
a room underneath a building, used for storing things. *a coal cellar.*

cello *noun* **cellos**
(*c-* in this word sounds like *ch-*)
a musical instrument like a big violin.

cement *noun*
something used in building to stick bricks together.

cemetery *noun* **cemeteries**
a place where dead people are buried.

centimetre *noun* **centimetres**
a measure for length. *My ruler is 30 centimetres long.*

centipede *noun* **centipedes**
a long, creeping creature with a lot of tiny legs.

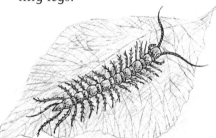

centre *noun* **centres**
1 the middle of something. *the centre of a circle.*
2 a place where you go to do certain things or to get certain things. *a sports centre, a garden centre.*

century *noun* **centuries**
a hundred years.

cereal *noun* **cereals**
1 any plant grown by farmers for its seed.
2 a food made from the seed of plants such as wheat and eaten at breakfast with milk.

ceremony *noun* **ceremonies**
something important and serious that is done in front of other people.

certain *adjective*
1 sure. *Are you certain?*
2 one in particular. *a certain person.*

certificate *noun* **certificates**
a piece of paper that says you have done something special.

chain *noun* **chains**
a line made of metal rings fastened together. *an anchor chain.*

chair *noun* **chairs**
a seat for one person.

chalk *noun* **chalks**
1 a kind of soft white rock. *chalk cliffs.*
2 a white stick used for writing on blackboards.

challenge *verb* **challenges, challenging, challenged**
to ask someone to try to do better than you at something. *He challenged me to a race.*

champion *noun* **champions**
someone who is the best in a sport or game, or who wins a competition. *a swimming champion.*

championship *noun* **championships**
a competition to decide who is the champion.

chance *noun* **chances**
1 a time when you can do something that you cannot do at other times. *This is our last chance to escape.*
2 the way things happen that have not been planned. *I saw him by chance on the bus.*

change *noun*
the money you get back when you give more money than you need to pay for something.

change *verb* **changes, changing, changed**
1 to make or become different. *Tadpoles change into frogs.*
2 to give something and get something in return. *They changed places with each other.*

channel *noun* **channels**
1 a narrow sea. *the English Channel.*
2 a groove in the ground that water moves along.
3 a television station. *Which channel shall we watch?*

chaos *noun*
(*ch-* in this word sounds like *k-*)
a very confused state. *There was chaos in the town when the traffic lights went out.*

chapel *noun* **chapels**
1 a kind of small church.
2 a small part of a church.

chapter *noun* **chapters**
a part of a book.
The book has ten chapters.

character *noun* **characters**
1 someone in a story.
2 the sort of person you are. *The twins look the same, but they have very different characters.*

charades *noun*
(*ch-* in this word sounds like *sh-*)
a party game in which you have to guess words from people's actions.

charcoal *noun*
a black substance made by burning wood very slowly. You can use it as a fuel in a barbecue.

charge *noun* **charges**
1 the cost of something.
2 a sudden rush.
to be in charge to have the job of organizing or looking after something. *Mum left me in charge of the washing-up.*

charge *verb* **charges, charging, charged**
1 to ask a certain price. *They charged £1 for an ice cream.*
2 to rush at something and attack it. *The bull charged.*

chariot *noun* **chariots**
a kind of cart with two wheels, pulled by horses.

charity *noun* **charities**
a group of people who raise money to help others.

charm *noun* **charms**
1 a magic spell.
2 a small ornament which you wear to bring good luck.

charm *verb* **charms, charming, charmed**
1 to cast a spell over someone or something.
2 to make people like you.

charming *adjective*
attractive, pretty.

chart *noun* **charts**
1 a big map. *Sailors use charts of the sea.*
2 a large sheet of paper with information on it. *a temperature chart.*

chase *verb* **chases, chasing, chased**
to run after and try to catch a person or animal. *I saw the cat chasing a mouse.*

chat *verb* **chats, chatting, chatted**
to talk in a friendly way about things that are not important.

chatter *verb* **chatters, chattering, chattered**
1 to talk a lot or very quickly.
2 to make a rattling noise. *His teeth chattered with fear.*

cheap *adjective* **cheaper, cheapest**
costing less than usual.
cheaply *adverb*

cheat *verb* **cheats, cheating, cheated**
1 to trick someone in order to get something from them.
2 to try to do well in a test or game by breaking the rules.

check *verb* **checks, checking, checked**
to go over something to make sure it is right. *Check your answers.*

checkout *noun* **checkouts**
the place in a shop where you pay.

cheek *noun* **cheeks**
1 the side of your face below the eye.
2 rude behaviour or speech.

cheeky *adjective* **cheekier, cheekiest**
rather rude, not showing respect.
Don't be cheeky to the teacher.
cheekily *adverb*

cheer *verb* **cheers, cheering, cheered**
to shout to show you are pleased or
that you want your team to win.

cheerful *adjective*
looking or sounding happy.

cheese *noun* **cheeses**
food made by stirring milk until it
becomes solid.

chemist *noun* **chemists**
someone whose job is to make or sell
medicines.

cheque *noun* **cheques**
a special piece of paper that a person
can sign and use instead of money.

cherry *noun* **cherries**
a small round red or black fruit with a
stone in it.

chest *noun* **chests**
1 a big, strong box.
2 the front part of your body between
the neck and the waist.

chestnut *noun* **chestnuts**
1 a kind of tree.
2 the shiny brown nut that grows on a
chestnut tree.

chew *verb* **chews, chewing, chewed**
to keep biting food while you eat it.

chick *noun* **chicks**
a young bird.

chicken *noun* **chickens**
a bird kept for its meat and eggs.

chicken-pox *noun*
an illness that gives you red spots that
itch.

chief *adjective*
the most important.

chief *noun* **chiefs**
the person in charge.

chilblain *noun* **chilblains**
an itchy swelling you get on your
hands or feet in cold weather.

child *noun* **children**
1 a young boy or girl.
2 a son or daughter.

childminder *noun* **childminders**
a person who looks after a child,
usually during the day.

chill *noun* **chills**
an illness that makes you shiver and
feel hot at the same time.

chill *verb* **chills, chilling, chilled**
to make something cold.

chime *verb* **chimes, chiming, chimed**
to make a sound like a bell. *The clock
chimed midnight.*

chimney *noun* **chimneys**
a tall pipe inside the wall of a house to
take away the smoke from a fire.

chimpanzee *noun* **chimpanzees**
an African animal like a large monkey
with long arms and no tail.

chin *noun* **chins**
the part of the face that is under the
mouth.

china *noun*
cups, saucers, and plates made of thin,
hard material. *China breaks easily.*

chip *noun* **chips**
1 a small piece broken off something.
2 a piece of fried potato.
3 a small electronic part in a computer
that makes it work. *a silicon chip.*

chip *verb* **chips, chipping, chipped**
to break or knock small pieces off
something. *This cup is chipped.*

chirp *verb* **chirps, chirping, chirped**
to make short, sharp sounds like a
bird.

chisel *noun* **chisels**
a tool with a short, sharp edge, for
cutting stone or wood.

chocolate *noun* **chocolates**
sweet food made from cocoa and
sugar.

choice *noun* **choices**
1 choosing. *You can have first choice.*
2 a number of different things to choose from. *There's a choice of vanilla, chocolate, or strawberry ice cream.*

choir *noun* **choirs**
a group of people who sing together.

choke *verb* **chokes, choking, choked**
1 to find it hard to get your breath because of something in your throat. *The smoke made him choke.*
2 to block up something. *The pond was choked with weeds.*

cholesterol *noun*
(*ch-* in this word sounds like *k-*)
a substance found in fat that can clog your arteries.

choose *verb* **chooses, choosing, chose, chosen**
to take one thing instead of another, because you want to. *He chose a chocolate cake. Which book have you chosen?*

chop *noun* **chops**
a small, thick slice of pork or lamb.

chop *verb* **chops, chopping, chopped**
to cut something with a knife or axe.

chopsticks *noun*
a pair of thin sticks held in one hand that Chinese and Japanese people use instead of a knife and fork.

chorus *noun* **choruses**
(*ch-* in this word sounds like *k-*)
the words repeated after every verse in a poem or song.

chose, chosen *verb* see **choose**

christen *verb* **christens, christening, christened**
to give a baby its name at a Christian ceremony in church.

Christian *noun* **Christians**
someone who believes in Jesus Christ.

Christmas *noun* **Christmases**
the 25th December when Jesus Christ's birthday is celebrated.

chrysalis *noun* **chrysalises**
(*ch-* in this word sounds like *k-*)
the cover a caterpillar makes round itself before it changes into a butterfly or moth.

chrysanthemum *noun* **chrysanthemums**
(*ch-* in this word sounds like *k-*)
an autumn flower with a lot of petals that grows in gardens.

chuckle *verb* **chuckles, chuckling, chuckled**
to laugh to yourself.

chunk *noun* **chunks**
a thick lump. *a chunk of cheese.*

church *noun* **churches**
a building where Christians worship.

churn *noun* **churns**
1 a large container for milk.
2 a machine for turning milk into butter.

cigar *noun* **cigars**
tobacco leaves that are rolled and then smoked.

cigarette *noun* **cigarettes**
a thin tube of paper with tobacco inside it for smoking.

a
b
c
d
e
f
g
h
i
j
k
l
m
n
o
p
q
r
s
t
u
v
w
x
y
z

cinders *noun*
the grey pieces left when coal has finished burning.

cinema *noun* **cinemas**
a place where people go to see films.

circle *noun* **circles**
1 a round shape like a ring or a wheel. The edge of a circle is always the same distance from the centre.
2 anything that makes this shape. *They danced in a circle.*

circle *verb* **circles, circling, circled**
to go in a circle.

circular *adjective*
like a circle. *A wheel is circular.*

circumference *noun* **circumferences**
the distance round the edge of a circle.

circumstances *noun*
the facts or details connected with something. *The police need to know the circumstances surrounding the accident.*

circus *noun* **circuses**
a show held in a big tent or building with animals, acrobats, and clowns.

citizen *noun* **citizens**
a person who belongs to a town, city, or country.

city *noun* **cities**
a big town.

claim *verb* **claims, claiming, claimed**
to ask for something that belongs to you. *She claimed her lost property.*

clamber *verb* **clambers, clambering, clambered**
to climb with difficulty, often using your hands to help. *They clambered over the rocks.*

clang *verb* **clangs, clanging, clanged**
to make a loud, deep ringing sound.

clank *verb* **clanks, clanking, clanked**
to make the hard sound that heavy metal chains make when they bang against each other.

clap *verb* **claps, clapping, clapped**
to make a noise by hitting the palm of one hand with the palm of the other.

clash *verb* **clashes, clashing, clashed**
1 to make the sound cymbals make.
2 to disagree with someone. *The girl and her mother clashed over which shoes to wear.*

clasp *verb* **clasps, clasping, clasped**
to hold tightly.

class *noun* **classes**
1 a group of children who learn things together.
2 a group of people or things that are the same in some way. *There are many classes of animals.*

classic *noun* **classics**
something that people remember because it is very good of its kind. *Mum says 'The Secret Garden' is a classic.*

classroom *noun* **classrooms**
a room where children have lessons.

clatter *noun*
a noise made when hard objects hit each other. *the clatter of horses' hooves.*

clatter *verb* **clatters, clattering, clattered**
to make the rattling sound a horse's hooves make on the road.

claw *noun* **claws**
one of the hard, sharp nails that some animals have on their feet. *The cat scratched me with her sharp claws.*

clay *noun*
a sticky kind of earth used for making things, because it keeps its shape and goes hard. *clay pots.*

clean *adjective* **cleaner, cleanest**
not dirty. **cleanly** *adverb*

clean *verb* **cleans, cleaning, cleaned**
to make something clean.

clear *adjective* **clearer, clearest**
1 easy to see through, not cloudy or dirty. *clear water.*
2 easy to see, understand, or hear. *a clear photograph, a clear voice.*
3 free from things you don't want. *a clear road.*

clear *verb* **clears, clearing, cleared**
1 to become clearer. *The water will clear when the mud settles.*
2 to get rid of things that are in the way. *Please clear the table.*

clench *verb* **clenches, clenching, clenched**
to close your teeth, fingers, or fist tightly.

clerk *noun* **clerks**
1 someone who writes letters in an office. *an office clerk.*
2 someone who deals with money in a bank. *a bank clerk.*

clever *adjective* **cleverer, cleverest**
if you are clever, you can learn things quickly and easily. **cleverly** *adverb*

click *verb* **clicks, clicking, clicked**
to make short, sharp sounds like the sound a light switch makes.

cliff *noun* **cliffs**
a steep hill made of rock close to the sea.

climate *noun* **climates**
the sort of weather that a place usually gets at different times of the year.

climax *noun* **climaxes**
the most exciting part of a story or an event, usually near the end.

climb *verb* **climbs, climbing, climbed**
to go up or down something high.

cling *verb* **clings, clinging, clung**
to hold tightly on to someone or something.

clinic *noun* **clinics**
a place where you can go to get help from doctors or nurses.

clip *noun* **clips**
1 a fastener for keeping things together or in place. *paper clips.*
2 a short piece from a film or TV programme.

clip *verb* **clips, clipping, clipped**
to cut with scissors or shears.

cloak *noun* **cloaks**
a very loose coat without sleeves.

cloakroom *noun* **cloakrooms**
the room where you hang your coat.

clock *noun* **clocks**
a machine that shows you what time it is.

clockwise *adverb*
the direction a clock's hands move in. *Turn the handle clockwise.*

clockwork *adjective*
worked by a spring which you have to wind up. *clockwork toys.*

clog *verb* **clogs, clogging, clogged**
to block up.

close *adjective* **closer, closest**
(rhymes with *dose*)
1 very near. *They got close to the fire.*
2 careful. *Keep a close watch on the puppy.*
closely *adverb*

close *verb* **closes, closing, closed**
(rhymes with *doze*)
1 to shut. *Please close the door.*
2 to stop being open so that people cannot go there.

cloth *noun*
material for making things like clothes and curtains.

clothes, clothing *noun*
things you wear to cover your body.

cloud *noun* **clouds**
1 something white, grey, or black that floats in the sky. Clouds are made of drops of water that often fall as rain.
2 dust or smoke that looks like a cloud.

a
b
c
d
e
f
g
h
i
j
k
l
m
n
o
p
q
r
s
t
u
v
w
x
y
z

39

cloudy *adjective* **cloudier, cloudiest**
1 full of clouds. *a cloudy sky.*
2 hard to see through. *cloudy water.*

clover *noun*
a plant with leaves like three small leaves joined together.

clown *noun* **clowns**
someone in a circus who wears funny clothes and make-up and makes people laugh.

club *noun* **clubs**
1 a group of people who meet together because they are interested in the same thing.
2 a thick stick used as a weapon.
3 a black clover leaf printed on some playing cards.
the ace of clubs.

clue *noun* **clues**
something that helps you to find the answer to a puzzle.

clump *noun* **clumps**
a group of trees or plants growing close together.

clumsy *adjective* **clumsier, clumsiest**
likely to knock things over or drop things, because you move badly.

clung *verb* see **cling**

cluster *noun* **clusters**
1 a group of things growing together. *a cluster of berries.*
2 a group of people, animals, or things gathered round something.

clutch *noun* **clutches**
part of a car which is worked by the pedal for your left foot.

clutch *verb* **clutches, clutching, clutched**
1 to snatch at something. *The drowning man clutched the rope.*
2 to hold tightly. *She was clutching her doll and would not let go.*

clutter *noun*
a lot of things in an untidy mess.

coach *noun* **coaches**
1 a bus that takes people on long journeys.
2 one of the separate parts of a train, where passengers sit.
3 someone who trains people in a sport.
a football coach.

coal *noun*
hard, black rock that is burned to make heat. *a coal fire.*

coarse *adjective* **coarser, coarsest**
1 not delicate or smooth, rough. *coarse material.*
2 in large pieces. *coarse sand.*

coast *noun* **coasts**
the edge of land next to the sea. *the west coast of Scotland. We went to the coast last Sunday.*

coat *noun* **coats**
1 a piece of clothing with sleeves that you wear on top of other clothes.
2 the hair or fur that covers an animal.
3 a covering. *a coat of paint.*

cobbler *noun* **cobblers**
someone whose job is to mend shoes.

cobweb *noun* **cobwebs**
a thin, sticky net spun by a spider to trap insects.

cockerel *noun* **cockerels**
a young, male bird kept with hens.

cocoa *noun*
a brown powder used to make a hot chocolate drink.

coconut *noun* **coconuts**
a big, round, hard seed that grows on palm trees. It is brown and hairy on the outside and it has a sweet white food and liquid inside.

cod *noun* **(the plural is the same)**
a large sea fish that can be eaten. *cod and chips.*

code *noun* **codes**
1 a set of signs or letters for sending messages secretly or quickly. *Morse code.*
2 a set of rules. *the Highway Code.*

coffee *noun* **coffees**
a hot drink made from roasted beans ground into a powder. *a cup of coffee, two coffees please.*

coffin *noun* **coffins**
the long box in which a dead person is put.

cogwheel *noun* **cogwheels**
a wheel with teeth round the edge, often used in machinery.

coil *verb* **coils, coiling, coiled**
to wind round and round in the shape of a circle or spiral. *The snake was coiled round a branch.*

coin *noun* **coins**
a piece of metal money.

cold *adjective* **colder, coldest**
not hot.

cold *noun* **colds**
an illness that makes you sneeze and blow your nose a lot.

collage *noun* **collages**
a picture made from small pieces of paper and material.

collapse *verb* **collapses, collapsing, collapsed**
to fall down. *The shed collapsed in the storm. People collapsed because it was so hot.*

collar *noun* **collars**
1 the part of your clothes that goes round your neck.
2 something that goes round the neck of an animal. *a dog's collar.*

collect *verb* **collects, collecting, collected**
1 to bring things together from different places. *I collect foreign coins.*
2 to go and get someone or something. *She collected the children from school.*

collection *noun* **collections**
1 a set of things that have been collected. *a stamp collection.*
2 money collected from many people for a special reason.

collector *noun* **collectors**
someone who collects things as a hobby or as a job.

college *noun* **colleges**
a place where you can go to study when you have left school.

collide *verb* **collides, colliding, collided**
to hit someone or something by accident, while you are moving. *The lorry collided with a bus.*

collision *noun* **collisions**
a crash between two moving things.

colon *noun* **colons**
a mark like this : that you use in writing

colour *noun* **colours**
any of the different effects you see from different kinds of light. Red, green, yellow, and blue are colours. *What is your favourite colour?*

colour *verb* **colours, colouring, coloured**
to use paint or crayon to put colour on something.

colourful *adjective*
1 full of bright colours.
2 lively, interesting. *Jo wrote a colourful description of the fair.*

column *noun* **columns**
1 things on a list each below the other.
2 a thick stone post that supports something or decorates a building. *Nelson's Column.*

comb *noun* **combs**
a strip of plastic, wood, or metal with a row of thin parts like teeth, for making hair tidy.

combine *verb* **combines, combining, combined**
to join or mix together.

combine harvester *noun* **combine harvesters**
a machine that cuts down corn and gets the seed out of it.

come *verb* **comes, coming, came**
1 to move here. *I came as soon as I could.*
2 to arrive. *Has the letter come yet?*

comedian *noun* **comedians**
someone who entertains people by making them laugh.

comedy *noun* **comedies**
a funny play.

comfort *verb* **comforts, comforting, comforted**
to be kind and helpful to someone who is hurt or ill or unhappy.

comfortable *adjective*
1 pleasant to use or to wear. *a comfortable chair, comfortable shoes.*
2 with no pain or worry. *Are you comfortable?*
comfortably *adverb*

comic *adjective*
funny.

comic *noun* **comics**
1 a paper with stories told in pictures.
2 a funny person.

comma *noun* **commas**
a mark like this , that you use in writing.

command *verb* **commands, commanding, commanded**
1 to tell someone to do something.
2 to be in charge of something.

comment *noun* **comments**
an opinion or a short explanation.

commentary *noun* **commentaries**
a description of what is going on. *a football commentary.*

commercial *noun* **commercials**
an advertisement on TV or radio.

commit *verb* **commits, committing, committed**
to do something. *to commit a crime.*

common *adjective* **commoner, commonest**
ordinary, usual.

commotion *noun*
a lot of noise and moving about.

communication *noun*
talking or writing to someone.

communications *noun*
ways of sending information from one place to another.

community *noun* **communities**
the people living in one place.

commuter *noun* **commuters**
a person who travels to work every day.

compact *adjective*
small and neat.
compact disc a kind of disc with music or other sounds recorded on it.

companion *noun* **companions**
a friend who is with you.

company *noun* **companies**
1 having an animal or another person with you so that you are not lonely. *The cat kept her company.*
2 a group of people who do things together. *a dance company.*

compare *verb* **compares, comparing, compared**
to try to see how like each other some things are.

compass *noun* **compasses**
an instrument with a needle that always points north. *The walkers used a compass to find their way home.*
a pair of compasses an instrument for drawing circles.

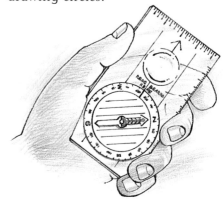

compel *verb* **compels, compelling, compelled**
to force someone to do something.

compete *verb* **competes, competing, competed**
to take part in a race or competition.

competition *noun* **competitions**
a test or game with a prize for the person who wins.

competitor *noun* **competitors**
a person who tries to win a competition.

complain *verb* **complains, complaining, complained**
to say that you are not pleased about something.
complaint *noun* **complaints**

complete *adjective*
whole, with nothing missing.
completely *adverb*

complete *verb* **completes, completing, completed**
1 to finish something. *You can play when you have completed your work.*
2 to make something whole. *I need one more piece to complete the jigsaw.*

complicated *adjective*
1 with a lot of different parts. *a complicated machine.*
2 difficult. *a complicated sum.*

compliment *noun* **compliments**
to pay someone a compliment to say something nice about someone.

composer *noun* **composers**
someone who writes music.

composition *noun* **compositions**
1 a piece of music.
2 a story you have made up and written down.

comprehensive school *noun* **comprehensive schools**
a school all children can go to when they are about eleven.

computer *noun* **computers**
a machine which stores information on tape or disk, organizes it and then produces it when someone needs it.

conceal *verb* **conceals, concealing, concealed**
to hide. *The money was concealed under the floor.*

conceited *adjective*
too proud of yourself and what you can do.

concentrate *verb* **concentrates, concentrating, concentrated**
to think hard about one thing. *I can't concentrate on my work!*
concentration *noun* Concentration is difficult when there is so much noise.

concern *verb* **concerns, concerning, concerned**
to be important or interesting to someone or something. *The information about the school trip concerned everyone.*

concerned *adjective*
worried. *When Katie was late home, her mother became very concerned.*

concert *noun* **concerts**
music played for a lot of people.

conclude *verb* **concludes, concluding, concluded**
1 to finish. *The festival concluded with a firework display.*
2 to form an opinion. *When you didn't arrive, we concluded that you'd missed the bus.*

conclusion *noun* **conclusions**
what you believe or decide after thinking carefully. *We came to the conclusion that you were right.*

concrete *noun*
a mixture of cement and sand used for making buildings, paths, and bridges.

condemn *verb* **condemns, condemning, condemned**
1 to say you don't like something. *We all condemn cruelty to animals.*
2 to say that someone is guilty. *The thief was condemned to spend three years in prison.*

condition *noun* **conditions**
1 the state something is in. *Is your bike in a safe condition?*
2 something you must agree to before something can happen. *You can go out to play on condition that you tidy your room first.*

conduct *verb* **conducts, conducting, conducted**
to stand in front of a band, choir, or orchestra and control the music the musicians play.

conductor *noun* **conductors**
1 someone who stands facing a band, choir, or orchestra and controls the music the musicians play.
2 someone who sells tickets on a bus.

cone *noun* **cones**
1 the shape of a witch's hat or an ice cream cornet.
2 a case for seeds on evergreen trees.

confess *verb* **confesses, confessing, confessed**
to say that you have done something wrong. *He confessed to breaking the window.*

confetti *noun*
tiny pieces of coloured paper that are thrown over a bride and bridegroom.

confident *adjective*
1 brave and not afraid. *Sam is a confident swimmer.*
2 sure about something. *Jo was confident that she knew the way.*
confidently *adverb*

conflict *noun* **conflicts**
a quarrel, a fight.

confuse *verb* **confuses, confusing, confused**
to mix people or things up. *He always confuses the names of the twins.*

congratulate *verb* **congratulates, congratulating, congratulated**
to tell someone how pleased you are about something special that has happened to them.
congratulations *noun Congratulations on winning the race!*

conjuror *noun* **conjurors**
someone who entertains people by doing tricks that look like magic.

conker *noun* **conkers**
the hard, brown nut that grows on a horse chestnut tree.

connect *verb* **connects, connecting, connected**
to join things together. *She connected the hose to the tap.*

conquer *verb* **conquers, conquering, conquered**
to beat an enemy in a battle or war.

conscience *noun*
a feeling inside you that tells you what is right and wrong. *Jo had a guilty conscience about breaking the window.*

conscious *adjective*
awake and able to understand what is happening around you. *After the operation he slowly became conscious.*

consent *verb* **consents, consenting, consented**
to agree to let someone do something.

conservation *noun*
taking good care of the world's air, water, plants, and animals. *conservation of the rain forest.*

consider *verb* **considers, considering, considered**
to think carefully about something.

considerable *adjective*
large. *These toys cost a considerable amount of money.*
considerably *adverb*

considerate *adjective*
kind and thoughtful in the way you behave.

consonant *noun* **consonants**
any letter of the alphabet except a, e, i, o, u and sometimes y.

constable *noun* **constables**
an ordinary policeman or policewoman.

constant *adjective*
going on all the time. *Constant chattering annoys the teacher.*
constantly *adverb*

construct *verb* **constructs, constructing, constructed**
to build. *a bridge constructed out of stone.*

consume *verb* **consumes, consuming, consumed**
to eat up, to use up.

contain *verb* **contains, containing, contained**
to have something inside. *The box contained toys.*

container *noun* **containers**
anything that you can put other things into. Buckets, cups, bags, boxes, and jars are all containers.

contented *adjective*
happy with what you have.
contentedly *adverb*

contents *noun*
what is inside a container or a book. *Be careful, the contents of this box are very fragile.*

contest *noun* **contests**
a competition.

continent *noun* **continents**
one of the seven very large areas of land in the world. *Asia is a continent.*

continual *adjective*
happening again and again. *continual interruptions.*
continually *adverb She is continually late for school.*

continue *verb* **continues, continuing, continued**
to go on doing something. *They continued the game after lunch.*

continuous *adjective*
going on without stopping. *a continuous noise.*
continuously *adverb It rained continuously for three hours.*

contradict *verb* **contradicts, contradicting, contradicted**
to say the opposite of what someone else has said. *I said it was her fault, but she contradicted me and said it was mine.*

contribute *verb* **contributes, contributing, contributed**
to give money or help to something.

control *verb* **controls, controlling, controlled**
to make someone or something do what you want. *I can't control my little sister.*

convenient *adjective*
easy to get at or use.
conveniently *adverb*

convent *noun* **convents**
a place where nuns live and work together.

conversation *noun* **conversations**
talking and listening to another person.

convince *verb* **convinces, convincing, convinced**
to make someone believe something. *He convinced her that ghosts were not real.*

cook *noun* **cooks**
someone whose job is to cook.

cook *verb* **cooks, cooking, cooked**
to get food ready to eat by heating it. *I'm learning to cook. I could smell something cooking in the kitchen.*

cookery *noun*
cooking food.

cool *adjective* **cooler, coolest**
not warm. *a cool wind.*

copper *noun*
a shiny brown or red metal. *The water pipes are made of copper.*

copy *verb* **copies, copying, copied**
1 to write down or draw what is already written down or drawn. *She copied the poem in her best writing.*
2 to do exactly the same as someone else. *She always copies what I wear.*

coral *noun*
a kind of rock made in the sea from the bodies of tiny creatures. Coral can be many colours.

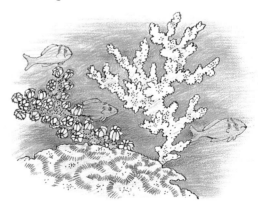

cord *noun* **cords**
thin rope.

core *noun* **cores**
the part in the middle of something. *an apple core.*

cork *noun* **corks**
a piece of the bark of a special kind of oak tree used as a stopper for a bottle.

corkscrew *noun* **corkscrews**
a tool for getting corks out of bottles.

corn *noun*
the seeds of plants such as wheat, barley, or oats, which we use as food.

corner *noun* **corners**
the point where two edges or streets meet.

cornet *noun* **cornets**
1 a wafer shaped like a cone, for holding ice cream.
2 a musical instrument made of brass, that you blow into.

coronation *noun* **coronations**
the time when someone is crowned as king or queen.

corpse *noun* **corpses**
a dead body.

correct *adjective*
without any mistakes.
correctly *adverb Have I spelt your name correctly?*

correct *verb* **corrects, correcting, corrected**
to show where the mistakes are in something and put it right. *The teacher corrected the homework.*

corridor *noun* **corridors**
a long narrow part of a building with rooms on each side of it.

cost *verb* **costs, costing, cost**
to have a certain price. *The bike cost £100.*

costly *adjective*
expensive, costing a lot.
costly repairs.

costume *noun* **costumes**
1 clothes worn for acting in plays or stories.
2 special clothes worn in a particular country. *the national costume of Japan.*

cosy *adjective* **cosier, cosiest**
warm and comfortable.
a cosy room.

cot *noun* **cots**
a small child's bed, with sides.

cottage *noun* **cottages**
a small house in the country.

cotton *noun*
1 thread for sewing.
2 cloth made from a plant that grows in hot countries.
cotton wool soft, white, fluffy stuff used for cleaning cuts, removing make-up, and other things.

couch *noun* **couches**
a long seat that you can sit or lie on.

cough *verb* **coughs, coughing, coughed**
to make a sudden, loud noise to get rid of something in your throat. Smoke and bad colds make people cough.

could *verb* see **can**

council *noun* **councils**
a group of people chosen to plan and decide what should be done in a place.

count *verb* **counts, counting, counted**
1 to say the numbers in order. *My little brother can count from 1 to 10.*
2 to use numbers to find out how many people or things there are. *I counted 10 fish in the pond.*

counter *noun* **counters**
1 the long table where you are served in a shop.
2 a small, round, flat piece of plastic used for playing some games.

country *noun* **countries**
1 a land with its own people and laws. England, Australia, and China are all countries.
2 land that is not in the town. *Do you live in the town or in the country?*

countryside *noun*
land with fields, woods, and farms away from towns. *We went for a picnic in the countryside.*

county *noun* **counties**
one of the large areas Britain and Ireland are divided into. *Devon and Cheshire are counties in England.*

couple *noun* **couples**
two people or things.
a couple of two. *I've only got a couple of sweets left.*

coupon *noun* **coupons**
a piece of paper which you can use to get something free or cheaper than usual, or to do something special. *If you collect ten coupons, you can send off for a free mug.*

courage *noun*
the feeling of not being afraid. *Katie showed a lot of courage when she had to go to hospital.*

course *noun* **courses**
1 the direction something goes in. *a ship's course.*
2 a piece of ground where some sport takes place. *a golf course.*
3 a series of lessons. *a swimming course.*

court *noun* **courts**
1 a piece of ground marked out for a game like netball or tennis.
2 the place where people decide whether someone is guilty of breaking the law. *a law court.*
3 the king and queen and the people who live with them. *the court of King Arthur.*

cousin *noun* **cousins**
the child of your aunt or uncle.

cover *noun* **covers**
a piece of material which goes over or round something. *The book has a picture of an elephant on the cover.*

cover *verb* **covers, covering, covered**
to put something over or round something else. *She covered him with a blanket.*

covering *noun* **coverings**
something which covers something else. *a covering of snow on the road.*

cow *noun* **cows**
a female animal kept by farmers for its milk.

coward *noun* **cowards**
someone who is afraid when they ought to be brave.

cowboy *noun* **cowboys**
a man who rides a horse and looks after the cattle on large farms in America.

crab *noun* **crabs**
an animal with a shell, claws, and ten legs that lives in or near the sea.

crack *noun* **cracks**
1 a narrow gap or thin line where something is nearly broken. *There is a crack in this glass.*
2 a sudden loud noise. *a crack of thunder.*

crack *verb* **cracks, cracking, cracked**
1 to get or make a crack.
This mug is cracked. Be careful not to crack the glass.
2 to make the sudden, sharp noise a dry twig makes when you break it.

cracker *noun* **crackers**
1 a paper tube with a toy and paper hat inside. It bangs when two people pull it apart.
Christmas crackers.
2 a thin biscuit that is not sweet.
You eat crackers with cheese.

crackle *verb* **crackles, crackling, crackled**
to make the cracking sounds burning wood makes.

cradle *noun* **cradles**
a baby's bed.

crafty *adjective* **craftier, craftiest**
clever in a sly sort of way.
craftily *adverb*

47

crane *noun* **cranes**
 1 a machine for lifting heavy things.
 2 a large bird with very long legs.

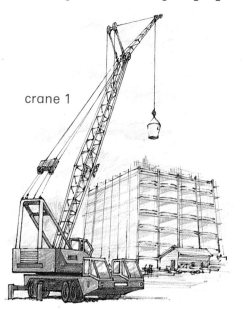

crane 1

crash *noun* **crashes**
 1 an accident in which a car, lorry, train, or plane crashes.
 2 the noise of something crashing. *I heard a loud crash as the tree fell.*

crash *verb* **crashes, crashing, crashed**
 to hit something with a loud noise.

crate *noun* **crates**
 a box for carrying bottles or other things.

crawl *noun*
 a way of swimming with your arms going over your head one at a time, and your legs kicking.

crawl *verb* **crawls, crawling, crawled**
 1 to move on your hands and knees. *Babies crawl before they can walk.*
 2 to move slowly. *The car crawled along in the fog.*

crayon *noun* **crayons**
 1 a stick of coloured wax used for drawing.
 2 a coloured pencil.

crazy *adjective* **crazier, craziest**
 likely to do strange or silly things.
 crazily *adverb*

creak *verb* **creaks, creaking, creaked**
 to make a rough, squeaking noise. *The door creaked as I opened it.*

cream *noun*
 the thick yellowish liquid that comes to the top of milk.

crease *verb* **creases, creasing, creased**
 to make a line in something by folding or pressing on it.

create *verb* **creates, creating, created**
 to make something no one else has made or can make.

creation *noun* **creations**
 something no one else has made or can make. *the creation of the world.*

creator *noun* **creators**
 someone who makes what no one else has made or can make.

creature *noun* **creatures**
 any animal.

credit card *noun* **credit cards**
 a piece of plastic with your name and a number on it that you can use to buy something and pay for it later.

creep *verb* **creeps, creeping, crept**
 1 to move along, keeping close to the ground. *We crept through the hole in the hedge.*
 2 to move quietly or secretly. *We crept away and nobody saw us.*

crept *verb* see **creep**

crescent *noun* **crescents**
 something shaped in a curve like a new moon.

crew *noun* **crews**
 a group of people who work together on a boat or aeroplane.

crib *noun* **cribs**
 a baby's cot.

cricket *noun*
 1 a game played in a field by two teams with a ball, two bats, and two wickets.
 2 an insect that makes a shrill sound.

cried *verb* see **cry**

crime *noun* **crimes**
 an activity such as stealing which is against the law.

criminal *noun* **criminals**
 someone who has done something bad that is against the law.

crimson *noun, adjective*
a deep red colour.

crinkle *verb* **crinkles, crinkling, crinkled**
to make small lines in skin or paper by creasing it.

cripple *verb* **cripples, crippling, crippled**
to hurt someone's legs so badly that they cannot walk. *She was crippled in an accident.*

crisp *adjective* **crisper, crispest**
1 very dry so that it breaks easily. *a crisp biscuit.*
2 firm and fresh. *a crisp apple.*

crisp *noun* **crisps**
a thin, crisp slice of fried potato.

criss-cross *adjective, adverb*
with lines that cross each other. *a criss-cross pattern.*

croak *verb* **croaks, croaking, croaked**
to make the hoarse sound a frog makes.

crocodile *noun* **crocodiles**
a large reptile that lives in rivers in some hot countries. It has short legs, a long body, and sharp teeth.

crocus *noun* **crocuses**
a small white, yellow, or purple spring flower.

crook *noun* **crooks**
1 someone who cheats or robs people.
2 a shepherd's stick with a curved top.

crooked *adjective*
not straight. *crooked teeth.*
crookedly *adverb*

crop *noun* **crops**
plants which are grown for food. *Wheat and potatoes are crops.*

cross *adjective* **crosser, crossest**
angry, in a bad temper.
crossly *adverb*.

cross *noun* **crosses**
a mark like x or +.

cross *verb* **crosses, crossing, crossed**
1 to move across something. *Take care when you cross the road.*
2 to make a shape like a cross. *Cross your arms.*
to cross something out to put a line through it.

crossing *noun* **crossings**
a place where you can cross a road or railway.

crossroads *noun*
a place where two roads cross.

crouch *verb* **crouches, crouching, crouches**
to lean forwards and bend your knees so that your bottom is almost touching the ground.

crow *noun* **crows**
a big, black bird.

crowd *noun* **crowds**
a large number of people.

crown *noun* **crowns**
a big ring of silver or gold worn on the head by a king or queen.

cruel *adjective* **crueller, cruellest**
very unkind.
cruelly *adverb*

cruise *noun* **cruises**
a holiday on a big ship.

crumb *noun* **crumbs**
a tiny bit of bread or cake.

49

crumble *verb* **crumbles, crumbling, crumbled**
to break or fall into small pieces.

crumple *verb* **crumples, crumpling, crumpled**
to make something very creased. *crumpled clothes.*

crunch *verb* **crunches, crunching, crunched**
to eat with the noise you make when you eat crisps.

crush *verb* **crushes, crushing, crushed**
to damage something by pressing it hard. *Carry the flowers carefully so you don't crush them.*

crust *noun* **crusts**
the hard part round the outside of bread.

crutch *noun* **crutches**
a stick that people who have hurt their legs can lean on when they are walking.

cry *verb* **cries, crying, cried**
1 to let tears fall from your eyes. *He was so upset that he cried.*
2 to shout.

crystal *noun* **crystals**
1 a material which is hard and clear like glass.
2 a small, hard, shiny piece of something. *crystals of ice.*

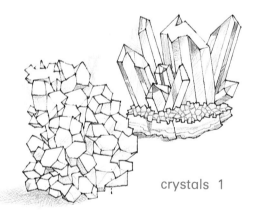

crystals 1

cub *noun* **cubs**
a young bear, lion, tiger, fox, or wolf.
Cub Scout a junior Scout.

cube *noun* **cubes**
the shape of dice or sugar lumps. Cubes have six square sides that are all the same size.

cuckoo *noun* **cuckoos**
a bird that lays its eggs in other birds' nests. It makes a sound like cuck-oo.

cucumber *noun* **cucumbers**
a long, green vegetable eaten raw.

cuddle *verb* **cuddles, cuddling, cuddled**
to put your arms round a person or animal that you love.

culprit *noun* **culprits**
the person who is guilty.

cunning *adjective*
crafty.
cunningly *adverb*

cup *noun* **cups**
a small bowl-shaped container with a handle, for drinking from.

cupboard *noun* **cupboards**
a piece of furniture or a space inside a wall. Cupboards have doors and usually some shelves.

cure *verb* **cures, curing, cured**
to make someone well again.

curiosity *noun*
a wish to find out about things. *Out of curiosity, he opened the letter.*

curious *adjective*
1 wanting to know about something, inquisitive. *Jo is curious to know what she'll get for her birthday.*
2 unusual. *a curious smell.*
curiously *adverb*

curl *noun* **curls**
a piece of hair twisted into rings.

curl *verb* **curls, curling, curled**
to twist or bend into the shape of a ring.
The cat curled up by the fire.

curly *adjective* **curlier, curliest**
with lots of curls. *curly hair.*

currant *noun* **currants**
a small, black, dried grape.

current *noun* **currents**
water, air, or electricity moving in one direction.

curriculum *noun* **curricula**
a statement of what schoolchildren are expected to learn. *the School National Curriculum.*

curry *noun* **curries**
a cooked food with a spicy flavour. *vegetable curry.*

cursor *noun* **cursors**
a mark which shows your position on a computer screen. *Move the cursor to the end of the line.*

curtain *noun* **curtains**
a piece of cloth pulled in front of a window or stage to cover it.

curtsy *verb* **curtsies, curtsying, curtsied**
to put one foot behind the other and bend the knees. *She curtsied to the Queen.*

curve *noun* **curves**
a line that is bent smoothly like the letter C.

cushion *noun* **cushions**
a cloth bag filled with soft material so that it is comfortable to sit on or rest against.

custard *noun*
a thick, sweet, yellow liquid poured over puddings.

custom *noun* **customs**
something that is usually done. *It is a custom to give presents at Christmas.*

customer *noun* **customers**
someone who uses a shop or a bank.

cut *noun* **cuts**
an opening in the skin made by something sharp.

cut *verb* **cuts, cutting, cut**
to divide something up, or make a hole in something, or change the look of something with scissors, a knife or something sharp.

cutlery *noun*
knives, forks, and spoons.

cycle *verb* **cycles, cycling, cycled**
to ride a bicycle. *Katie cycles to school every day.*

cygnet *noun* **cygnets**
(*c-* in this word sounds like *s-*)
a young swan.

cylinder *noun* **cylinders**
(*c-* in this word sounds like *s-*)
the shape of a tin of soup or a toilet roll.

cymbals *noun*
(*c-* in this word sounds like *s-*)
a musical instrument that is two round pieces of metal that you bang together.

Dd

dad, daddy *noun* **dads, daddies**
(*informal*) father.

daffodil *noun* **daffodils**
a yellow flower that grows from a bulb in spring.

dagger *noun* **daggers**
a very short sword with two sharp edges.

daily *adjective, adverb*
every day, happening every day.

dairy *noun* **dairies**
a place where people make cheese, butter, and other things from milk.

daisy *noun* **daisies**
a small flower with white or pink petals.

dam *noun* **dams**
a wall built to hold water back.

damage *verb* **damages, damaging, damaged**
to harm something, to break or spoil it.
The house was badly damaged in the fire.

damp *adjective* **damper, dampest**
a little wet, not quite dry. *Don't sit on the damp grass.*

dance *noun* **dances**
1 movements that you do to music.
2 a party where people dance.

dance *verb* **dances, dancing, danced**
to move about to music.

dancer *noun* **dancers**
somebody who moves to music.

dandelion *noun* **dandelions**
a wild plant which has yellow flowers, and balls of white feathery seeds which blow away.

danger *noun* **dangers**
1 the chance that something dangerous or nasty might happen. *That boy is in danger of falling off the wall.*
2 a person or thing that is dangerous. *Cats are a danger to baby birds.*

dangerous *adjective*
likely to kill or hurt you. *a dangerous road.*
dangerously *adverb*

dangle *verb* **dangles, dangling, dangled**
to hang loosely. *She sat on the fence with her legs dangling.*

dare *verb* **dares, daring, dared**
1 to be brave enough or rude enough to do something. *How dare you shout at me like that!*
2 to ask someone to do something to show how brave they are. *I dare you to climb that tree.*

daring *adjective*
very brave.

dark *adjective* **darker, darkest**
1 without any light. *a dark night.*
2 nearly black. *dark hair.*
3 not faint in colour. *dark red.*
darkly *adverb*
darkness *noun*

darling *noun* **darlings**
someone you love very much.

darn *verb* **darns, darning, darned**
to mend a hole in clothing with criss-cross stitches.

dart *noun* **darts**
a thing like a short arrow that you throw at a round board in the game of **darts**

dart *verb* **darts, darting, darted**
to move suddenly and quickly. *The cat darted across the road.*

dash *noun* **dashes**
1 a hurried rush. *We made a dash for the bus.*
2 a long mark like this —.

dash *verb* **dashes, dashing, dashed**
to move very quickly. *She dashed into the house.*

data *noun*
facts or information, especially information for use in a computer.

date *noun* **dates**
1 the day, month, and year when something happens. *What date is your birthday?*
2 an arrangement to go out with someone. *My sister had a date with her boyfriend last night.*
3 a sweet brown fruit that grows on a palm tree.

dates 3

daughter *noun* **daughters**
someone's female child.

dawdle *verb* **dawdles, dawdling, dawdled**
to walk too slowly. *Stop dawdling! We're late!*

dawn *noun*
the time of day when the sun rises.

day *noun* **days**
1 the twenty-four hours between midnight and the next midnight.
2 the part of the day when it is light.

dazzle *verb* **dazzles, dazzling, dazzled**
to be so bright that it hurts your eyes to look. *I was dazzled by the car's lights.*

dead *adjective*
not alive, not living.

deadly *adjective* **deadlier, deadliest**
likely to kill someone. *deadly poison.*

deaf *adjective* **deafer, deafest**
not able to hear.

deal *noun*
a good deal a great deal a lot

deal *verb* **deals, dealing, dealt**
to give out. *I dealt the cards last time.*
to deal with something to do what needs to be done with it.

dear *adjective* **dearer, dearest**
1 loved. *a dear friend.*
2 costing a lot of money. *Those trainers are too dear.*

death *noun* **deaths**
the end of life, dying.

debt *noun* **debts**
money that you owe someone.

decade *noun* **decades**
ten years.

decay *verb* **decays, decaying, decayed**
to go bad, or to rot.

deceit *noun*
making someone believe something you know is not true.

deceive *verb* **deceives, deceiving, deceived**
to make someone believe something which you know is not true.

December *noun*
the twelfth and last month of the year.

decide *verb* **decides, deciding, decided**
to make up your mind about something, to make a choice. *They decided to go to the park.*

decimal *adjective*
using tens. *the decimal system.*
the decimal point the dot you put after whole numbers when you write fractions like this: 2·5.

decision *noun* **decisions**
what you have decided.

deck *noun* **decks**
a floor in a ship or bus.

declare *verb* **declares, declaring, declared**
to say something out loud for everyone to hear. *The country declared war on its enemy.*

decorate *verb* **decorates, decorating, decorated**
1 to make something look smart or pretty. *We decorated the Christmas tree.*
2 to put paint or wallpaper on the walls of a room. *I'm helping to decorate my bedroom.*

decrease *verb* **decreases, decreasing, decreased**
to make or become less. *The car decreased speed to go round the bend. Temperature decreases as night falls.*

deed *noun* **deeds**
something special that you do. *a good deed.*

deep *adjective* **deeper, deepest**
going a long way down from the top. *deep water, a deep hole.*

deer *noun* **(the plural is the same)**
an animal that eats grass and can run fast. Male deer have horns called **antlers**

defeat *verb* **defeats, defeating, defeated**
to beat someone in a game or battle.

defend *verb* **defends, defending, defended**
to keep someone or something safe from attack.
defender *noun*

definite *adjective*
1 certain. *Is it definite that you can come?*
2 clear. *There is a definite improvement in your work.*
definitely *adverb I'm definitely going swimming tomorrow.*

defy *verb* **defies, defying, defied**
to say or show that you will not obey someone.
She defied her parents and stayed out late.

degree *noun* **degrees**
a unit of measurement for temperature or angles. You can write it using the sign °.
The temperature is 22° today. This angle measures 45°.

delay *verb* **delays, delaying, delayed**
1 to make someone or something late. *The train was delayed by heavy snow.*
2 to put off doing something until later. *We'll have to delay giving out the prizes until everyone is here.*

deliberate *adjective*
done on purpose.
a deliberate mistake.
deliberately *adverb*

delicate *adjective*
1 soft and fine. *a delicate flower.*
2 likely to get ill or broken.
a delicate child, a delicate vase, delicate machinery.
delicately *adverb*

delicious *adjective*
tasting or smelling very pleasant.
a delicious cake.

delight *verb* **delights, delighting, delighted**
to please very much. *The surprise gift delighted her.*

deliver *verb* **delivers, delivering, delivered**
to bring things like milk or newspapers to someone's house.

delivery *noun* **deliveries**
delivering something.
We're waiting for a delivery of bread.

demand *verb* **demands, demanding, demanded**
to ask for something that you think you ought to have.

demolish *verb* **demolishes, demolishing, demolished**
to knock something down and break it up. *The old house was demolished.*

demon *noun* **demons**
a wicked spirit.

demonstrate *verb* **demonstrates, demonstrating, demonstrated**
to show. *She's demonstrating how the computer works.*

demonstration *noun* **demonstrations**
1 showing people how to do something or how something works. *I'll give you a demonstration.*
2 a lot of people marching through the streets to show what they think about something.

den *noun* **dens**
1 a place where you can hide.
2 a place where a wild animal lives.

dense *adjective* **denser, densest**
thick. *dense fog, a dense crowd.*

dent *verb* **dents, denting, dented**
to make a hollow in something hard, by hitting it. *Cars are often dented in accidents.*

dentist *noun* **dentists**
someone whose job is to look after teeth. A dentist can take out bad teeth or fill them.

deny *verb* **denies, denying, denied**
to say that something is not true. *She denied breaking the cup.*

deodorant *noun* **deodorants**
something that removes smell.

depart *verb* **departs, departing, departed**
to go away. *The next train departs from platform 1.*

depend *verb* **depends, depending, depended**
to trust someone or something to give you the help you need. *The blind man depends on his guide dog.*

depress *verb* **depresses, depressing, depressed**
to make someone feel sad.

depth *noun* **depths**
how deep something is. *Measure the depth of the hole.*

descend *verb* **descends, descending, descended**
to go down. *The plane started to descend. He descended the stairs slowly.*

describe *verb* **describes, describing, described**
to say what something or someone is like. *Can you describe her?*

description *noun* **descriptions**
words that tell you about someone or something. *Write a description of your house.*

desert *noun* **deserts**
dry land where very few plants can grow.

deserted *adjective*
left by everyone. *a deserted house.*

deserve *verb* **deserves, deserving, deserved**
to have done something that makes people think you should get a reward or a punishment. *He was so brave he deserves a medal.*

design *verb* **designs, designing, designed**
to draw a plan or pattern for something.

desirable *adjective*
worth having or worth doing.

desire *verb* **desires, desiring, desired**
to want very much.

desk *noun* **desks**
a kind of table where you can read, write, and keep books.

despair *verb* **despairs, despairing, despaired**
to give up hope.

desperate *adjective*
wanting something very much. *She was desperate for a drink of water.*
desperately *adverb*

dessert *noun* **desserts**
sweet food eaten after the main part of a meal. *We had ice cream for dessert.*

destination *noun* **destinations**
the place you are travelling to. *It took all day to reach our destination.*

destroy *verb* **destroys, destroying, destroyed**
to break or spoil something so badly that it cannot be used again. *The house was destroyed by fire.*

destruction *noun*
the destroying of something. *the destruction of the rain forest.*

detail *noun* **details**
a tiny piece of information about something.
She could remember every detail about the house.

detective *noun* **detectives**
someone who tries to find out who did a crime.

detergent *noun* **detergents**
a kind of washing powder or liquid.

determined *adjective*
with your mind firmly made up. *determined to win.*

detest *verb* **detests, detesting, detested**
to hate.

develop *verb* **develops, developing, developed**
to grow or to become bigger or better. *Acorns develop into oak trees.*

device *noun* **devices**
something that has been made for a special purpose. *A tin-opener is a useful device.*

devil *noun* **devils**
a wicked spirit.

devoted *adjective*
caring and loving. *The little boy was devoted to his pet dog.*

dew *noun*
tiny drops of water that form during the night on things outside.

diagonal *noun* **diagonals**
a slanting line drawn from one corner of something to the opposite corner.

diagram *noun* **diagrams**
a kind of picture that explains something. *The car book had a diagram of an engine.*

dial *noun* **dials**
a circle with numbers round it, on things like clocks or speedometers.

a
b
c
d
e
f
g
h
i
j
k
l
m
n
o
p
q
r
s
t
u
v
w
x
y
z

dial *verb* **dials, dialling, dialled**
to make a telephone call by turning a dial or pressing buttons. *He dialled 999 and asked for an ambulance.*

diameter *noun* **diameters**
the distance across a circle, through the centre.

diamond *noun* **diamonds**
1 a very hard jewel like clear glass.
2 a shape with four sloping sides that are the same length. Some playing cards have red diamonds printed on them.

diarrhoea *noun*
an illness which makes you go to the toilet very often.

diary *noun* **diaries**
a book where you can write down what happens every day. *She kept a diary of her holiday.*

dice *noun*
small cubes with each side marked with a different number of dots, from one to six. You use dice in various games. *Throw the dice.*

dictionary *noun* **dictionaries**
a book where you can find out what a word means and how to spell it.

did *verb* see **do**

die *verb* **dies, dying, died**
to stop living.

diesel *noun* **diesels**
a kind of engine which uses oil as fuel.

diet *noun* **diets**
special meals that some people must have to be healthy. *She went on a diet to lose weight.*

difference *noun* **differences**
how different one thing is from another thing. *Can you spot the difference between these two pictures?*

different *adjective*
not like someone or something else. *She's very different from her sister.*

difficult *adjective*
not easy. *a difficult question.*

difficulty *noun* **difficulties**
something difficult.
with difficulty not easily.

dig *verb* **digs, digging, dug**
to move soil away to make a hole in the ground.

digest *verb* **digests, digesting, digested**
to change the food in your stomach so that your body can use it.
digestion *noun*

dignified *adjective*
looking serious and important. *a dignified old lady.*

dilute *verb* **dilutes, diluting, diluted**
to make a liquid weaker or thinner by adding water. You dilute orange squash before you drink it.

dim *adjective* **dimmer, dimmest**
not bright. *a dim light.*
dimly *adverb*

din *noun*
a loud, annoying noise. *Stop making such a din!*

dinghy *noun* **dinghies**
a small sailing boat.

dining room *noun* **dining rooms**
the room where people have their meals.

dinner *noun* **dinners**
the main meal of the day.

dinosaur *noun* **dinosaurs**
an animal like a huge lizard that lived millions of years ago.

dip *verb* **dips, dipping, dipped**
to put something into a liquid for a short time. *I dipped my toe into the water.*

direct *adjective*
as straight or as quick as it can be. *We walked the direct way home. This train goes direct from Oxford to London.*
directly *adverb* *We went out directly after lunch.*

direct *verb* **directs, directing, directed**
1 to show someone the way. *Can you direct me to the station?*
2 to be in charge of something. *to direct a play or film.*

direction *noun* **directions**
the way you go to get somewhere. *Which direction is your house?*

director *noun* **directors**
a person who is in charge of something.

dirt *noun*
dust or mud.

dirty *adjective* **dirtier, dirtiest**
marked with dirt or stains. *a dirty face.*

disabled *adjective*
not able to do some of the things other people can do, because you are ill, or because you have been injured.

disagree *verb* **disagrees, disagreeing, disagreed**
to think that someone else is wrong and that you are right.

disappear *verb* **disappears, disappearing, disappeared**
to go away and not be seen any more. *The kitten disappeared under the sofa.*

disappoint *verb* **disappoints, disappointing, disappointed**
to make someone sad by not doing what they hoped.
disappointing *adjective*

disappointed *adjective*
sad because something was not as good as you had hoped. *She was disappointed because she did not win first prize.*

disapprove *verb* **disapproves, disapproving, disapproved**
to have a poor opinion of someone or something.

disaster *noun* **disasters**
something very bad that happens suddenly.

disc *noun* **discs**
1 any round, flat object.
2 a record. *a compact disc.*
3 see **disk.**

discs 2

disciple *noun* **disciples**
a person who follows a religious leader.

discipline *noun*
behaviour which shows that you have been trained to be obedient.
Our teacher likes to have discipline in the classroom.

disco *noun* **discos**
a party where you dance to pop music on records.

discord *noun* **discords**
an ugly clash of sounds in music.

discourage *verb* **discourages, discouraging, discouraged**
to try to stop someone doing something by telling them how difficult or bad it is.
She discouraged her children from smoking.

discover *verb* **discovers, discovering, discovered**
to find out about something.

discovery *noun* **discoveries**
finding out about something.
Scientists have made an important new discovery.

discuss *verb* **discusses, discussing, discussed**
to talk about something with people who have different ideas about it.
discussion *noun* **discussions**

disease *noun* **diseases**
illness.

a
b
c
d
e
f
g
h
i
j
k
l
m
n
o
p
q
r
s
t
u
v
w
x
y
z

disgraceful *adjective*
so bad that it makes people ashamed of you. *disgraceful behaviour.*
disgracefully *adverb*

disguise *verb* **disguises, disguising, disguised**
to make yourself look different so that people will not recognize you. *The thief disguised himself as a policeman.*

disgust *verb* **disgusts, disgusting, disgusted**
to be so nasty that people hate it.
disgusting *adjective*

dishonest *adjective*
not honest.
dishonestly *adverb*

disk *noun* **disks**
a device for storing data for a computer.
disk drive a device for reading the data on a computer disk.

disk drive

dislike *verb* **dislikes, disliking, disliked**
to feel that you do not like someone or something.

dismal *adjective*
gloomy. *dismal weather.*
dismally *adverb*

dismiss *verb* **dismisses, dismissing, dismissed**
to send someone away. *The teacher dismissed the class at the end of the day.*

disorder *noun*
things in an untidy, confused state.

display *noun* **displays**
a show or exhibition.

display *verb* **displays, displaying, displayed**
to show, to make a display.

disposable *adjective*
made to be thrown away after being used. *disposable nappies.*

dissolve *verb* **dissolves, dissolving, dissolved**
to mix something in liquid so that it becomes part of the liquid. *You can dissolve sugar in hot tea.*

distance *noun* **distances**
the amount of space between two places.

distant *adjective*
far away.

distinct *adjective*
1 easy to see or hear. *The sound of the cuckoo was quite distinct.*
2 different. *The two teams wear distinct colours.*
distinctly *adverb*

distinguish *verb* **distinguishes, distinguishing, distinguished**
to see or hear the difference between two things or people. *Most people can't distinguish between me and my twin sister.*

distress *noun*
a strong feeling of sadness or worry.

distribute *verb* **distributes, distributing, distributed**
to share out, to give out.

district *noun* **districts**
part of a town, city, county, or country.

disturb *verb* **disturbs, disturbing, disturbed**
1 to stop someone from doing something. *Don't disturb the baby. She's asleep.*
2 to worry someone. *She was disturbed by the bad news.*

disturbance *noun* **disturbances**
something that upsets someone's peace or rest.

ditch *noun* **ditches**
a long, narrow hole dug to take away water from land.

dive *verb* **dives, diving, dived**
to jump head first into water.

divide *verb* **divides, dividing, divided**
1 to share something out. *Divide the sweets equally between you.*
2 to split something into smaller parts. *The cake was divided into eight pieces.*
3 to find out how many times one number goes into another. Six divided by two is three, 6 ÷ 2 = 3.

division *noun* **divisions**
dividing things or numbers into smaller amounts.

divorce *noun* **divorces**
the ending of a marriage.

Diwali *noun*
an important Hindu festival at which lamps are lit. It is held in October or November.

dizzy *adjective* **dizzier, dizziest**
feeling as if everything is spinning round you.

do *verb* **does, doing, did, done**
1 to carry out an action.
Jo does lots of jobs around the house, but her sister doesn't. What are you doing now?
2 to finish.
I did my work before I went out to play. Have you done your homework?

dock *noun* **docks**
a place where ships and boats are loaded, unloaded, or mended.

doctor *noun* **doctors**
someone whose job is to help sick people to get better.

dodge *verb* **dodges, dodging, dodged**
to move quickly to get out of the way of something.

doe *noun* **does**
a female deer, rabbit, or hare.

does *verb* see **do**

dog *noun* **dogs**
an animal that can bark, often kept as a pet.

dole *noun*
money paid to a person who cannot get a job.

doll *noun* **dolls**
a toy in the shape of a person.

dollar *noun* **dollars**
an amount of money. Dollars are used in the United States of America, Australia, and some other countries.

dolphin *noun* **dolphins**
an animal with warm blood that lives in the sea.

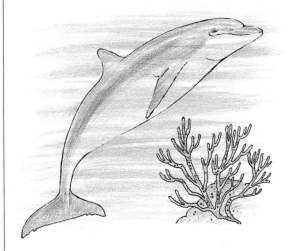

dome *noun* **domes**
a roof shaped like the top half of a ball.

domino *noun* **dominoes**
a small, oblong piece of wood with spots on it, used in the game called **dominoes**

done *verb* see **do**

donkey *noun* **donkeys**
an animal that looks like a small horse with long ears.

a b c **d** e f g h i j k l m n o p q r s t u v w x y z

59

door *noun* **doors**
something that opens or closes the way in to something. *a car door, the bathroom door.*

dose *noun* **doses**
the amount of medicine someone has to take.

dot *noun* **dots**
a small spot, like a full stop.

double *adjective*
twice as much or as many.

doubt *noun* **doubts**
the feeling you have when you are not sure about something. *If you are in doubt, ask your teacher.*

doubt *verb* **doubts, doubting, doubted**
to feel not sure about something. *I doubt that he will come to the party.*

doubtful *adjective*
not sure.
doubtfully *adverb*

dough *noun*
a mixture of flour and water. Dough is used for making bread and cakes.

doughnut *noun* **doughnuts**
a small cake that is fried and covered in sugar.

dove *noun* **doves**
a bird that looks like a small pigeon.

down *adverb, preposition*
to somewhere lower. *Run down the hill.*

down *noun*
very soft feathers.

downward, downwards *adverb*
moving to somewhere lower. *The bird flew downwards.*

doze *verb* **dozes, dozing, dozed**
to be nearly asleep.

dozen *noun* **dozens**
a set of twelve.
one dozen eggs.

drag *verb* **drags, dragging, dragged**
to pull something heavy along.

dragon *noun* **dragons**
a monster with wings, that you read about in stories.

dragonfly *noun* **dragonflies**
a brightly coloured insect that lives near water.

drain *verb* **drains, draining, drained**
to get rid of water or other liquid from something. *The water drained down the sink. We washed the plates and left them to drain.*

drake *noun* **drakes**
a male duck.

drama *noun*
acting in a play or story.

drank *verb* see **drink**

draught *noun* **draughts**
1 cold air that blows into a room.
2 one of twenty-four round pieces used in the game of **draughts**

draw *verb* **draws, drawing, drew, drawn**
1 to do a picture with a pen, pencil, or crayon.
2 to pull, to attract. *The pony was drawing a small cart. The fair drew a large crowd.*
3 to end a game with the same score on both sides. *We drew 1–1 on Saturday.*

drawbridge *noun* **drawbridges**
a bridge over the water round a castle. It can be pulled up to stop people getting into the castle.

drawer *noun* **drawers**
a box without a lid, that slides into a piece of furniture.

dread *noun*
great fear. *Cats have a dread of water.*

dreadful *adjective*
very bad. *a dreadful storm.*
dreadfully *adverb*

dream *noun* **dreams**
things you seem to see while you are asleep.

dream *verb* **dreams, dreaming, dreamed** or **dreamt**
to have dreams.

dress *noun* **dresses**
a garment for women or girls which has a skirt and also covers the top half of your body.

dress *verb* **dresses, dressing, dressed**
to put clothes on.

drew *verb* see **draw**

dribble *verb* **dribbles, dribbling, dribbled**
1 to let liquid come out of your mouth without meaning to. Babies often dribble.
2 to keep kicking a ball as you run along, so that the ball stays close to your feet.

drift *verb* **drifts, drifting, drifted**
to be carried gently along by water or air.
The empty boat drifted along on the sea.

drill *noun* **drills**
a tool for making holes.

drink *verb* **drinks, drinking, drank, drunk**
to swallow liquid. *Have you drunk your milk?*

drip *verb* **drips, dripping, dripped**
to let drops of liquid fall off.

drive *verb* **drives, driving, drove, driven**
1 to control a car, bus, train, or lorry.
Sam is learning to drive.
2 to make someone or something move.
We drove the cows into the field.

driver *noun* **drivers**
a person who drives a car, bus, train, or lorry.

drizzle *noun*
very light rain.

droop *verb* **droops, drooping, drooped**
to hang down weakly. *a drooping flower.*

drop *noun* **drops**
a tiny amount of liquid.
drops of rain.

drop *verb* **drops, dropping, dropped**
to fall or to let something fall.

drove *verb* see **drive**

drown *verb* **drowns, drowning, drowned**
to die because you are under water and cannot breathe.

drug *noun* **drugs**
1 a substance used to help you if you are ill or in pain.
2 a substance which affects your mind as if you were drunk.

drum *noun* **drums**
a hollow musical instrument that you bang with a stick or with your hands.

drunk *adjective*
not able to control what you say or do because you have drunk too much alcohol.

drunk *verb* see **drink**

dry *adjective* **drier, driest**
not damp or wet. *dry land.*

dual carriageway *noun* **dual carriageways**
a wide road with a strip of grass or concrete along the middle to separate traffic going one way from traffic going the other way.

duck *noun* **ducks**
a bird that lives near water. It has a wide, flat beak.

due *adjective*
expected. *The train is due now.*
due to caused by. *The accident was due to the thick fog.*

duel *noun* **duels**
a fight between two people using the same kind of weapon. *a duel with swords.*

dug *verb* see **dig**

dull *adjective* **duller, dullest**
1 not interesting. *a dull book.*
2 not bright. *a dull colour.*
3 not sharp. *a dull pain.*

dumb *adjective*
not able to speak.

dummy *noun* **dummies**
1 a piece of rubber made for a baby to suck.
2 a model of a person. You often see dummies in shop windows.

dump *noun* **dumps**
a place where people leave rubbish.

dump *verb* **dumps, dumping, dumped**
1 to leave something you want to get rid of.
I hate to see people dumping rubbish in a ditch.
2 to put something down quickly or carelessly.
I dumped my things on the table.

dungeon *noun* **dungeons**
a prison underneath a castle.

during *preposition*
while something else is going on.
I fell asleep during the film.

dusk *noun*
the dim light at the end of the day, before it gets dark.

dust *noun*
dry dirt that is like powder.

dustbin *noun* **dustbins**
a large container with a lid, for rubbish.

duty *noun* **duties**
what you ought to do.
It is your duty to look after your little brother on your way home from school.

duvet *noun* **duvets**
a cover for a bed instead of blankets.

dwarf *noun* **dwarfs**
a very small person.

dye *verb* **dyes, dyeing, dyed**
to change the colour of something by putting it in a special liquid.

dying *verb* see **die**

dynamite *noun*
something very powerful that is used for blowing things up.

Ee

each *adjective, pronoun*
every. *She gave each child a present.*

eager *adjective*
if you are eager to do something you want to do it very much.
eager to begin.
eagerly *adverb*

eagle *noun* **eagles**
a large bird that hunts and eats small animals.

ear *noun* **ears**
the part of the body used for hearing.

early *adjective, adverb* **earlier, earliest**
1 near the beginning.
early in the day.
2 sooner than we expected.
She came early.

earn *verb* **earns, earning, earned**
to get money by working for it.

earth *noun*
1 the planet that we all live on.
2 the ground or soil in which plants grow.

earthquake *noun* **earthquakes**
a time when the ground suddenly shakes. Strong earthquakes can destroy buildings.

easel *noun* **easels**
a stand for holding a blackboard or a picture while you work at it.

east *noun, adjective*
the direction where the sun rises in the morning.

Easter *noun*
the day when Christians specially remember that Jesus Christ came back from the dead.

easy *adjective* **easier, easiest**
1 if something is easy, you can do it or understand it without any trouble. *an easy sum.*
2 comfortable. *easy chairs.*
easily *adverb*

eat *verb* **eats, eating, ate, eaten**
to put food in your mouth and swallow it. *Have you eaten all the sweets?*

echo *noun* **echoes**
a sound that you hear again as it bounces back off something solid. You often hear echoes in caves and tunnels.

edge *noun* **edges**
the part along the end or side of something.
the edge of the cliff.

edit *verb* **edits, editing, edited**
1 to get a newspaper, magazine, or book ready for printing.
2 to put a story, film, or tape-recording in the order you want.

editor *noun* **editors**
the person in charge of a newspaper, magazine, or comic. Editors decide which stories and pictures will be printed.

educate *verb* **educates, educating, educated**
to teach people things they need to know like reading and writing.

education *noun*
the teaching and training you get in a school or college.

eel *noun* **eels**
a fish that looks like a snake.

effect *noun* **effects**
anything that happens because of something else. The effect of acid rain is to make trees die.

effort *noun* **efforts**
hard work at something you are trying to do.

egg *noun* **eggs**
1 an oval object with a thin shell, made by a hen and used as food.
2 one of the oval objects that baby birds, fish, insects, or snakes live inside until they are big enough to be born.

eight *noun* **eights**
the number 8.
eighth *adjective*

eighteen *noun*
the number 18.
eighteenth *adjective*

eighty *noun*
the number 80.
eightieth *adjective*

either *pronoun*
one or the other of two people or things. *There are two cakes. You can have either.*

elastic *noun*
a strip of material that can stretch and then go back to its usual size.

elbow *noun* **elbows**
the bony part in the middle of the arm where it bends.

elderly *adjective*
rather old. *an elderly man.*

elect *verb* **elects, electing, elected**
to choose somebody who will be in charge of something. *We elected a new captain of the football team.*

election *noun* **elections**
a time when people can vote to choose who will be in charge of their town or country.

electric, electrical *adjective*
worked by electricity. *an electric cooker.*

electricity *noun*
the power or energy used to give light and heat and to work machines. It comes along wires or from batteries.

electronic *adjective*
using electrical signals. TV sets, computers, and automatic washing machines have electronic devices inside them.

elephant *noun* **elephants**
a very big grey animal with tusks and a very long nose called a trunk.

eleven *noun*
the number 11.
eleventh *adjective*

elf *noun* **elves**
a kind of fairy.

else *adverb*
different, other. *Ask someone else. Let's do something else.*

embankment *noun* **embankments**
earth piled up to make a raised way for a road or railway, or to make the bank of a river stronger.

embark *verb* **embarks, embarking, embarked**
to get on a ship at the beginning of a journey.

embarrass *verb* **embarrasses, embarrassing, embarrassed**
to make someone feel shy and upset.
embarrassed *adjective*
embarrassing *adjective*

embrace *verb* **embraces, embracing, embraced**
to put your arms round someone to show you love them.

embroidery *noun*
pretty sewing that decorates something.

emerge *verb* **emerges, emerging, emerged**
to come out, to appear.

emergency *noun* **emergencies**
something very dangerous that suddenly happens. *Call the doctor, it's an emergency.*

emigrate *verb* **emigrates, emigrating, emigrated**
to go and live in another country.

empire *noun* **empires**
a group of countries ruled over by one person.

employ *verb* **employs, employing, employed**
to pay someone to work for you.

empty *adjective*
with nothing in it or on it. *an empty box.*

empty *verb* **empties, emptying, emptied**
to take everything out of something. *He emptied his pocket.*

emulsion paint *noun*
a kind of paint to go on walls and ceilings.

enchantment *noun* **enchantments**
magic, or a magic spell.

encourage *verb* **encourages, encouraging, encouraged**
to make someone brave and full of hope so that they will do something. *He encouraged me to dive from the diving board.*

encyclopedia *noun* **encyclopedias**
a book or set of books that tells you about all kinds of things.

end *noun* **ends**
the last part of something, the place where something stops.

end *verb* **ends, ending, ended**
to finish, to come to the end.

enemy *noun* **enemies**
1 someone who wants to hurt you.
2 the people fighting against you.

energetic *adjective*
full of the strength you need to do a lot of things.

energy *noun*
1 the strength to do something.
2 the power that comes from coal, electricity, and gas. It makes machines work and gives us heat and light.

engine *noun* **engines**
a machine that can make things move. *Most cars have petrol engines.*

engineer *noun* **engineers**
someone who makes machines, or plans the building of roads and bridges.

enjoy *verb* **enjoys, enjoying, enjoyed**
to like watching, listening to, or doing something. *Did you enjoy the film?*

enormous *adjective*
very big.

enough *adjective, noun*
as much as is needed. *enough money. I have had enough.*

enter *verb* **enters, entering, entered**
1 to come or go in.
2 to take part in a race or a competition.

enterprising *adjective*
willing to take a risk and try something new.

entertain *verb* **entertains, entertaining, entertained**
to make time pass very pleasantly for people. *The clown entertained the children.*

entertainment *noun* **entertainments**
anything that entertains people. Shows, circuses, plays, and films are entertainments.

enthusiasm *noun* **enthusiasms**
a very great interest in something.

enthusiastic *adjective*
so interested in something that you spend a lot of time doing it or talking about it.
enthusiastically *adverb*

entire *adjective*
whole.
The entire class was ill.
entirely *adverb*

entrance *noun* **entrances**
the way into a place.

entry *noun* **entries**
1 a way into a place.
2 going or coming into a place. *No entry!*
3 a person, animal, or thing in a competition. *There were many entries for the competition.*

envelope *noun* **envelopes**
a paper cover for a letter. *You write the address on the envelope.*

envious *adjective*
full of envy. If you feel envious, you want something that someone else has. *I'm envious because my brother has got a new bike.*
enviously *adverb*

environment *noun* **environments**
the world we live in, especially the plants, animals, and things around us which can make our lives nicer or nastier.
Jo thinks that planting more trees will improve our environment.

envy *noun*
a feeling you get when you would like to have something that someone else has.

episode *noun* **episodes**
one programme in a radio or TV serial. *We must wait until next week to see the next episode.*

equal *adjective*
the same as something else in amount, size, or value. *Everyone had an equal share of the cake.*
equally *adverb*

equator *noun*
an imaginary line round the middle of the earth. Countries near the equator are very hot.

equipment *noun*
the things you need for doing something. *sports equipment.*

errand *noun* **errands**
a short journey to take a message or fetch something for someone.

error *noun* **errors**
a mistake.

escalator *noun* **escalators**
a moving staircase.

escape *verb* **escapes, escaping, escaped**
1 to get free. *The prisoner escaped.*
2 to get away. *They escaped from the rain by going into a café.*

especially *adverb*
more than anything else. *I hate going to bed early, especially in the summer.*

essential *adjective*
necessary.

estate *noun* **estates**
1 an area of land with a lot of houses on it. *a housing estate.*
2 a large area of land that belongs to one person.

estimate *verb* **estimates, estimating, estimated**
to guess the amount, size, or price of something. *Estimate how much pocket money you can save.*

eve *noun* **eves**
the day or night before a special day. *Christmas Eve.*

even *adjective*
1 level or equal. *At half time the scores were even.*
2 that two will go into. 4, 6, and 8 are even numbers.
evenly *adverb Spread the butter evenly.*

evening *noun* **evenings**
the time at the end of the day before people go to bed.

event *noun* **events**
something important that happens. *Your birthday is a big event.*

eventually *adverb*
in the end.

ever *adverb*
at any time. *Have you ever climbed this tree?*
for ever always.

evergreen *noun* **evergreens**
any tree that has green leaves all through the year. *A Christmas tree is an evergreen.*

yew

spruce

everlasting *adjective*
lasting for ever.

every *adjective*
each. *I go swimming every week.*

everybody, everyone *pronoun*
every person.

everything *pronoun*
all things.

everywhere *pronoun*
in all places. *We've looked everywhere for the ball.*

evidence *noun*
anything that shows that something is true. *There was plenty of evidence that he was guilty.*

evil *adjective*
wicked.

ewe *noun* **ewes**
(rhymes with *you*)
a female sheep.

exact *adjective*
just right. *Add the exact amount of water.*
exactly *adverb*

exaggerate *verb* **exaggerates, exaggerating, exaggerated**
to say that something is bigger, better, larger, or more impressive than it really is.

exam, examination *noun* **exams, examinations**
an important test.

examine *verb* **examines, examining, examined**
to look at something very carefully.

example *noun* **examples**
1 anything that shows how something works or what it is like. *I copied the example from the book.*
2 a person or thing that should be copied. *He behaves so well he sets a good example.*

excellent *adjective*
very good.
excellently *adverb*

except *preposition*
not including, apart from. *Everyone got a prize except me.*

exchange *verb* **exchanges, exchanging, exchanged**
  to give something and get something in return.

excite *verb* **excites, exciting, excited**
  to give someone very strong feelings, to make someone excited.

excited *adjective*
  very lively, interested, and eager. *We're getting very excited about the party.*

excitement *noun*
  an excited feeling.

exclaim *verb* **exclaims, exclaiming, exclaimed**
  to make a sudden sound because you are surprised or excited. *'I don't believe it!' she exclaimed.*

exclamation mark *noun*
  exclamation marks
  a mark like this ! put after words to show that they have been shouted or are surprising.

excuse *noun* **excuses** (rhymes with *goose*)
  words that try to explain why you have done wrong so that you will not get into trouble. *Her excuse for being late was that she had missed the bus.*

excuse *verb* **excuses, excusing, excused**
  (rhymes with *choose*)
  1 to forgive. *Please excuse our dog's bad behaviour.*
  2 to allow someone not to do something. *I was excused from swimming because I had a cold.*

execute *verb* **executes, executing, executed**
  to kill someone as a punishment.

exercise *noun* **exercises**
  1 work that makes your body healthy and strong. *Take exercise to keep fit.*
  2 a piece of work that you do to make yourself better at something.

exhaust *noun*
  1 the gases that come out from an engine.
  2 the pipe that these gases come out of.

exhausted *adjective*
  tired out.

exhausting *adjective*
  making you very tired.

exhibition *noun* **exhibitions**
  a group of things put on show so that people can come to see them. *an exhibition of paintings.*

exist *verb* **exists, existing, existed**
  1 to be real, not imaginary. *Do fairies exist?*
  2 to live. *Camels exist in the desert.*

exit *noun* **exits**
  the way out of a place.

expand *verb* **expands, expanding, expanded**
  to get bigger. A balloon expands when you blow air into it.

expect *verb* **expects, expecting, expected**
  to think something is very likely to happen. *It is so cold I expect it will snow.*

expedition *noun* **expeditions**
  a journey made for a special reason. *a shopping expedition.*

expel *verb* **expels, expelling, expelled**
  to force a person to leave. *She was expelled from school.*

expensive *adjective*
  costing a lot of money.

experience *noun* **experiences**
  1 what you learn from things that you see and do. *The experience of living on a farm has made him fond of animals.*
  2 something that has happened to you. *a frightening experience.*

experiment *noun* **experiments**
  a test to find out whether an idea works. *a scientific experiment.*

expert *noun* **experts**
  someone who does something very well or knows a lot about something.

explain *verb* **explains, explaining, explained**
to make something clear to people so that they understand it.

explanation *noun* **explanations**
something said or written to help people to understand.

explode *verb* **explodes, exploding, exploded**
to make something burst or blow up with a loud bang.

explore *verb* **explores, exploring, explored**
to look carefully round a place for the first time. *Let's explore the cave.*

explosion *noun* **explosions**
a loud bang made by something bursting or blowing up.

explosive *noun* **explosives**
anything used for making things blow up.

expression *noun* **expressions**
the look on someone's face. *a happy expression.*

extent *noun*
the length or area or amount of something.

exterminate *verb* **exterminates, exterminating, exterminated**
to destroy completely.

extinct *adjective*
no longer existing. *Dinosaurs are extinct.*

extinguish *verb* **extinguishes, extinguishing, extinguished**
to put out a fire.

extra *adjective*
more than usual.

extract *verb* **extracts, extracting, extracted**
to pull out. *The dentist extracted one of my teeth.*

extraordinary *adjective*
very unusual. *The camel is an extraordinary animal. It stores water in its hump.*

extravagant *adjective*
spending more money or using more of something than people think you should.

extreme *adjective*
1 very great. *extreme cold.*
2 the furthest away. *the extreme corner of the playground.*
extremely *adverb*

eye *noun* **eyes**
1 the part of the head used for seeing.
2 the small hole in a needle.

eye 1

eyebrow *noun* **eyebrows**
the curved line of hair above each eye.

eyelash *noun* **eyelashes**
one of the short hairs that grow in a fringe around each eye.

Ff

fable *noun* **fables**
a story about animals that teaches people something.

fabulous *adjective*
(*informal*) wonderful.

face *noun* **faces**
1 the front part of your head
2 the front or side of something. *a clock face.*

face *verb* **faces, facing, faced**
1 to have your face towards something. *Can you all face the front of the class, please?*
2 to have the front towards something. *Jo's house faces the park.*

fact *noun* **facts**
something that we know is true. *It's a fact that the earth travels around the sun.*

factory *noun* **factories**
a building where people make things with machines. *a car factory.*

fade *verb* **fades, fading, faded**
to get paler or quieter so that it is harder to see or hear.

fail *verb* **fails, failing, failed**
1 not to do something you should do, or something you want to do. *Our team failed to win the match.*
2 not to pass a test or exam. *My brother failed his driving test.*

failure *noun* **failures**
someone or something that has failed.

faint *adjective* **fainter, faintest**
weak, hard to see or hear. *faint cries for help, a faint mark.*
faintly *adverb*

faint *verb* **faints, fainting, fainted**
to feel dizzy and become unconscious for a short time.

fair *adjective* **fairer, fairest**
1 light in colour. *fair hair.*
2 someone or something that is fair treats people equally or in the right way. *It's not fair if she gets more sweets than me.*
3 quite good but not very good. *She has a fair chance of winning.*

fair *noun* **fairs**
a place outside where you can go on rides and roundabouts and try to win things.

fairly *adverb*
to some extent but not a lot. *It's fairly warm today.*

fairy *noun* **fairies**
one of the tiny, magic people in stories.

faith *noun*
feeling sure that someone or something is good, right, and honest.

faithful *adjective*
always ready to help your friends and do what you promised to do.
faithfully *adverb*

fake *noun* **fakes**
something not valuable that is made to look valuable. *The painting was a fake.*

fall *verb* **falls, falling, fell, fallen**
to go down quickly, to drop. *She fell downstairs and broke her arm.*

false *adjective*
1 not real. *false teeth.*
2 not true. *He gave a false name to the police.*
falsely *adverb*

familiar *adjective*
well known to you. *a familiar face.*

family *noun* **families**
1 a parent or parents with a child or children.
2 a group of people or things who are closely related. *Lions belong to the cat family.*

famine *noun* **famines**
a time when there is very little food. *There is famine in many parts of Africa.*

famous *adjective*
very well known.

fan *noun* **fans**
1 something that blows air.
2 a person who supports someone or something. *Sam is a fan of our local football team.*

fancy *adjective*
decorated, pretty. *fancy cakes.*
fancy dress unusual clothes you dress up in for fun. *She went to the fancy dress party dressed as a witch.*

fang *noun* **fangs**
a long, sharp tooth. *the fangs of a wolf.*

fantastic *adjective*
(*informal*) very good, wonderful.
fantastically *adverb*

a b c d e **f** g h i j k l m n o p q r s t u v w x y z

fantasy *noun* **fantasies**
something you imagine, something that is more like a dream than real life.

far *adverb* **farther, farthest**
a long way. *Do you live far from the shops? Jo lives farther from the shops than I do.*

fare *noun* **fares**
the money people have to pay to travel on trains, buses, boats, or aeroplanes.

farewell *interjection*
goodbye.

farm *noun* **farms**
a piece of land where someone grows crops and keeps animals for food.

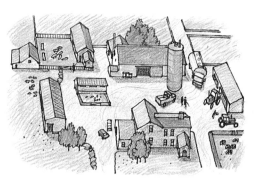

farmer *noun* **farmers**
someone who keeps a farm.

farther, farthest *adverb* see **far**

fashion *noun* **fashions**
the up-to-date way of dressing most people like and try to copy.

fast *adjective, adverb* **faster, fastest**
1 moving quickly. *a fast train. He can run fast.*
2 showing a time that is later than the right time. *My watch is fast.*

fasten *verb* **fastens, fastening, fastened**
1 to close something so that it will not come open. *Fasten the seat belt.*
2 to join something. *Fasten a badge to your jacket.*

fastener *noun* **fasteners**
something used for fastening things. *a zip fastener.*

fat *adjective* **fatter, fattest**
1 with a large, round body. *a fat person.*
2 having too much fat. *fat meat.*

fat *noun*
1 the white, greasy part of meat.
2 one of the greasy things you use in cooking, such as butter or margarine.

fatal *adjective*
causing death. *a fatal accident.*
fatally *adverb* **fatally wounded.**

father *noun* **fathers**
a male parent.

fault *noun* **faults**
1 something wrong that spoils a person or thing.
2 if something bad is your fault, you made it happen. *It's your fault we missed the bus.*

favour *noun* **favours**
something kind that you do for someone.
Please do me a favour and post those letters for me.

favourite *adjective*
liked the most. *Cats are my favourite animals.*

fax *noun* **faxes**
a copy of a letter or a picture sent using telephone lines and a machine called a **fax machine**

fear *noun* **fears**
the feeling you get when you think something bad is going to happen.

fear *verb* **fears, fearing, feared**
to be afraid of someone or something. *There is no need to fear the dark.*

feast *noun* **feasts**
a special meal for a lot of people.

feat *noun* **feats**
something you do that is brave or difficult. *Climbing Mount Everest was an amazing feat.*

feather *noun* **feathers**
one of the many light, soft things that cover a bird instead of hair or fur and help it to fly.

February *noun*
the second month of the year.

fed *verb* see **feed**

feeble *adjective* **feebler, feeblest**
weak.
feebly *adverb*

feed *verb* **feeds, feeding, fed**
1 to give food to a person or animal. *I fed the cat last night.*
2 to eat. *The pigs are feeding now.*

feel *verb* **feels, feeling, felt**
1 to touch something to find out what it is like. *The cat's fur feels soft.*
2 to know something inside yourself. *I feel happy.*

feeling *noun* **feelings**
something that you feel inside yourself, like anger or love.

feet *noun* see **foot**

fell *verb* see **fall**

felt *noun*
a thick cloth made from wool that has been pressed flat.

felt *verb* see **feel**

female *noun* **females**
any person or animal that can become a mother.

feminine *adjective*
belonging to women, like women, suitable for women.

fence *noun* **fences**
a kind of wall made of wood or posts and wire. Fences are put round gardens and fields.

fern *noun* **ferns**
a plant with leaves like feathers and no flowers.

ferocious *adjective*
fierce and dangerous. *a ferocious dog.*
ferociously *adverb*

ferret *noun* **ferrets**
a small animal used for catching rats and rabbits.

ferry *noun* **ferries**
a boat that takes people from one side of a piece of water to the other.

fertile *adjective*
able to grow a lot of healthy plants. *fertile land.*

fertilizer *noun* **fertilizers**
something you add to the soil to feed plants and make them grow better.

festival *noun* **festivals**
a time when people do special things to show that they are happy about something.

fetch *verb* **fetches, fetching, fetched**
to go and get. *Please fetch my coat.*

fête *noun* **fêtes**
a kind of party in the open air with competitions and stalls selling different things.

fever *noun* **fevers**
an illness that makes your body get hotter than it should.

fib *noun* **fibs**
(*informal*) a lie.

fibre *noun* **fibres**
1 a very thin thread. *cotton fibres.*
2 a substance in some foods which we need to digest things properly and make us healthy inside.

fiddle *noun* **fiddles**
(*informal*) a violin.

fiddle *verb* **fiddles, fiddling, fiddled**
to play with something with your fingers. *Stop fiddling with your hair!*

fidget *verb* **fidgets, fidgeting, fidgeted**
to keep moving about in an annoying way. *Please don't fidget!*

field *noun* **fields**
a piece of ground with a fence around it and crops or grass growing on it. *a field of corn.*

fierce *adjective* **fiercer, fiercest**
angry and dangerous. *Tigers are fierce animals.*
fiercely *adverb*

fifteen *noun*
the number 15.
fifteenth *adjective*

fifty *noun*
the number 50.
fiftieth *adjective*

fight *verb* **fights, fighting, fought**
to take part in a struggle, battle, or war.

figure *noun* **figures**
1 one of the signs for numbers, such as 1, 2, and 3.
2 the shape of a body. *a tall thin figure.*

file *noun* **files**
1 a line of people one behind the other. *Line up in single file.*
2 a flat tool that you rub against things to make them smooth. *a nail file.*
3 a box or cover that you keep papers in.
4 a collection of information on a computer.

fill *verb* **fills, filling, filled**
to make someone or something full. *Jo filled the jug with milk.*

film *noun* **films**
1 the thin roll of plastic you put in a camera for taking photographs.
2 moving pictures which tell a story, like those you see at a cinema or on television.

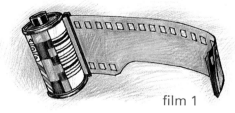
film 1

filthy *adjective* **filthier, filthiest**
very dirty.

fin *noun* **fins**
one of the thin, flat parts that stand out from a fish's body and help it swim.

final *adjective*
coming at the end. *The final word in this dictionary is zoom.*
finally *adverb*

find *verb* **finds, finding, found**
to see or get or come across something, either by chance or because you have been looking for it. *I found 50 pence on the ground.*

fine *adjective* **finer, finest**
1 very thin, very small. *fine hair, fine sand.*
2 dry and sunny. *fine weather.*
3 very good. *a fine piece of work.*

fine *noun* **fines**
money someone has to pay as a punishment.

finger *noun* **fingers**
one of the five separate parts at the end of the hand.

fingernail *noun* **fingernails**
the hard part at the end of each finger.

fingerprint *noun* **fingerprints**
the mark left on a surface by the tip of a finger.

finish *verb* **finishes, finishing, finished**
to end, to come to the end. *I've finished my work.*

fir *noun* **firs**
a tall tree that has cones, and leaves shaped like needles.

fire *noun* **fires**
1 something which is burning.
2 something which gives us heat. *a gas fire.*

fire *verb* **fires, firing, fired**
to shoot. *to fire a gun.*

fire engine *noun* **fire engines**
a large vehicle that carries firemen to put out fires.

firefighter *noun* **firefighters**
a person whose job is to put out fires.

fireman *noun* **firemen**
a person whose job is to put out fires.

fireplace *noun* **fireplaces**
the part of a room where you can have a fire.

firework *noun* **fireworks**
a thing that burns or explodes with loud bangs and coloured lights.

firm *adjective* **firmer, firmest**
something that is firm is hard and does not move easily. *That shelf is not very firm so don't put too many books on it.*
firmly *adverb*

first *adjective, adverb*
before all others.
A is the first letter of the alphabet.
I came first in the race.

first aid *noun*
help that you give to a person who is hurt, before a doctor comes.

fish *noun* **fishes** or **fish**
any animal with scales and fins that lives and breathes in water.

fish *verb* **fishes, fishing, fished**
to try to catch fish.

fisherman *noun* **fishermen**
a person who tries to catch fish.

fist *noun* **fists**
a tightly-closed hand.

fit *adjective* **fitter, fittest**
1 healthy, strong. *Swimming helps to keep you fit.*
2 good enough. *Is this old bread fit to eat?*

fit *verb* **fits, fitting, fitted**
to be the right size and shape. *These jeans don't fit me anymore.*

five *noun* **fives**
the number 5.
fifth *adjective*

fix *verb* **fixes, fixing, fixed**
1 to join firmly to something.
Fix the shelf onto the wall.
2 to mend.
She fixed the broken toy.

fizzy *adjective* **fizzier, fizziest**
with a lot of tiny bubbles that keep bursting.
fizzy drinks.

flag *noun* **flags**
a piece of cloth, often with a coloured design on it, used as a sign or signal. *Every country has its own flag.*

Union Flag
Scotland
China
United States
Australia
New Zealand
Italy
Wales
Eire
Pakistan
India
Barbados
Japan
Germany
France

flame *noun* **flames**
fire shaped like a pointed tongue. *a candle flame.*

flannel *noun* **flannels**
a piece of soft cloth used for washing yourself.

flap *noun* **flaps**
a flat piece of something joined along one edge so that it covers an opening. *The flap of an envelope.*

flap *verb* **flaps, flapping, flapped**
to move up and down like a bird's wings, or from side to side. *The sails of the boat flapped in the wind.*

flash *verb* **flashes, flashing, flashed**
1 to shine suddenly and brightly. *The lights flashed on and off.*
2 to appear for a very short time. *The cars flashed past.*

flask *noun* **flasks**
a container that keeps hot drinks hot and cold drinks cold.

flat *adjective* **flatter, flattest**
with no bumps or holes.

flat *noun* **flats**
a set of rooms to live in, which is part of a bigger building. *a block of flats.*

flatten *verb* **flattens, flattening, flattened**
to make something flat.

flatter *verb* **flatters, flattering, flattered**
to praise someone too much.

flavour *noun* **flavours**
the taste of something. *ten different flavours of ice cream.*

flavour *verb* **flavours, flavouring, flavoured**
to add something to food to make it taste different. *strawberry flavoured milk.*

flea *noun* **fleas**
a small jumping insect that sucks blood.

flee *verb* **flees, fleeing, fled**
to run away.

fleece *noun* **fleeces**
the wool that covers a sheep.

flesh *noun*
the soft part of your body between the bones and skin.

flew *verb* see **fly**

flight *noun* **flights**
1 a journey through the air made by a bird or an aeroplane. *a flight from London to New York.*
2 an escape.
a flight of stairs a set of stairs.

flimsy *adjective* **flimsier, flimsiest**
thin, not very strong. *a dress made of flimsy material.*

fling *verb* **flings, flinging, flung**
to throw something as hard as you can.

flipper *noun* **flippers**
1 a limb used by water animals for swimming. *Seals and penguins have flippers.*
2 something you can wear on your foot to help you to swim.

float *verb* **floats, floating, floated**
to stay on the surface of a liquid or in the air.
Wood floats on water.

flock *noun* **flocks**
a large group of sheep or birds. *a flock of seagulls.*

flood *noun* **floods**
a lot of water that spreads over land that is usually dry.

flood *verb* **floods, flooding, flooded**
to flow over its banks. *The river burst its banks and flooded.*

floor *noun* **floors**
the part of a building or room that people walk on.

flop *verb* **flops, flopping, flopped**
1 to drop down suddenly. *She flopped into a chair, feeling exhausted.*
2 to hang loosely. *My hair keeps flopping into my eyes.*

floppy disk *noun* **floppy disks**
a piece of flat plastic that stores information for a computer.

flour *noun*
a powder made from wheat and used for making bread, pastry, and cakes.

flourish *verb* **flourishes, flourishing, flourished**
to grow well. *The plants flourished.*

flow *verb* **flows, flowing, flowed**
to move along like a river.

flower *noun* **flowers**
the part of a plant that has petals and produces seeds.

flown *verb* see **fly**

flu *noun*
an illness that gives you a cold and makes you ache all over and feel very hot.

fluff *noun*
light, soft stuff that comes off wool, hair, or feathers.

fluffy *adjective*
light and soft like fluff.

fluid *noun* **fluids**
any substance that can flow, any liquid or gas.

flung *verb* see **fling**

fluoride *noun*
a substance which some people think helps to keep your teeth healthy.

flute *noun* **flutes**
a musical instrument which you hold to the side of your face and play by blowing across a hole.

flutter *verb* **flutters, fluttering, fluttered**
to make quick flapping movements. *The baby bird fluttered its wings.*

fly *noun* **flies**
a small insect with wings.

fly *verb* **flies, flying, flew, flown**
to move along through the air. *A blackbird flew across the garden.*

flyover *noun* **flyovers**
a bridge which takes one road over another.

foal *noun* **foals**
a young horse.

foam *noun*
1 a lot of small bubbles on top of a liquid.
2 a soft substance with a lot of small holes in it like a sponge.

focus *verb* **focuses, focusing, focused**
to set the lens of a camera, telescope or projector so that you get a clear picture.

fog *noun* **fogs**
damp air that looks like thick smoke and is difficult to see through.

foil *noun* **foils**
a sheet of metal as thin as paper.

fold *verb* **folds, folding, folded**
to bend one part of something on top of another part. *Fold up your clothes neatly please.*

folder *noun* **folders**
a large cover made of card for keeping your work in.

folk *noun*
people. *country folk.*

follow *verb* **follows, following, followed**
1 to go after.
A dog followed me.
2 to go along.
Follow this road.
3 to understand.
Did you follow what she said?

fond *adjective* **fonder, fondest**
liking someone or something a lot. *She's very fond of her pet dog.*

food *noun* **foods**
anything that you eat to help you grow and be healthy.

fool *noun* **fools**
someone who is very silly.

foolish *adjective*
silly.
foolishly *adverb*

foot *noun* **feet**
1 the part of the body at the end of the leg that you stand on.
2 a measure of length. There are 12 inches in one foot.

football *noun*
a game played by two teams who kick a ball and try to score goals.

for *preposition*
THIS WORD HAS SEVERAL USES. HERE ARE SOME OF THE WAYS YOU CAN USE IT: *This present is for me. This knife is for peeling potatoes. I bought some sweets for 50 pence.*

forbid *verb* **forbids, forbidding, forbade, forbidden**
to say that someone must not do something. *Walking on the grass is forbidden.*

force *noun* **forces**
1 strength, power, violence. *They had to use force to open the door.*
2 an organized group of people, such as police or an army.

force *verb* **forces, forcing, forced**
to use power or violence to make a person or thing do what you want. *They forced him to give them the money.*

forecast *noun* **forecasts**
a statement about what someone thinks is going to happen. *a weather forecast.*

forehead *noun* **foreheads**
the part of the face above the eyebrows.

foreign *adjective*
belonging to another country. *a foreign language.*

foreigner *noun* **foreigners**
a person who comes from another country.

forest *noun* **forests**
a lot of trees growing together.

forge *verb* **forges, forging, forged**
to copy something because you want to trick people.
He was put in prison for forging £10 notes.

forgery *noun* **forgeries**
a forged copy of something. *This £10 note is a forgery.*

forget *verb* **forgets, forgetting, forgot, forgotten**
to fail to remember.
I forgot my money. I have forgotten her name.

forgive *verb* **forgives, forgiving, forgave, forgiven**
to stop being angry with someone.
I forgave him when he said sorry.

forgot, forgotten *verb* see **forget**

fork *noun* **forks**
a tool with three or four thin pointed parts called prongs.

form *noun* **forms**
1 the shape something has. *a birthday cake in the form of a train.*
2 a long wooden seat without a back.
3 one of the classes in a school.
4 a printed paper with spaces where you have to write.

formal *adjective*
being very correct in what you say, do, or wear, because something important is happening.

fort *noun* **forts**
a strong building with soldiers in it, made to protect a place against enemies.

fortnight *noun* **fortnights**
two weeks. *We are going on holiday for a fortnight.*

fortress *noun* **fortresses**
a big fort.

fortunate *adjective*
lucky.
fortunately *adverb*

fortune *noun* **fortunes**
1 a lot of money.
2 luck. *By good fortune, I met her in town.*

forty *noun*
the number 40.
fortieth *adjective*

forward, forwards *adverb*
in the direction that is in front of you.
to look forward to wait for something with pleasure.

fossil *noun* **fossils**
part of a dead plant or animal that has been in the ground for millions of years and has become hard like rock.

foster *verb* **fosters, fostering, fostered**
to care for someone else's child as if he or she was one of your own family.

fought *verb* see **fight**

foul *adjective* **fouler, foulest**
1 dirty and nasty. *a foul smell.*
2 (*informal*) bad. *foul weather.*
3 against the rules. *foul play.*

found *verb* see **find**

foundations *noun*
the solid part under the ground that a building is built on.

fountain *noun* **fountains**
water that shoots up into the air.

four *noun* **fours**
the number 4.
fourth *adjective*

fourteen *noun*
the number 14.
fourteenth *adjective*

fox *noun* **foxes**
a wild animal that looks like a dog and has a long, furry tail.

fraction *noun* **fractions**
1 a number that is not a whole number. $\frac{1}{2}$, $\frac{5}{3}$, and $\frac{1}{4}$ are fractions.
2 a small part of something.

fracture *noun* **fractures**
a place where something is broken, especially a bone.

fragile *adjective*
easily broken. *Glass is fragile.*

fragment *noun* **fragments**
a small piece that has been broken off.

frail *adjective* **frailer, frailest**
not strong or healthy.

frame *noun* **frames**
1 a structure made of rods or bars, often to support something.
2 something that fits round a picture or round the lenses of a pair of glasses.

fraud *noun* **frauds**
a trick or a person who tries to cheat someone.

freckle *noun* **freckles**
one of the small brown spots people sometimes get on their skin, when they have been in the sun.

free *adjective* **freer, freest**
1 able to do what you want or go where you want.
2 not costing anything.
a free gift.

free *verb* **frees, freeing, freed**
to let a person or animal go free after being shut in somewhere.

freeze *verb* **freezes, freezing, froze, frozen**
1 to change into ice.
2 to be very cold. *Your hands will be frozen if you don't wear gloves.*

freezer *noun* **freezers**
a large refrigerator used for keeping food very cold for a long time.

frequent *adjective*
happening often.
frequent showers.
frequently *adverb*

fresh *adjective* **fresher, freshest**
1 new. *fresh bread.*
2 clean and cool. *fresh air.*
3 not tired. *fresh after a rest.*
freshly *adverb*

Friday *noun* **Fridays**
the sixth day of the week.

friend *noun* **friends**
someone you like who likes you. Friends like doing things together.

friendly *adjective* **friendlier, friendliest**
behaving like a friend.

frieze *noun* **friezes**
a wide strip of pictures along the top of a wall.

fright *noun* **frights**
sudden fear. *That loud noise gave me a fright.*

frighten *verb* **frightens, frightening, frightened**
to make someone afraid. *He's frightened of spiders.*
frightened *adjective*
frightening *adjective*

frill *noun* **frills**
a strip of material with folds in it. Frills are stitched to the edges of things to decorate them.

fringe *noun* **fringes**
1 an edge.
2 short hair that hangs over your forehead.

frog *noun* **frogs**
a small animal with a smooth, wet skin. Frogs live near water and jump.

front *noun* **fronts**
the side that people usually see first. *the front of the house.*

frost *noun* **frosts**
ice that looks like powder and covers things when the weather is very cold.

froth *noun*
a lot of small bubbles on the top of a liquid.

frown *verb* **frowns, frowning, frowned**
to have lines on your forehead because you are angry or worried.

froze, frozen *verb* see **freeze**

fruit *noun* **fruits** or **fruit**
the part of a plant which contains seeds and is often used as food.

fry *verb* **fries, frying, fried**
to cook in hot fat in a pan on top of a stove. *fried eggs.*

frying pan *noun* **frying pans**
a large, shallow pan.

fudge *noun*
a kind of soft, very sweet toffee.

fuel *noun* **fuels**
anything that is burnt to make heat. *Coal is a fuel.*

full *adjective* **fuller, fullest**
holding as much as possible. *The bus was full. A cup full of milk.*
full stop the dot which you put at the end of every sentence.

fumes *noun*
gases and smoke, which usually smell nasty. *car fumes.*

fun *noun*
amusement, enjoying yourself. *We had great fun on the beach.*

fund *noun* **funds**
money that will be used for something special.

funeral *noun* **funerals**
the ceremony when a dead person is buried or burned.

fungus *noun* **fungi**
a kind of plant that is not green and grows in damp places. Mushrooms and toadstools are both **fungi**

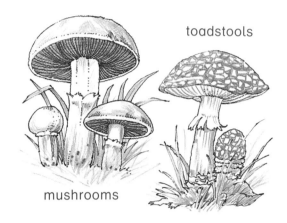
toadstools
mushrooms

funnel *noun* **funnels**
1 a chimney on a ship or steam engine.
2 a tube with one very wide end to help you pour things into bottles.

funny *adjective* **funnier, funniest**
1 a person or thing that is funny, makes you laugh, or makes you smile. *a funny joke.*
2 strange. *a funny smell.*

fur *noun* **furs**
the soft hair that covers some animals.

furious *adjective*
very angry.
furiously *adverb*

furniture *noun*
things such as beds and tables that you need inside a house.

furrow *noun* **furrows**
the straight, narrow hollow made in the ground by a plough.

furry *adjective* **furrier, furriest**
covered in fur.

further *adjective, adverb*
to a greater distance. *I swam further than you.*

fuse *noun* **fuses**
1 a safety device fitted in electrical equipment. Plugs usually have fuses in them.
2 a thing used to set off an explosion.

fuss *verb* **fusses, fussing, fussed**
to worry and bother too much about something that is not important.

fussy *adjective* **fussier, fussiest**
hard to please, always fussing.

future *noun*
the time that will come. *Nobody knows what will happen in the future.*

fuzzy *adjective* **fuzzier, fuzziest**
not clear.
The TV picture is fuzzy.

Gg

gadget *noun* **gadgets**
a small, useful tool.
A penknife is a useful gadget.

gain *verb* **gains, gaining, gained**
to get something that you need or that you did not have before.
We gained more points than the other team.

galaxy *noun* **galaxies**
a large group of stars and planets. The Milky Way is a galaxy.

gale *noun* **gales**
a very strong wind.

gallery *noun* **galleries**
a building or long room where paintings are shown. *an art gallery.*

gallon *noun* **gallons**
a measure for liquids. There are eight pints in one gallon.

gallop *verb* **gallops, galloping, galloped**
to go at the fastest speed a horse can go.

gamble *verb* **gambles, gambling, gambled**
to attempt to win money by playing a game that needs luck.

game *noun* **games**
something that you play at that has rules. *a game of tennis, a card game.*

gander *noun* **ganders**
a male goose.

gang *noun* **gangs**
a group of people who do things together.

gangster *noun* **gangsters**
someone who belongs to a gang that robs and kills people.

gaol *noun* **gaols** (say *jail*)
prison.

gap *noun* **gaps**
an empty space or time between two things. *We went through a gap in the fence.*

gape *verb* **gapes, gaping, gaped**
1 to open your mouth wide with surprise. *Sam just gaped at us when we told him he'd won.*
2 to be wide open. *He fell down a big gaping hole in the ground.*

garage *noun* **garages**
1 the building where a car or bus is kept.
2 a place that sells petrol and mends cars.

garden *noun* **gardens**
a piece of ground where flowers, fruit, or vegetables are grown.

gargle *verb* **gargles, gargling, gargled**
to wash your throat by moving liquid around inside it then spitting it out.

garment *noun* **garments**
any piece of clothing. Shirts, coats, and jeans are all garments.

gas *noun* **gases**
1 any substance that can move about like air.
2 a gas that we burn to make heat. *a gas fire.*

gash *noun* **gashes**
a deep cut. *She fell over and got a nasty gash on her forehead.*

gasp *verb* **gasps, gasping, gasped**
to breathe in noisily and quickly because you are surprised or ill, or because you have been running. *'I can't run any further,' she gasped.*

a
b
c
d
e
f
g
h
i
j
k
l
m
n
o
p
q
r
s
t
u
v
w
x
y
z

gate *noun* **gates**
a kind of door in a wall or fence round a piece of land.

gather *verb* **gathers, gathering, gathered**
1 to come together.
A crowd gathered to watch the fight.
2 to bring together, to collect.
We gathered information for our project.

gave *verb* see **give**

gaze *verb* **gazes, gazing, gazed**
to look at something for a long time.

gear *noun* **gears**
1 part of a bicycle or car. Gears help to control the speed of the wheels so that it is easier to go up and down hills.
2 the things needed for a job or sport.
hockey gear.

gem *noun* **gems**
a valuable or beautiful stone.

general *adjective*
1 concerning most people or things.
All grown-ups can vote in a general election.
2 not going into details.
He gave us a general idea of what he wanted.
generally *adverb*

general *noun* **generals**
an important officer in the army.

generous *adjective*
always ready to give or share what you have.
generously *adverb*

gentle *adjective* **gentler, gentlest**
quiet and kind, not rough.
gently *adverb*

gentleman *noun* **gentlemen**
a polite name for a man.

genuine *adjective*
real.
genuine gold.

geography *noun*
the study of the earth, with its mountains, rivers, countries, and the people who live in them.

geranium *noun* **geraniums**
a plant with red, pink, or white flowers that is often grown in a pot.

gerbil *noun* **gerbils**
a small, brown animal with long back legs, often kept as a pet.

germ *noun* **germs**
a tiny living thing, too small to see. Germs sometimes cause diseases.

get *verb* **gets, getting, got**
1 to receive, buy, or earn. *What did you get for your birthday? I'm going to the shop to get some food. Jo got £2 for washing the car.*
2 to become. *I got cold waiting outside.*

ghost *noun* **ghosts**
the shape of a dead person that people think they have seen.

giant *noun* **giants**
a very big person.

giddy *adjective* **giddier, giddiest**
dizzy.

gift *noun* **gifts**
a present. *a birthday gift.*

gigantic *adjective*
very big.

giggle *verb* **giggles, giggling, giggled**
to laugh in a silly way.

gill *noun* **gills**
the part on each side of a fish that it breathes through.

ginger *noun*
a spice with a strong, hot taste.

gingerbread *noun*
a kind of cake or biscuit made with ginger.

giraffe *noun* **giraffes**
a very tall African animal with a very long neck.

girl *noun* **girls**
a female child or young person.

give *verb* **gives, giving, gave, given**
to let someone have something. *I gave Sam a present.*

glacier *noun* **glaciers**
a river of ice that moves very slowly down a mountain.

glad *adjective*
happy.
gladly *adverb*

glance *verb* **glances, glancing, glanced**
to look at something quickly.

glare *verb* **glares, glaring, glared**
1 to shine very brightly. *The sun glared down on us.*
2 to look angrily at someone. *They stood glaring at each other.*

glass *noun* **glasses**
1 a very hard substance that you can see through, used for making windows.
2 a kind of cup without a handle, made of glass.

glasses *noun*
a pair of lenses held in front of the eyes by a frame that fits over your nose and ears. Glasses help you see better.

glide *verb* **glides, gliding, glided**
to move very smoothly. *gliding on skates.*

glider *noun* **gliders**
a kind of aeroplane without an engine.

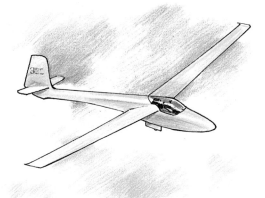

glimpse *verb* **glimpses, glimpsing, glimpsed**
to see something for only a few seconds. *She glimpsed the pony from the window of the train.*

glisten *verb* **glistens, glistening, glistened**
to shine like something with drops of water on it. *The grass glistened with dew.*

glitter *verb* **glitters, glittering, glittered**
to shine with a bright light that keeps coming and going. *glittering jewels.*

globe *noun* **globes**
a ball with the map of the whole world on it.

gloomy *adjective* **gloomier, gloomiest**
1 dark. *a gloomy room.*
2 sad. *a gloomy face.*

glory *noun*
1 great fame. *the glory of winning the Olympics.*
2 great beauty. *the glory of the woods in autumn.*

glossy *adjective* **glossier, glossiest**
smooth and shiny.

glove *noun* **gloves**
a covering for the hand with separate parts for the thumb and each finger.

a b c d e f **g** h i j k l m n o p q r s t u v w x y z

glow *verb* **glows, glowing, glowed**
to shine with a warm light.

glue *noun* **glues**
a substance used for sticking things together.

glutton *noun* **gluttons**
someone who eats too much.

gnarled *adjective*
(*gn-* in this word sounds like *n-*)
twisted like the trunk of an old tree.

gnat *noun* **gnats**
(*gn-* in this word sounds like *n-*)
a thin fly that sucks blood.

gnaw *verb* **gnaws, gnawing, gnawed**
(*gn-* in this word sounds like *n-*)
to keep biting something hard like a bone.

gnome *noun* **gnomes**
(*gn-* in this word sounds like *n-*)
a kind of ugly fairy.

go *verb* **goes, going, went, gone**
1 to move, to travel. *I go to school by bus.*
2 to work. *Is your watch going?*
3 to become. *She went very quiet when she heard the bad news.*

goal *noun* **goals**
1 the two posts the ball must go between to score a point in games like football.
2 a point scored in football, netball, and other games.

goat *noun* **goats**
a farm animal with horns, kept for its milk.

gobble *verb* **gobbles, gobbling, gobbled**
to eat quickly and greedily.

goblin *noun* **goblins**
a kind of bad, ugly fairy.

god *noun* **gods**
a person or thing that people worship.

gold *noun*
a valuable, shiny, yellow metal.

golden *adjective*
coloured like gold.
golden hair.

goldfish *noun* **(goldfishes** or **goldfish)**
a small orange fish often kept as a pet.

golf *noun*
a game played by hitting small, white balls with sticks called clubs.

gone *verb* see **go**

gong *noun* **gongs**
a large metal disc which makes an echoing sound when you hit it.

good *adjective* **better, best**
1 what people like and praise. *a good story.*
2 kind and true. *a good friend.*
3 well behaved. *a good boy.*

goodbye *interjection*
the word you say when you are leaving someone.

goods *noun*
things that can be bought and sold.

goose *noun* **geese**
a large bird that is kept for its meat nd eggs.

gooseberry *noun* **gooseberries**
a green berry that grows on a bush with thorns.

gorgeous *adjective*
very good, wonderful. *a gorgeous day.*

gorilla *noun* **gorillas**
an African animal like a very large monkey with long arms and no tail.

gorse *noun*
a prickly bush with small yellow flowers.

gossip *verb* **gossips, gossiping, gossiped**
to talk a lot about other people, sometimes in an unkind way.

got *verb* see **get**

govern *verb* **governs, governing, governed**
to be in charge of a country or a group of people.

government *noun* **governments**
the group of people who govern a country.

grab *verb* **grabs, grabbing, grabbed**
to take hold of something suddenly. *She grabbed her coat and ran.*

graceful *adjective*
moving in an attractive way. *a graceful dancer.*
gracefully *adverb*

grain *noun*
the seed that grows in plants like corn and is used for making food.

grains *noun*
tiny bits of something like sand or salt.

gram *noun* **grams**
a measure of weight. 1,000 grams make 1 kilogram.

grammar *noun*
the rules for using words properly.

grand *adjective* **grander, grandest**
large, important.

grandchild *noun* **grandchildren**
a child of your son or daughter. Granddaughters and grandsons are grandchildren.

grandparent *noun* **grandparents**
a parent of your mother or father. Grandmothers and grandfathers are grandparents. A grandmother is often called grandma or granny. A grandfather is often called grandpa or grandad.

grant *verb* **grants, granting, granted**
to agree to give someone what they have asked for. *The fairy granted three wishes.*

grape *noun* **grapes**
a small, soft green or purple fruit that grows in bunches.

grapefruit *noun* **grapefruits**
a sour-tasting fruit that looks like a big orange, but is yellow.

graph *noun* **graphs**
a diagram that helps you to compare different numbers or amounts of things.
We drew a graph showing how much rain fell in each month of the year.

graphics *noun*
pictures, patterns, or designs. *computer graphics.*

grasp *verb* **grasps, grasping, grasped**
to get hold of something and hold it tightly. *She grasped my arm to stop herself from falling.*

grass *noun* **grasses**
a green plant with flat, narrow leaves that can be eaten by cattle and other animals.

grasshopper *noun* **grasshoppers**
an insect that makes a shrill sound and can jump a long way.

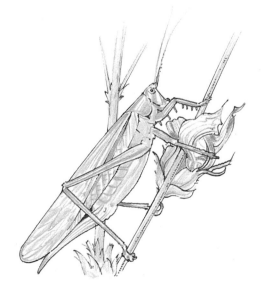

grate *noun* **grates**
a frame of metal bars for holding coal or wood in a fire.

grate *verb* **grates, grating, grated**
1 to rub something against a rough surface so that it makes small pieces. *to grate cheese.*
2 to make a nasty, annoying noise.

grateful *adjective*
wanting to thank someone for what they have done. *I was grateful for her help.*
gratefully *adverb*

grave *adjective* **graver, gravest**
very serious. *a grave illness.*
gravely *adverb*

grave *noun* **graves**
a place where a dead person is buried in the ground.

gravel *noun*
tiny stones.
a gravel path.

gravity *noun*
the force that pulls everything towards the earth.

gravy *noun*
a kind of hot brown sauce you pour over meat before you eat it.

graze *verb* **grazes, grazing, grazed**
1 to hurt the skin by rubbing hard against something.
2 to eat grass. *The sheep were grazing in the field.*

grease *noun*
thick, slippery stuff like oil.

greasy *adjective* **greasier, greasiest**
covered in grease, full of grease. *greasy hair.*

great *adjective* **greater, greatest**
1 big, impressive. *a great storm.*
2 admired by many people. *a great musician.*
3 (*informal*) very good. *We had a great time.*
greatly *adverb*

greedy *adjective* **greedier, greediest**
wanting more food or money than you need.
greedily *adverb*

green *noun, adjective*
the colour of grass.

greengrocer *noun* **greengrocers**
a shopkeeper who sells fruit and vegetables.

greenhouse *noun* **greenhouses**
a glass building for growing plants in.

greet *verb* **greets, greeting, greeted**
to welcome someone or say hello.

grew *verb* see **grow**

grey *noun, adjective*
the colour of the sky on a cloudy day.

grief *noun*
a very sad feeling.

grill *verb* **grills, grilling, grilled**
to cook food on metal bars put under or over heat.
grilled steak.

grim *adjective* **grimmer, grimmest**
not kind, not pleased or cheerful. *She looked grim.*
grimly *adverb*

grin *verb* **grins, grinning, grinned**
to smile showing your teeth.

grind *verb* **grinds, grinding, ground**
to crush into tiny bits. *The wheat was ground into flour.*

grip *verb* **grips, gripping, gripped**
to hold tightly.
He gripped the handlebars as he went downhill.

gristle *noun*
tough bits in meat that are hard to chew.

grit *noun*
tiny bits of stone or sand.

groan *verb* **groans, groaning, groaned**
to make a low sound because you are in pain or trouble.

grocer *noun* **grocers**
a shopkeeper who sells tea, sugar, jam, and other kinds of food.

groceries *noun*
food that you buy in packets, tins, and jars.

groom *noun* **grooms**
1 a person who looks after horses.
2 another word for a bridegroom.

groom *verb* **grooms, grooming, groomed**
to make an animal look smart by cleaning and brushing it. *to groom a horse.*

groove *noun* **grooves**
a long, narrow cut in something.

grope *verb* **gropes, groping, groped**
to try to find something by feeling for it when you cannot see. *In the dark she groped for the door.*

grotto *noun* **grottoes**
a cave, a place like a cave.

ground *noun* **grounds**
1 the earth.
2 a piece of land to play on. *a football ground.*
the grounds of a house the land round it which belongs to it.

ground *verb* see **grind**

group *noun* **groups**
1 a number of people, animals, or things that belong together in some way.
a group of teenagers.
2 people who play music together.
a pop group.

grow *verb* **grows, growing, grew, grown**
1 to become bigger. *You've grown very quickly.*
2 to plant something in the ground and look after it. *We grew onions and radishes last year.*

growl *verb* **growls, growling, growled**
to make a deep, angry sound. *Angry dogs growl.*

grown-up *noun* **grown-ups**
a man or woman who is not a child any more.

growth *noun*
getting bigger, growing. *We measured the growth of the plants.*

grub *noun* **grubs**
a tiny creature that will become an insect.

grubby *adjective* **grubbier, grubbiest**
dirty.
grubby hands.

grudge *noun* **grudges**
a bad feeling you have against someone, because you think they have harmed you.

gruesome *adjective*
horrible, disgusting.

gruff *adjective* **gruffer, gruffest**
with a deep, rough voice.
gruffly *adverb*

grumble *verb* **grumbles, grumbling, grumbled**
to complain, to be bad-tempered about something.

grunt *verb* **grunts, grunting, grunted**
to make the sound a pig makes.

guarantee *noun* **guarantees**
(*gu-* in this word sounds like *g-*)
a promise to mend or replace something if it goes wrong.

guard *verb* **guards, guarding, guarded**
to keep someone or something safe from other people. *The dog was guarding the house.*

guardian *noun* **guardians**
a person who is in charge of a child whose parents cannot look after him or her.

guess *verb* **guesses, guessing, guessed**
to say what you think the answer is when you do not really know. *Did you guess the right answer?*

guest *noun* **guests**
a person who is invited to a party, or is making a visit to someone else's home.

guide *noun* **guides**
someone or something that shows you where to go or what to look at. *The tourist guide took us round the castle.*
Guide a member of the Girl Guides Association.
guide dog a dog trained to help a blind person.

guilty *adjective* **guiltier, guiltiest**
1 responsible for doing something wrong. *He was guilty of stealing.*
2 feeling or looking as if you were guilty. *He had a guilty look.*

guinea pig *noun* **guinea pigs**
a furry animal that has no tail.

guitar *noun* **guitars**
a musical instrument with strings across it that you play with your fingers.

a
b
c
d
e
f
g
h
i
j
k
l
m
n
o
p
q
r
s
t
u
v
w
x
y
z

gull *noun* **gulls**
a kind of sea bird.

gulp *verb* **gulps, gulping, gulped**
to swallow very quickly. *Don't gulp your food!*

gum *noun* **gums**
1 the hard pink part of the mouth that holds the teeth.
2 a sweet that you chew. *chewing gum.*

gun *noun* **guns**
a weapon that fires bullets or shells from a metal tube.

gunpowder *noun*
a black powder that explodes.

gurgle *verb* **gurgles, gurgling, gurgled**
to make the noise water makes as it goes down the plughole in a bath.

gush *verb* **gushes, gushing, gushed**
to move like water rushing out of a tap.

gust *noun* **gusts**
a sudden rush of wind or air.

gutter *noun* **gutters**
a long, narrow hollow at the side of a street or along the edge of a roof to take away rainwater.

gym *noun* **gyms**
gym is short for gymnastics and gymnasium.

gymnastics *plural noun*
exercises for the body usually carried out in a **gymnasium**

gypsy *noun* **gypsies**
one of a group of people who travel from place to place in caravans. Gypsies are also called travellers.

Hh

habit *noun* **habits**
anything that you do without thinking, because you have done it so often.

had *verb* see **have**

haddock *noun* **(the plural is the same)**
a sea fish.

hail *noun*
small pieces of ice that fall from the sky like rain.

hair *noun* **hairs**
a soft covering that grows on the heads and bodies of people and animals.

hairdresser *noun* **hairdressers**
someone whose job is to cut people's hair, wash it, or fix it in a special way.

hairy *adjective* **hairier, hairiest**
covered with hair.

half *noun* **halves**
one of the two equal parts something can be divided into. It can also be written as $\frac{1}{2}$. *Two halves make a whole.*

hall *noun* **halls**
1 the part inside a house near the front door.
2 a very big room. *a school hall.*
3 a large, important building or house. *the Town Hall.*

hallo, hello *interjection*
the word you say when you meet someone.

Hallowe'en *noun*
the 31st October when some people think that witches and ghosts appear.

halt *verb* **halts, halting, halted**
to stop. *The train halted at the red light.*

halter *noun* **halters**
a rope or strap put round an animal's head or neck so that it can be controlled.

ham *noun*
meat from a pig's leg.

hamburger *noun* **hamburgers**
a round flat cake of minced beef.

hammer *noun* **hammers**
a heavy tool used for hitting nails.

hammock *noun* **hammocks**
a bed made of cloth or rope that you hang up at the two ends.

hamster *noun* **hamsters**
a small brown animal that has smooth fur and is kept as a pet.

hand *noun* **hands**
the part of the body at the end of your arm.

handbag *noun* **handbags**
a small bag which women sometimes carry money and other belongings in.

handcuffs *noun*
a pair of metal rings used for locking someone's wrists together.

handicap *noun* **handicaps**
anything that makes it more difficult for you to do something. *a school for children with physical handicaps.*

handicapped *adjective*
having some kind of handicap.

handkerchief *noun* **handkerchiefs**
a square of material you use for blowing your nose.

handle *noun* **handles**
the part of a thing specially made for you to hold it or work it by.

handle *verb* **handles, handling, handled**
to touch, feel, hold, or use something with your hands. *Please wash your hands before you handle the food.*

handsome *adjective*
attractive. You usually use this word to describe men or boys.

hang *verb* **hangs, hanging, hung**
to fix the top part of something to a hook or nail. *I hung up my coat and went in. The towels were hanging on hooks.*

hangar *noun* **hangars**
a big shed for keeping an aeroplane in.

hanger *noun* **hangers**
something used for hanging up things. *coat hangers.*

happen *verb* **happens, happening, happened**
1 to take place. *How did the accident happen?*
2 to do something by chance. *I just happened to see it.*

happiness *noun*
the feeling you have when you are very pleased or enjoying yourself.

happy *adjective* **happier, happiest**
full of happiness.
happily *adverb*

harbour *noun* **harbours**
a place where boats can stay safely when they are not out at sea.

hard *adjective* **harder, hardest**
1 not soft. *hard ground.*
2 difficult. *hard sums.*
3 severe. *a hard punishment.*

hard *adverb*
a lot.
She works hard.

hardly *adverb*
not easily. *After the accident I could hardly walk.*

hardware *noun*
1 tools, nails, wire, and other things made of metal. *a hardware shop.*
2 the machinery of a computer.

hare *noun* **hares**
an animal like a big rabbit with very long ears, that can move very quickly.

harm *verb* **harms, harming, harmed**
to hurt or spoil someone or something.

harmful *adjective*
likely to do harm, bad for you.
Too much sun can be harmful to the skin.

harness *noun* **harnesses**
the set of straps put over a horse's head and round its neck so that it can be controlled.

harp *noun* **harps**
a musical instrument. It has a large frame with strings stretched across it that are played with the fingers.

harsh *adjective* **harsher, harshest**
not kind or gentle. *a harsh voice.*
harshly *adverb*

harvest *noun* **harvests**
the time when farmers gather in the fruit, corn, or vegetables they have grown.

haste *noun*
being too quick and not careful. *Yasmin forgot her books in her haste.*

hasty *adjective* **hastier, hastiest**
quick and not careful, hurrying.
hastily *adverb*

hat *noun* **hats**
something that you wear to cover the top of your head.

hatch *verb* **hatches, hatching, hatched**
to break out of an egg. Baby birds, insects, fish, and snakes hatch.

hate *verb* **hates, hating, hated**
to have a very strong feeling against someone or something you do not like.

haul *verb* **hauls, hauling, hauled**
to pull something heavy. *They hauled the boat out of the river.*

haunted *adjective*
often visited by ghosts. *a haunted house.*

have *verb* **has, having, had**
THIS WORD HAS SEVERAL USES. HERE ARE SOME OF THE WAYS YOU CAN USE IT:
1 to own. *Jo has a new kitten.*
2 to include, to contain. *Hamid's class has thirty pupils.*
3 to enjoy, to suffer. *I was having a good time, but Sam had a cold.*
4 to receive, to get. *I had lots of presents for my birthday.*

hawk *noun* **hawks**
a bird that hunts and eats smaller animals.

hay *noun*
dry grass used to feed animals.

hazel *noun* **hazels**
a small nut tree.

hazy *adjective* **hazier, haziest**
misty, not clear.
hazy sunshine.

head *noun* **heads**
1 the part of a person or animal that contains the brain, eyes, and mouth.
2 the person in charge.

headache *noun* **headaches**
a pain in the head that goes on hurting.

heading *noun* **headings**
words you write as a title at the top of a piece of writing.

headline *noun* **headlines**
words in large print at the top of a piece of writing in a newspaper.
the headlines the most important news, given in a few words.

headquarters *noun*
the place from which the people organizing something send out orders.

headteacher *noun* **headteachers**
the person in charge of all the teachers and children in a school, sometimes called the **headmaster** or **headmistress**

heal *verb* **heals, healing, healed**
1 to become well again. *The cut on my foot healed slowly.*
2 to make someone well again. *The doctor healed the sick man.*

health *noun*
how well your body is, how you are feeling.

healthy *adjective* **healthier, healthiest**
1 not ill or injured in any way. *healthy children.*
2 good for your health. *healthy food.*

heap *noun* **heaps**
an untidy pile.
Don't throw your clothes in a heap on the floor!

hear *verb* **hears, hearing, heard**
to take in sounds through the ears. *I heard you shout so I came.*

heart *noun* **hearts**
1 the part of the body that makes the blood go round inside.
2 your feelings. *She has a kind heart.*

hearth *noun* **hearths**
the part of the floor where the fire is.

heat *noun*
the feeling you get from a fire or from the rays of the sun.

heat *verb* **heats, heating, heated**
to make something hot. *Heat up some milk.*

heath *noun* **heaths**
wild, flat land with small bushes, but no trees.

heather *noun* **heathers**
a low bush with small purple, pink, or white flowers. Heather grows on heaths and moors.

heave *verb* **heaves, heaving, heaved**
to lift or pull something heavy. *We heaved the box of books onto the table.*

heaven *noun*
1 God's home.
2 a very happy place.

heavy *adjective* **heavier, heaviest**
weighing a lot, hard to lift.

hedge *noun* **hedges**
a kind of wall made by bushes growing close together.

hedgehog *noun* **hedgehogs**
a small animal covered in spines like sharp needles.

heel *noun* **heels**
the back part of your foot.

height *noun* **heights**
how high something is. *We measured the height of the door.*

heir *noun* **heirs**
(sounds like *air*)
the person who will be given money, property, or a title when their owner dies.
The princess was heir to the throne.

held *verb* see **hold**

helicopter *noun* **helicopters**
a flying machine with a big propeller that spins round on its roof.

hell *noun*
a place where some people believe wicked people are punished after they die.

helmet *noun* **helmets**
a strong covering that protects the head. *Motorcyclists must wear a crash helmet.*

help *verb* **helps, helping, helped**
to do something useful for someone else.
helper *noun* **helpers**

helping *noun* **helpings**
an amount of food put on your plate at one time. *Granny gave us big helpings of pudding.*

helpless *adjective*
not able to look after yourself.
helplessly *adverb*

helter-skelter *noun* **helter-skelters**
a tall slide at a fair. You go round and round as you slide down it.

hem *noun* **hems**
the edge of a piece of cloth, that is folded under and sewn down. *The hem of her skirt is coming undone.*

hemisphere *noun* **hemispheres**
1 one half of the earth.
2 a shape like half a ball.

a b c d e f g **h** i j k l m n o p q r s t u v w x y z

89

hen *noun* **hens**
1 a female bird. *a hen pheasant.*
2 one of the birds which lay the eggs we eat.

her *adjective*
belonging to the woman or girl you are talking about. *Is that her coat?*

herb *noun* **herbs**
a plant used in cooking to make the food taste good. Parsley and mint are herbs.

herd *noun* **herds**
a group of animals that live and feed together. *a herd of cattle, deer, elephants.*

here *adverb*
in, at, or to this place. *Come here! Here's my book.*

hermit *noun* **hermits**
someone who lives alone and keeps away from people.

hero *noun* **heroes**
a boy or man who has done something very brave.

heroine *noun* **heroines**
a girl or woman who has done something very brave.

herring *noun* (**herrings** or **herring**)
a sea fish that can be eaten.

herself *pronoun*
she and no one else. *She told me herself.*
by herself on her own. *She walked home by herself.*

hesitate *verb* **hesitates, hesitating, hesitated**
to wait a little before you do or say something, because you are not sure about it.

hexagon *noun* **hexagons**
a shape with six sides.

hibernate *verb* **hibernates, hibernating, hibernated**
to sleep for a long time during the cold weather. Bats, tortoises, and hedgehogs all hibernate.

hiccup *verb* **hiccups, hiccuping, hiccuped**
to make a sudden, sharp gulping sound. You sometimes hiccup when you eat or drink too quickly.

hide *verb* **hides, hiding, hid, hidden**
1 to go to a place where people cannot see you.
I was hiding behind a tree.
2 to put something in a secret place.
He hid his money under the carpet.

hide-and-seek *noun*
a game in which someone hides and other people try to find them.

hiding place *noun* **hiding places**
a place where someone or something is hidden.

high *adjective, adverb* **higher, highest**
1 going a long way up.
a high mountain.
2 a long way above the ground.
high clouds.
3 measuring from top to bottom.
The door is two metres high.
4 above what you expect.
high prices.
5 of a sound that is not deep or low.
a high voice.

highwayman *noun* **highwaymen**
a man on a horse, who stopped people on the roads and robbed them.

hijack *verb* **hijacks, hijacking, hijacked**
to seize control of an aeroplane or other vehicle and make it go somewhere else.

hill *noun* **hills**
ground that is higher than the ground around it.

himself *pronoun*
he and no one else.
He told me himself.
by himself on his own.
He walked home by himself.

hinder *verb* **hinders, hindering, hindered**
to get in someone's way so that it is difficult for them to do something.
Don't hinder your mother in the kitchen.

Hindu *noun* **Hindus**
someone who follows the religion of Hinduism.

Hinduism *noun*
one of the religions in India.

hinge *noun* **hinges**
a metal fastener that joins a door to a wall and lets the door swing open and close.

hint *noun* **hints**
1 an idea that someone suggests without being very definite about it. *Jo gave me a hint that she wanted a book for her birthday.*
2 a useful idea. *He gave us some hints on how to draw people.*

hint *verb* **hints, hinting, hinted**
to give someone a hint.

hip *noun* **hips**
1 the bony part of the body that sticks out where your leg joins the side of your body.
2 a red berry on a rose.

hippopotamus *noun* **hippopotamuses**
a very large, heavy, African animal that lives near water. It is sometimes called a **hippo** for short.

hire *verb* **hires, hiring, hired**
to pay to get the use of something. *You can hire skates at the ice rink.*

his *adjective*
belonging to him. *his boat.*

hiss *verb* **hisses, hissing, hissed**
to make the long sss sound that snakes make.

history *noun*
finding out about things that happened in the past.

hit *verb* **hits, hitting, hit**
to knock, to touch something roughly or violently.

hive *noun* **hives**
a kind of box for keeping bees in.

hoard *noun* **hoards**
a secret store of money or other things.

hoarse *adjective* **hoarser, hoarsest**
sounding rough and deep. *a hoarse voice.*
hoarsely *adverb*

hobble *verb* **hobbles, hobbling, hobbled**
to walk with difficulty because there is something wrong with your leg or foot.

hobby *noun* **hobbies**
something interesting that people like doing in their spare time. *My hobbies are reading and swimming.*

hoe *noun* **hoes**
a tool for getting rid of weeds.

hold *verb* **holds, holding, held**
1 to have something in your hands. *Jo held the ladder while Dad climbed up.*
2 to have room inside for something. *The box held six books.*
holder *noun* **holders**

hole *noun* **holes**
a gap or opening made in something.

holiday *noun* **holidays**
time off from school or work.

hollow *adjective*
with an empty space inside. *a hollow tree.*
hollow *noun* **hollows**

holly *noun* **hollies**
a tree that has shiny, prickly leaves and red berries in the winter.

holy *adjective* **holier, holiest**
special because it belongs to God.

home *noun* **homes**
the place where you live.

a b c d e f g **h** i j k l m n o p q r s t u v w x y z

homesick *adjective*
sad because you are away from home.

honest *adjective*
not stealing, cheating, or telling lies.
honestly *adverb*

honey *noun*
sweet, sticky food made by bees.

honour *noun*
great respect.

hood *noun* **hoods**
the part of a coat that you put over
your head in bad weather.

hoof *noun* **hoofs** or **hooves**
the hard part round a horse's foot.

hook *noun* **hooks**
a bent or curved piece of metal or other
material, for hanging things on or for
catching hold of things.

hoop *noun* **hoops**
a big wooden or metal ring used in
games.

hoot *verb* **hoots, hooting, hooted**
to make a sound like an owl or the
horn of a car.
hooter *noun* **hooters**

hop *verb* **hops, hopping, hopped**
1 to jump on one foot.
2 to move by jumping. *The blackbird
hopped across the lawn.*

hope *verb* **hopes, hoping, hoped**
to want something that you think is
likely to happen. *I'm hoping for a bike
for my birthday.*

hopeful *adjective*
if you are hopeful, you think that
something you want will happen.
hopefully *adverb*

hopeless *adjective*
1 very bad at doing something. *He was
hopeless at swimming.*
2 impossible, without hope. *It was
hopeless trying to drive through the snow.*

hopscotch *noun*
a game where you hop and throw or
kick a stone into squares drawn on the
ground.

horizon *noun*
the line where the sky and the land or
sea seem to meet. *I can see a ship on the
horizon.*

horizontal *adjective*
flat and level like the horizon, the
opposite of vertical.

horn *noun* **horns**
1 a kind of pointed bone that grows on
the heads of some animals.
2 a brass musical instrument that you
blow into.

horrible *adjective*
1 nasty. *a horrible taste.*
2 frightening. *a horrible shock.*
horribly *adverb*

horrid *adjective*
horrible, unkind.

horror *noun*
very great fear.

horse *noun* **horses**
a big animal with hooves that can
carry people and pull things.

horse chestnut *noun* **horse chestnuts**
a big tree that conkers grow on.

horseshoe *noun* **horseshoes**
a piece of metal shaped like the letter
U, fixed on the bottom of a horse's
hoof.

hosepipe *noun* **hosepipes**
a long plastic or rubber tube that water can go through.

hospital *noun* **hospitals**
a place where people who are ill or hurt are looked after.

hostage *noun* **hostages**
a person who is kept as a prisoner or threatened with harm until a demand is met.

hostile *adjective*
unfriendly, acting like an enemy.

hot *adjective* **hotter, hottest**
very warm, giving off a lot of heat. *hot weather, a hot fire.*

hotel *noun* **hotels**
a building where you can pay to stay the night and to have meals.

hound *noun* **hounds**
a dog used for hunting.

hour *noun* **hours**
a measure of time. *60 minutes in 1 hour.*

house *noun* **houses**
a building where people live.

housework *noun*
the jobs you have to do in the house, like cleaning and cooking.

hover *verb* **hovers, hovering, hovered**
1 to stay in one place in the air. *The helicopter hovered overhead.*
2 to wait near someone or something and have nothing to do. *She hovered about by the house waiting for the car.*

hovercraft *noun* **(the plural is the same)**
a vehicle without wheels that can carry people or goods just above the surface of land or water.

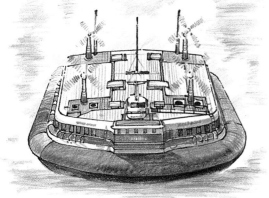

how *adverb*
1 a word that you use to ask questions.
How old are you?
How are you? Very well, thank you.
2 in what way.
Show me how to do it.

howl *verb* **howls, howling, howled**
to give a long, loud cry like an animal in pain.

hub *noun* **hubs**
the part at the centre of a wheel, where the spokes meet.

huddle *verb* **huddles, huddling, huddled**
to keep close to others in a group because you are cold or frightened.

hug *verb* **hugs, hugging, hugged**
to hold someone in your arms to comfort them or show you love them.

huge *adjective*
very big.

hum *verb* **hums, humming, hummed**
to sing a tune with your lips closed.

human, human being *noun*
humans, human beings
any man or woman or child.

humble *adjective* **humbler, humblest**
not proud.
humbly *adverb*

humorous *adjective*
funny, amusing. *a humorous story.*

humour *noun*
a mood.
She's in a good humour.
a sense of humour the ability to see the funny side of things.

hump *noun* **humps**
a bump, a round lump. *A camel has a hump on its back.*

hundred *noun* **hundreds**
the number 100.
hundredth *adjective*

hung *verb* see **hang**

hunger *noun*
the need for food.

hungry *adjective* **hungrier, hungriest**
feeling the need for food.
hungrily *adverb*

a
b
c
d
e
f
g
h
i
j
k
l
m
n
o
p
q
r
s
t
u
v
w
x
y
z

hunt *verb* **hunts, hunting, hunted**
1 to go after an animal because you
want to kill it. *Young lions have to learn
to hunt.*
2 to look carefully for something. *I've
hunted everywhere for my keys but I can't
find them.*
hunter *noun* **hunters**

hurl *verb* **hurls, hurling, hurled**
to throw something as far as you can.

hurrah, hurray *interjection*
a word that you shout when you are
very glad about something.

hurricane *noun* **hurricanes**
a storm with a very strong wind.

hurry *verb* **hurries, hurrying, hurried**
1 to move quickly. *She hurried away to
catch her bus.*
2 to try to do something quickly. *He
hurried to finish before the bell.*

hurt *verb* **hurts, hurting, hurt**
1 to make a person or animal feel pain.
Stop hurting me!
2 to feel pain.
My leg hurts.

hurtle *verb* **hurtles, hurtling, hurtled**
to move very quickly. *The rocket
hurtled through space.*

husband *noun* **husbands**
a man married to someone.

hush *verb* **hushes, hushing, hushed**
to tell someone to be quiet. *Hush!
Don't wake the baby!*

hut *noun* **huts**
a small building made of wood.

hutch *noun* **hutches**
a box for keeping a rabbit in.

hymn *noun* **hymns**
(sounds like *him*)
a song that praises God.

hyphen *noun* **hyphens**
a mark like this - that you use in
writing to join parts of words
together, such as grown-up.

hypnotize *verb* **hypnotizes, hypnotizing,
hypnotized**
to send someone into a state like a
deep sleep, so that you can control
what they do.
hypnotist *noun* **hypnotists**

94

Ii

ice *noun*
water that has frozen hard.

iceberg *noun* **icebergs**
a very big piece of ice floating in the
sea.

ice cream *noun* **ice creams**
a sweet frozen food that is made from
milk.

icicle *noun* **icicles**
a thin, pointed piece of ice hanging
down.

icing *noun*
a mixture of sugar and other things
which you sometimes spread over
cakes to decorate them.

icy *adjective* **icier, iciest**
1 very cold. *an icy wind.*
2 slippery, covered with ice. *icy roads.*

idea *noun* **ideas**
1 something you have thought of. *I've
got an idea. Let's go to the beach.*
2 a picture in your mind. *The film gives
you an idea of what Iceland is like.*

ideal *adjective*
just what you want. *ideal weather for a
picnic.*

identical *adjective*
exactly the same. *identical twins.*

idiot *noun* **idiots**
a very stupid person.

idle *adjective* **idler, idlest**
doing nothing. *idle hands.*

idol *noun* **idols**
1 someone or something that people worship as a god.
2 a famous person that people love. *a pop idol.*

igloo *noun* **igloos**
a round house made of blocks of hard snow.

ignition key *noun* **ignition keys**
the key used to start the engine of a car.

ignorant *adjective*
if you are ignorant, you do not know about something. *He's very ignorant about computers.*

ignore *verb* **ignores, ignoring, ignored**
to take no notice of someone. *I said hello to her, but she ignored me.*

ill *adjective*
not well, in bad health. *I feel too ill to go to school.*

illegal *adjective*
against the law. *It is illegal to drive a car if you are under 17.*

illness *noun* **illnesses**
something that makes people ill. Measles, chicken-pox, and colds are illnesses.

illuminations *noun*
a lot of bright, coloured lights used to decorate streets, buildings, or parks.

illustrate *verb* **illustrates, illustrating, illustrated**
to add pictures to show something more clearly. *a book illustrated with colour photographs.*

illustration *noun* **illustrations**
a picture in a book.

imaginary *adjective*
not real, existing only in your mind. *Dragons are imaginary animals.*

imagination *noun*
the power to imagine things. *You have to use your imagination to write stories.*

imagine *verb* **imagines, imagining, imagined**
to make a picture in your mind of something you cannot see.
I closed my eyes and tried to imagine I was on the beach.

imitate *verb* **imitates, imitating, imitated**
to copy a person or animal. *He imitated the teacher's voice.*

imitation *noun* **imitations**
a copy that is not as valuable as the real thing.
It's not a real diamond, it's only a glass imitation.

immediate *adjective*
happening or done straight away.
immediately *adverb* *Come here immediately!*

immense *adjective*
very big.

immersion heater *noun* **immersion heaters**
a kind of electric heater inside a hot water tank.

imp *noun* **imps**
a small devil.

impatient *adjective*
not patient, not wanting to wait.
Don't be so impatient! It's your turn next.
impatiently *adverb*

imperfect *adjective*
not perfect.

impertinent *adjective*
rude, cheeky.

implore *verb* **implores, imploring, implored**
to beg someone to do something.

impolite *adjective*
rude, not polite.

important *adjective*
1 well known and special. *an important person.*
2 If something is important, you must think about it carefully and seriously. *an important message.*

impossible *adjective*
not possible.
It's impossible to undo this knot.

a b c d e f g h **i** j k l m n o p q r s t u v w x y z

impress *verb* **impresses, impressing, impressed**
to make people think you are very good at something. *She impressed her friends with her new clothes.*

impression *noun* **impressions**
a vague idea or feeling. *I get the impression he doesn't like us.*

impressive *adjective*
so wonderful that you will always remember it. *an impressive firework display.*

imprison *verb* **imprisons, imprisoning, imprisoned**
to put someone in prison.

improve *verb* **improves, improving, improved**
1 to become better. *Her cold is improving.*
2 to make something better. *He improved his handwriting.*

improvement *noun* **improvements**
a change that makes something better. *There has been a lot of improvement in Sam's work this term.*

inaccurate *adjective*
not accurate, not exact.

inch *noun* **inches**
a measure of length. Twelve inches make one foot.

include *verb* **includes, including, included**
to make something part of a group of other things. *The children included the new girl in all their games.*

income *noun* **incomes**
the money which a person gets to live on.

inconvenient *adjective*
if something is inconvenient, it happens when you want to do something else. *My friend came round at an inconvenient time. We were having lunch.*

incorrect *adjective*
not correct, wrong. *an incorrect answer.*

increase *verb* **increases, increasing, increased**
to become bigger or greater, or to make something bigger or greater. *The number of children in my class has increased from 30 to 32.*

incredible *adjective*
not to be believed. *His story about dinosaurs was incredible.*

indeed *adverb*
really. *He's very rich indeed.*

index *noun* **indexes**
a list at the back of a book, arranged in alphabetical order. It tells you what things are in the book and where to find them.

indicator *noun* **indicators**
1 one of the flashing lights on a car that show other drivers which way you are going to turn.
2 something that points things out or gives you information.

indignant *adjective*
angry because someone has said or done something unfair. *I was very indignant when she said I was lazy.*
indignantly *adverb*

indistinct *adjective*
not easy to see or hear.
indistinctly *adverb*

individual *adjective*
for one person or thing. *He had individual lessons to help him to read.*

individual *noun* **individuals**
one single person.

indoors *adverb*
inside a building.

industrial *adjective*
with a lot of factories.

industry *noun* **industries**
1 work done in factories.
2 all the companies that make the same thing. *Japan has a big car industry.*

infant *noun* **infants**
a young child.

infectious *adjective*
likely to spread to others. *an infectious illness.*

inflation *noun*
a general rise in prices.

influence *verb* **influences, influencing, influenced**
to have the power to change what someone thinks or does.

inform *verb* **informs, informing, informed**
to tell someone something. *You should inform the police of the accident.*

informal *adjective*
not formal, not strict. *informal clothes, an informal party.*
Words in this dictionary marked 'informal' are used when you talk to friends and at other times when you don't need to be very proper.

information *noun*
facts, news, words that tell you about something. *We are gathering information about rain forests.*

infuriate *verb* **infuriates, infuriating, infuriated**
to make very angry.

ingenious *adjective*
clever at thinking of new ways to do things.

ingredient *noun* **ingredients**
one of the things you mix together when you cook something. *Flour is one of the ingredients of sponge cake.*

inhabit *verb* **inhabits, inhabiting, inhabited**
to live in a place.

initial *noun* **initials**
the first letter of a name. *William Brown's initials are W. B.*

injection *noun* **injections**
a prick in the skin made by a hollow needle filled with medicine so that the medicine goes into the body.

injure *verb* **injures, injuring, injured**
to harm, to damage. *A cat injured a baby bird.*

injury *noun* **injuries**
damage done to part of your body, such as a cut or a broken bone.

ink *noun* **inks**
a coloured liquid used for writing with a pen.

inland *adjective, adverb*
in a part of the country that is not near the sea.

inn *noun* **inns**
a kind of hotel.

innings *noun* **(the plural is the same)**
a turn at batting in cricket.

innocent *adjective*
not guilty, not doing wrong.
innocently *adverb*

inoculation *noun* **inoculations**
an injection or medicine which protects you from getting ill.

input *noun*
the information that is put into the memory of a computer.

inquiry *noun* **inquiries**
a question that you ask to find out about something. *The police are making inquiries about the robbery.*

inquisitive *adjective*
always wanting to find out about things, fond of asking questions.
inquisitively *adverb*.

inscription *noun* **inscriptions**
words written or carved somewhere for people to see, like the words carved on a monument.

insect *noun* **insects**
a tiny creature with six legs. Flies, ants, butterflies, mosquitoes, and bees are all insects.

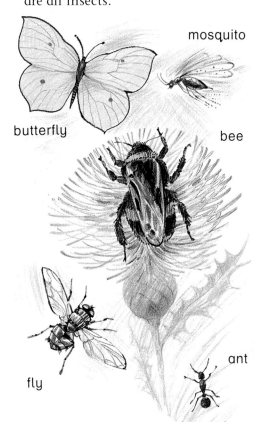

mosquito

butterfly

bee

fly

ant

insert *verb* **inserts, inserting, inserted**
to put something into a hole or a slot. *He inserted a disk into the computer.*

inside *adjective, adverb, preposition*
in something. *Come inside, it's raining.*

insist *verb* **insists, insisting, insisted**
to be very firm in asking, saying, or doing something. *He insists on coming with us.*

insolent *adjective*
very rude, very cheeky. *insolent behaviour.*
insolently *adverb*

inspect *verb* **inspects, inspecting, inspected**
to look carefully at people or things. *The detectives inspected the room for fingerprints.*

inspector *noun* **inspectors**
1 an important policeman.
2 someone whose job is to check that things are done properly. *a ticket inspector.*

instalment *noun* **instalments**
1 a part of a story that is told in parts. *a serial told in instalments.*
2 an amount of money people pay every week or every month in order to buy something.

instant *adjective*
made or done very quickly.
instant coffee coffee you can make quickly just by adding hot water.

instantly *adverb*
immediately, without waiting.

instead *adverb, preposition*
in place of something else. *They made tea instead of coffee.*

instinct *noun* **instincts**
something that makes people and animals do things they have not learnt to do – they can just do them. *Spiders spin webs by instinct.*
instinctive *adjective Animals have an instinctive fear of fire.*

instruct *verb* **instructs, instructing, instructed**
1 to tell someone how to do something.
2 to give orders to someone.

instructions *noun*
words that tell you how to do something. *Read the instructions before using this glue.*

instructor *noun* **instructors**
a person who instructs you to do something. *a swimming instructor.*

instrument *noun* **instruments**
1 a tool or something else used for doing a job. *A microscope is an instrument for looking at very tiny things.*
2 something used for making musical sounds. *Violins and flutes are musical instruments.*

insult *verb* **insults, insulting, insulted**
to hurt someone's feelings by being rude. *She insulted me by saying I was stupid.*

intelligent *adjective*
clever, able to learn and understand things easily.
intelligently *adverb*

intend *verb* **intends, intending, intended**
to mean to do something. *Did you intend to push me?*

intense *adjective*
very great. *intense heat.*

intentional *adjective*
done on purpose.

interest *verb* **interests, interesting, interested**
to make someone want to find out more, look, or listen.
interested *adjective*

interesting *adjective*
making you want to find out more, making you want to look or listen.

interfere *verb* **interferes, interfering, interfered**
to take part in something that has nothing to do with you.

international *adjective*
of or between different countries. *international travel.*

interrupt *verb* **interrupts, interrupting, interrupted**
to stop someone from carrying on with what they are saying or doing. *Don't interrupt me while I'm doing my homework.*

interval *noun* **intervals**
the time between parts of a play or film.

interview *verb* **interviews, interviewing, interviewed**
to ask someone questions to find out what they are like, or what they think, or what they know.
interviewer *noun a television interviewer.*

introduce *verb* **introduces, introducing, introduced**
to make someone or something known to other people. *Jo introduced me to her friend.*

introduction *noun* **introductions**
1 being introduced to someone.
2 a short part at the beginning of a book or piece of music.

invade *verb* **invades, invading, invaded**
1 to go into another country to try to capture it.
2 to go where you are not supposed to go and make trouble. *The crowd invaded the football pitch.*
invasion *noun*

invalid *noun* **invalids**
someone who is weak because they are ill or injured.

invent *verb* **invents, inventing, invented**
1 to be the first person to make or think of a new thing. *The telephone was invented by Alexander Graham Bell.*
2 to make something up. *He invented the whole story.*
inventor *noun*

inverted commas *noun*
the marks like this ' ' or this " " that you use in writing to show what someone has said.

investigate *verb* **investigates, investigating, investigated**
to try to find out as much as you can about something.

invisible *adjective*
not able to be seen. *invisible ink.*

invitation *noun* **invitations**
words that ask you politely to come. *a party invitation.*

invite *verb* **invites, inviting, invited**
to ask someone politely to come or do something.

iron *noun* **irons**
1 a strong, heavy metal.
2 a flat piece of metal with a handle. It is heated and used for making clothes smooth and flat.

ironmonger *noun* **ironmongers**
someone who keeps a shop that sells tools, nails, and other metal things.

irritable *adjective*
easily annoyed.

irritate *verb* **irritates, irritating, irritated**
to keep annoying someone. *The buzzing fly irritated the horse.*

Islam *noun*
the religion of Muslim people. People who follow Islam call God Allah.
Islamic *adjective*

island *noun* **islands**
a piece of land with water all round it.

issue *verb* **issues, issuing, issued**
to give out.
The teacher issued one pencil to each child.

italics *noun*
sloping letter printed *like this.*

itch *verb* **itches, itching, itched**
to have a feeling in your skin that makes you want to scratch.

item *noun* **items**
any one thing in a list or group of things.
The first item on the shopping list is cheese.

its *adjective*
belonging to it. *The dog chased its tail.*

it's
1 it is. *It's raining.*
2 it has. *I think it's stopped raining.*

itself *pronoun*
it and nothing else. *The cat was washing itself.*
by itself on its own. *The central heating comes on by itself before we get up.*

ivory *noun*
a hard substance that has come from the tusks of elephants. It has a pale cream colour.

ivy *noun* **ivies**
a climbing plant with shiny leaves.

Jj

jab *verb* **jabs, jabbing, jabbed**
to poke at someone or something roughly, often with something sharp. *She jabbed me in the ribs with her elbow.*

jack *noun* **jacks**
1 a tool for lifting up a car when you want to change a wheel.
2 the card between the ten and the queen in a pack of cards. *the jack of hearts.*

jackdaw *noun* **jackdaws**
a kind of black bird.

jacket *noun* **jackets**
a short coat.

jagged *adjective*
with a sharp, uneven edge. *jagged rocks.*

jail *noun* **jails**
a prison.

jam *noun* **jams**
1 fruit boiled with sugar until it is thick. *raspberry jam.*
2 a lot of people or cars crowded together so that it is difficult to move. *a traffic jam.*

jam *verb* **jams, jamming, jammed**
to become stuck tight so that it is hard to move. *Our back door keeps getting jammed.*

January *noun*
the first month of the year.

jar *noun* **jars**
a container like the glass ones used for jam.

jaw *noun* **jaws**
1 the lower part of the face.
2 one of the bones that hold the teeth.

jazz *noun*
a kind of music first played and sung by black people in America.

jealous *adjective*
unhappy because someone else has more or does better than you. *I was very jealous of Yasmin's new bicycle.*

jeans *noun*
trousers usually made of strong blue cotton cloth.

jeer *verb* **jeers, jeering, jeered**
to laugh at someone in a rude, scornful way.

jelly *noun* **jellies**
a sweet, slippery food that shakes when you move it.

jellyfish *noun* **(the plural is the same)**
a sea animal that looks rather like jelly.

jerk *verb* **jerks, jerking, jerked**
to move suddenly or clumsily.

jersey *noun* **jerseys**
a warm piece of clothing with sleeves for the top half of your body.

jet *noun* **jets**
1 a liquid or gas coming quickly out of a small opening. *A jet of water spurted out of the broken pipe.*
2 a fast aeroplane.

Jew *noun* **Jews**
1 a person descended from the ancient tribes of Israel.
2 a person who follows the Jewish religion, called Judaism.

jewel *noun* **jewels**
a valuable and beautiful stone. *Diamonds and rubies are jewels.*

jewellery *noun*
necklaces, bracelets, rings, and brooches.

Jewish *adjective*
belonging to the Jewish people.

jigsaw puzzle *noun* **jigsaw puzzles**
a set of small pieces of cardboard or wood that fit together to make a picture.

job *noun* **jobs**
1 the work that a person does to earn money. *Sam has a job in the supermarket at weekends.*
2 a particular piece of work you have to do. *It's my job to wash up.*

jockey *noun* **jockeys**
someone who rides horses in races.

jog *verb* **jogs, jogging, jogged**
1 to run slowly.
2 to push against something. *He jogged my elbow and I spilled my drink.*

join *verb* **joins, joining, joined**
1 to put or fix two things together.
2 to become a member of a group. *I've joined a swimming club.*

joint *noun* **joints**
1 the place where two parts fit together. The ankle is the joint between the foot and the leg.
2 a large piece of meat. *a joint of beef.*

joke *noun* **jokes**
something you say or do to make people laugh.

joke *verb* **jokes, joking, joked**
to make jokes.
joker *noun* **jokers**

jolly *adjective* **jollier, jolliest**
happy and cheerful.

jolt *noun* **jolts**
a sudden movement. *The bus started with a jolt.*

jolt *verb* **jolts, jolting, jolted**
to move or move something quickly and suddenly.

journey *noun* **journeys**
the travelling people do to get from one place to another place. *We went on a long train journey from London to Edinburgh.*

joy *noun*
happiness.

joyful *adjective*
happy, cheerful.
joyfully *adverb.*

joystick *noun* **joysticks**
a lever that you move forwards, backwards, or sideways to control a computer game or a machine.

judge *noun* **judges**
a person who judges.

judge *verb* **judges, judging, judged**
1 to say whether someone is guilty or not guilty.
2 to say whether something is good or bad, right or wrong.

jug *noun* **jugs**
a container with a handle, used for holding and pouring water or other liquids. *a milk jug.*

juggle *verb* **juggles, juggling, juggled**
to keep two or more things in the air by throwing and catching them quickly. *The clown juggled three oranges.*

juggler *noun* **jugglers**
a person who juggles.

juice *noun* **juices**
the liquid in fruit and vegetables. *orange juice.*

July *noun*
the seventh month of the year.

jumble *noun*
a lot of different things all mixed up.
jumble sale a sale of second-hand clothes and other things.

jump *verb* **jumps, jumping, jumped**
to move up suddenly from the ground into the air.

jumper *noun* **jumpers**
a warm piece of clothing with sleeves for the top half of your body. *a woollen jumper.*

a b c d e f g h i **j** k l m n o p q r s t u v w x y z

junction *noun* **junctions**
a place where roads or railway lines meet.

June *noun*
the sixth month of the year.

jungle *noun* **jungles**
a forest in a very hot, damp country.

junior *adjective*
younger, for younger children. *a junior school.*

junk *noun*
1 useless things that people do not want any more.
2 a Chinese sailing boat.

junk 2

just *adjective*
right and fair, what the law says ought to happen. *a just punishment.*

just *adverb*
1 exactly. *It's just what I want.*
2 hardly. *I just caught the bus.*
3 recently. *She has just gone.*
4 only. *I'll just be a minute.*

Kk

kaleidoscope *noun* **kaleidoscopes**
a thick tube you look through to see coloured patterns.

kangaroo *noun* **kangaroos**
an Australian animal that jumps. Female kangaroos have pouches in which they carry their babies.

karate *noun*
a style of fighting originally from Japan. People do karate as a sport.

kebab *noun* **kebabs**
pieces of meat and other food cooked on a long spike called a skewer.

keen *adjective* **keener, keenest**
1 very interested in something. *Sam is keen on pop music.*
2 sharp or strong. *Dogs have a keen sense of smell.*

keep *verb* **keeps, keeping, kept**
1 to have something as your own and not get rid of it. *He kept the money he found.*
2 to make something stay as it is. *Try to keep your clothes clean.*
3 to look after something. *She keeps rabbits.*

kennel *noun* **kennels**
a little hut for keeping a dog in.

kerb *noun* **kerbs**
the blocks of stone along the edge of the pavement.

kernel *noun* **kernels**
the part that you can eat inside the shell of a nut.

ketchup *noun*
a kind of sauce.
tomato ketchup.

kettle *noun* **kettles**
a container specially made to boil water in.

key *noun* **keys**
1 a piece of metal shaped so that it fits into a lock.
2 a small lever pressed with the finger. Pianos, typewriters, and computers have keys.

keyboard *noun* **keyboards**
1 a set of keys arranged in rows, like those on a piano or computer.
2 an electronic musical instrument with a keyboard like the one on a piano.

kick *verb* **kicks, kicking, kicked**
to hit with your foot.

kid *noun* **kids**
1 a young goat.
2 (*informal*) a child.

a b c d e f g h i j k l m n o p q r s t u v w x y z

kidnap *verb* **kidnaps, kidnapping, kidnapped**
to take someone away and keep them prisoner until you get what you want.

kill *verb* **kills, killing, killed**
to cause the death of someone or something.
killer *noun* **killers**

kilogram *noun* **kilograms**
a measure of weight. One kilogram = 1000 grams.

kilometre *noun* **kilometres**
a measure of length. One kilometre = 1000 metres.

kilt *noun* **kilts**
a skirt with pleats. *Men in Scotland sometimes wear tartan kilts.*

kind *adjective* **kinder, kindest**
friendly, ready to help other people.

kind *noun* **kinds**
a sort, a type. *A terrier is a kind of dog.*

king *noun* **kings**
a man who has been crowned as ruler of a country.

kingdom *noun* **kingdoms**
a land that is ruled by a king or queen.

kingfisher *noun* **kingfishers**
a bright blue bird that lives near water and catches fish.

kiosk *noun* **kiosks**
1 a telephone box.
2 a small stall that sells newspapers, sweets, and tobacco.

kiss *verb* **kisses, kissing, kissed**
to touch someone with your lips because you are fond of them.

kitchen *noun* **kitchens**
the room where food is cooked.

kite *noun* **kites**
a light frame covered in cloth or paper and flown in the wind at the end of a long piece of string.

kitten *noun* **kittens**
a very young cat.

knee *noun* **knees**
the bony part in the middle of the leg where it bends.

kneel *verb* **kneels, kneeling, kneeled**
to get down on your knees.

knew *verb* see **know**

knickers *noun*
pants worn by women and girls.

knife *noun* **knives**
a tool with a long, sharp edge for cutting things.

knight *noun* **knights**
1 a man who has been given the title, Sir.
Sir Francis Drake.
2 a man in armour who rode into battle on a horse.

knit *verb* **knits, knitting, knitted**
to use wool and a pair of long needles to make clothes.

knob *noun* **knobs**
the round handle on a door or drawer.

knock *verb* **knocks, knocking, knocked**
to hit something hard.
to knock someone out to make them unconscious by hitting them.

knot *noun* **knots**
the twisted part where pieces of string, rope, cotton, or ribbon have been tied together.

know *verb* **knows, knowing, knew, known**
1 to have something in your mind.
Sam knows the names of all the football teams.
2 to be able to remember or recognize someone or something.
I don't know that girl. Who is she?

knowledge *noun*
things that you know and understand.
He has a lot of knowledge about animals.

knuckle *noun* **knuckles**
one of the places where the fingers bend.

koala *noun* **koalas**
a furry Australian animal that lives in trees and looks like a small bear.

Koran *noun*
the holy book of Islam.

a
b
c
d
e
f
g
h
i
j
k
l
m
n
o
p
q
r
s
t
u
v
w
x
y
z

Ll

label *noun* **labels**
a piece of material, card, or sticky paper put on something to show what it is, whose it is, or where it is going.

laboratory *noun* **laboratories**
a room or building where scientific work is done.

labour *noun*
1 hard work.
2 the time when a woman is giving birth to a baby.

lace *noun* **laces**
1 thin, pretty material with a pattern of holes in it. *a lace collar.*
2 a piece of thin cord used to tie up a shoe.

lack *verb* **lacks, lacking, lacked**
to be without something. *The team lacked a goalkeeper.*

ladder *noun* **ladders**
two long bars with short bars between them (called **rungs**) that you can climb up or down.

ladle *noun* **ladles**
a big, deep spoon used for serving soup.

lady *noun* **ladies**
a polite name for a woman.

ladybird *noun* **ladybirds**
a red or yellow insect with black spots on it that can fly.

lag *verb* **lags, lagging, lagged**
to be behind because you are moving too slowly. *If you lag behind you might miss the bus.*

laid *verb* see **lay**

lain *verb* see **lie** *verb*

lair *noun* **lairs**
(rhymes with *hair*)
a wild animal's home.

lake *noun* **lakes**
a large area of water with land all around it.

lamb *noun* **lambs**
a young sheep.

lame *adjective*
not able to walk properly. *The horse is lame.*

lamp *noun* **lamps**
something that gives light where you want it. *a street lamp.*

lance *noun* **lances**
a long spear like the ones used by knights long ago.

land *noun* **lands**
1 the dry part of the earth's surface.
2 a country. *foreign lands.*

land *verb* **lands, landing, landed**
to arrive by boat or aeroplane. *The plane landed at Heathrow airport.*

landing *noun* **landings**
a flat place at the top of stairs.

landlady, landlord *noun* **landladies, landlords**
1 the owner of a house or flat that someone pays rent to live in.
2 a person who looks after a pub or hotel.

lane *noun* **lanes**
1 a narrow road.
a quiet country lane.
2 a strip of road for one line of traffic.
Some motorways have six lanes.

language *noun* **languages**
words spoken or written by people. *foreign languages.*

lantern *noun* **lanterns**
a container for a light, which the light can shine through without being blown out by the wind.

lap *noun* **laps**
1 the level place you make with the top of your legs when you sit down. *The cat sat on my lap.*
2 once round a race course.

lap *verb* **laps, lapping, lapped**
to drink with the tongue, as a cat does. *The cat lapped up all the milk.*

lard *noun*
white fat used in cooking.

larder *noun* **larders**
a cool cupboard or small room where food is kept.

large *adjective* **larger, largest**
big, more than average in size.

lark *noun* **larks**
a small brown bird that sings while flying high in the air.

lasagne *noun*
food made of sheets of pasta with minced meat and sauce between.

laser *noun* **lasers**
a thing that makes a narrow beam of very strong light. Some lasers are used to cut metal.

lash *verb* **lashes, lashing, lashed**
1 to tie tightly to something.
2 to hit hard, as if with a whip. *The rain lashed against the window.*

lasso *noun* **lassoes**
a long rope with a loop at the end, tied so that the loop can get bigger or smaller. Cowboys use lassoes for catching cattle.

last *adjective*
coming after all the others. *Will the last person close the door?*

last *verb* **lasts, lasting, lasted**
to go on, to continue. *The film lasted two hours.*

latch *noun* **latches**
a fastener on a gate or door.

late *adjective* **later, latest**
1 after the expected time. *The bus was late.*
2 near the end of a day, month, or year. *We arrived late afternoon.*

lately *adverb*
not long ago, recently. *Have you seen Jo lately?*

lather *noun*
soap bubbles on the top of water.

laugh *verb* **laughs, laughing, laughed**
to make sounds that show that you are happy or think something is funny.

laughter *noun*
the sound of laughing.

launch *noun* **launches**
a large boat with an engine.

launch *verb* **launches, launching, launched**
1 to put a boat into the water.
2 to send off a rocket or spaceship.

launderette *noun* **launderettes**
a place with washing machines that people can pay to use.

laundry *noun* **laundries**
1 clothes that need to be washed.
2 a place where people send dirty clothes and sheets to be washed.

lavatory *noun* **lavatories**
a place where you get rid of the waste from your body, a toilet.

lavender *noun*
a bush with pale purple flowers that smell very sweet.

law *noun* **laws**
a rule or set of rules that everyone in a country must keep.

lawn *noun* **lawns**
the part of a garden that is covered with short grass.

lawyer *noun* **lawyers**
a person who has studied the law and who helps people or talks for them in a court of law.

lay *verb* **lays, laying, laid**
1 to put something down. *I laid the papers out on the desk.*
2 to produce an egg. *Hens lay eggs.*
to lay the table to get the table ready for a meal by putting out knives, forks, and other things you need.

lay-by *noun* **lay-bys**
a space for vehicles to stop by the side of a main road.

layer *noun* **layers**
something flat that lies over or under another surface. *a layer of icing on the cake.*

lazy *adjective* **lazier, laziest**
a person who is lazy does not want to work.
lazily *adverb*

lead *noun* (rhymes with *bed*)
a very heavy, grey metal.

lead *noun* **leads** (rhymes with *seed*)
a strap you fasten to a dog's collar so that you can control it.

lead *verb* **leads, leading, led**
1 to go in front. *You lead and we'll follow you.*
2 to be in charge of other people. *The captain led her team with great skill.*
leader *noun* **leaders**

leaf *noun* **leaves**
one of the flat green parts that grow on trees and other plants.

league *noun* **leagues**
a group of teams that play matches against each other.

leak *verb* **leaks, leaking, leaked**
to have a hole or crack that liquid or gas can get through. *The bottle is leaking.*

lean *adjective* **leaner, leanest**
not fat. *lean meat.*

lean *verb* **leans, leaning, leaned** or **leant**
1 to bend your body towards something. *I leant forward.*
2 to rest against something. *Lean against me if you are tired.*
3 to make something slope. *Lean your bike against the wall.*

leap *verb* **leaps, leaping, leaped** or **leapt**
to jump. *They leapt into the swimming pool.*

learn *verb* **learns, learning, learned** or **learnt**
1 to find out about something. *We're learning about the Aztecs in history.*
2 to find out how to do something. *I learnt to swim last year.*

leash *noun* **leashes**
a dog's lead.

least *adjective, adverb, pronoun*
less than all the others, the smallest in amount. *It was the least expensive coat in the shop. Yasmin has lots of money, Sam has less and Julie has the least.*

leather *noun*
a strong material made from the skins of animals.

leave *verb* **leaves, leaving, left**
1 to go from a person or place. *What time do you leave for school?*
2 to let something stay where it is. *I've left my book at home.*

lecture *noun* **lectures**
a talk to an audience by a teacher or an expert.

led *verb* see **lead** *verb*

ledge *noun* **ledges**
a narrow shelf like the one that sticks out under a window.

leek *noun* **leeks**
a long, white vegetable with green leaves that tastes like onion.

left *verb* see **leave**

left *adjective, adverb*
on the side opposite the right.

left-handed *adjective*
If you are left-handed you use the left hand to write and do other important things.

leg *noun* **legs**
1 one of the parts of the body an animal uses to stand, walk, and run.
2 one of the upright pieces that support a table or chair.

legal *adjective*
allowed by the law. *It is not legal to steal.* **legally** *adverb*

legend *noun* **legends**
an old story handed down from the past. *the legend of Robin Hood.*

leisure *noun*
time when you can do what you want because you do not have to work.

lemon *noun* **lemons**
a yellow fruit with a sour taste.

lemonade *noun*
a drink made from lemons, sugar, and water.

lend *verb* **lends, lending, lent**
to let someone have something of yours for a short time. *Sam lent me his bike yesterday.*

length *noun*
how long something is.

lens *noun* **lenses**
a curved piece of glass or plastic that makes light go where it is needed. Glasses, cameras, and telescopes have lenses.

leopard *noun* **leopards**
a big, wild cat found in Africa and Asia. It has yellow fur with black spots on it.

leotard *noun* **leotards**
a piece of clothing worn by dancers and people doing exercises.

less *adjective*
smaller in amount. *Please make less noise.*

lessen *verb* **lessens, lessening, lessened**
to become less or to make something less. *The medicine will help to lessen the pain.*

lesson *noun* **lessons**
1 the time when someone is teaching you. *a history lesson.*
2 something that you have to learn. *Road safety is an important lesson for everyone.*

let *verb* **lets, letting, let**
1 to allow someone to do something. *Sam let me ride his bike.*
2 to allow someone to use a house or building if they pay money. *She lets the cottage to people on holiday.*

letter *noun* **letters**
1 one of the signs used for writing words, such as **a**, **b**, or **c**.
2 a written message sent to another person.

lettuce *noun* **lettuces**
a vegetable with large green leaves that you eat in salads.

level *adjective*
1 flat and smooth. *level ground.*
2 equal. *The two teams are level with 10 points each.*

lever *noun* **levers**
a bar that is pulled down to lift something heavy or make a machine work.

liar *noun* **liars**
someone who tells lies.

library *noun* **libraries**
a building or room where a lot of books are kept for people to use.

licence *noun* **licences**
a printed paper that says that you can do, own, or use something.

lick *verb* **licks, licking, licked**
to move your tongue over something.

lid *noun* **lids**
a cover for a box or jar.

lie *noun* **lies**
something you say that you know is not true. *Don't tell lies.*

lie *verb* **lies, lying, lied**
to say something that you know is not true.

lie *verb* **lies, lying, lay, lain**
1 to rest with your body flat, as it is in bed. *We lay on the bed and went to sleep.*
2 to be or stay on something. *Snow lay on the ground.*

life *noun* **lives**
being alive, the time between birth and death. *The doctor saved her life.*

lifeboat *noun* **lifeboats**
a boat that goes out to sea in bad weather to save people's lives.

lifelike *adjective*
looking like a real person. *The wax models were very lifelike.*

lifetime *noun*
all the time that you are alive. *There have been a lot of changes in my grandmother's lifetime.*

lift *noun* **lifts**
1 a machine for taking people or things up and down inside a building.
2 a free ride in someone's car.

lift *verb* **lifts, lifting, lifted**
1 to move something up to a higher level. *Lift the box onto the shelf.*
2 to pick up. *Jo lifted the baby out of the pram.*

light *adjective* **lighter, lightest**
1 not heavy, not weighing a lot.
a light suitcase.
2 not dark, with plenty of light.
a light room.
3 pale.
light colours.

light *noun* **lights**
1 what you need to be able to see things. Light comes from the sun, the stars, fires, and lamps.
2 any device which provides light. *electric lights.*

light *verb* **lights, lighting, lit**
1 to provide light so that you can see something. *At Christmas they lit the church with candles.*
2 to start something burning. *We tried to light the bonfire.*

light-hearted *adjective*
cheerful, not worried.

lighthouse *noun* **lighthouses**
a tower with a bright light that warns ships of rocks or other dangers.

lightning *noun*
the bright light that flashes in the sky in a thunderstorm.

like *preposition, conjunction*
nearly the same as another person or thing. *Jo looks like her mother.*

like *verb* **likes, liking, liked**
to think someone or something is nice. *Do you like ice cream?*

likely *adjective* **likelier, likeliest**
probable, expected to happen or to be true. *It is likely to rain.*

lily *noun* **lilies**
a beautiful white flower grown in gardens.

limb *noun* **limbs**
a leg, arm, or wing.

limit *noun* **limits**
a line or point that people cannot or should not pass. *a speed limit.*

limp *adjective* **limper, limpest**
not stiff, drooping. *The cardboard went limp when it got wet.*

limp *verb* **limps, limping, limped**
to walk with difficulty because you have hurt your leg or foot.

line *noun* **lines**
1 a long mark like this ————.
2 a row of people or things.
3 the set of metal rails a train moves along.
4 all the words that are beside each other on a page. *I don't know the next line of the poem.*

linen *noun*
strong cloth used for making sheets and tablecloths.

liner *noun* **liners**
a big ship for taking people on long journeys.

linger *verb* **lingers, lingering, lingered**
to be slow to leave. *Don't linger in the playground after school.*

lining *noun* **linings**
a layer you put inside something to make it thicker or to protect it.

link *noun* **links**
one of the rings in a chain.

link *verb* **links, linking, linked**
to join things together.

lino, linoleum *noun*
a stiff, shiny covering for the floor.

lion *noun* **lions**
a large, light brown wild cat found in Africa and India.

lioness *noun* **lionesses**
a female lion.

lip *noun* **lips**
one of the parts of your face which make the top and bottom edges of your mouth.

lipstick *noun*
colour that you put on your lips.

liquid *noun* **liquids**
anything that is like water or oil.

liquorice *noun*
a black sweet that you get in sticks and other shapes.

list *noun* **lists**
a group of things or names written down one after the other.

listen *verb* **listens, listening, listened**
to pay attention in order to hear something.

lit *verb* see **light** *verb*

literature *noun*
books, plays, and poetry.

litre *noun* **litres**
a measure for liquid. *a litre of paint.*

litter *noun* **litters**
1 paper, empty packets, bottles, and other rubbish, dropped or left lying about.
2 all the young animals born to the same mother at the same time.

little *adjective* **littler, littlest**
1 not big. *a little village.*
2 not much. *I've got very little money.*

live *adjective* (rhymes with *dive*)
alive, living. *live animals in a zoo.*

live *verb* **lives, living, lived**
1 to be alive, so that you can feed and develop as animals and plants should do.
2 to have your home somewhere.

lively *adjective* **livelier, liveliest**
full of life and energy. *a lively kitten.*

lizard *noun* **lizards**
an animal with skin like a snake and four legs.

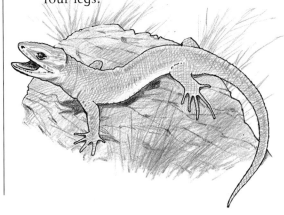

a
b
c
d
e
f
g
h
i
j
k
l
m
n
o
p
q
r
s
t
u
v
w
x
y
z

109

load *noun* **loads**
things that you carry or deal with at one time. *The lorry brought another load of sand. He was carrying loads of books.*

load *verb* **loads, loading, loaded**
1 to put things on to something that will carry them. *Load the suitcases into the car boot.*
2 to put bullets into a gun. *Load the gun.*
3 to put film into a camera.

loaf *noun* **loaves**
bread in the shape it was baked in.

loan *noun* **loans**
anything that is lent to someone.

lobster *noun* **lobsters**
a sea creature with a shell, two large claws, eight legs, and a tail.

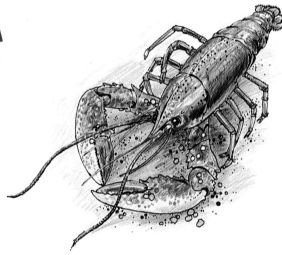

local *adjective*
of a place near you. *We go to the local school.*

loch *noun* **lochs**
a lake in Scotland.

lock *noun* **locks**
1 a fastening for a door, gate, or box which is opened with a key.
2 a piece of hair.

lock *verb* **locks, locking, locked**
to fasten with a key.

locomotive *noun* **locomotives**
the engine that pulls a train.

lodger *noun* **lodgers**
a person who pays to live in another person's home.

loft *noun* **lofts**
a room in the roof, where things can be kept.

logical *adjective*
sensible, reasonable.

loiter *verb* **loiters, loitering, loitered**
to stand about with nothing to do.

lollipop *noun* **lollipops**
a big sweet on the end of a stick.

lolly *noun* **lollies**
ice on a stick, usually with a fruity taste.

lonely *adjective* **lonelier, loneliest**
1 sad because you are on your own.
2 far from others. *a lonely house.*

long *adjective* **longer, longest**
1 measuring a lot from one end to the other.
a long road.
2 taking a lot of time.
a long holiday.

long *verb* **longs, longing, longed**
to want something which you have to wait for.
I longed for a drink.

loo *noun* **loos**
(*informal*) a lavatory.

look *verb* **looks, looking, looked**
1 to use your eyes, to turn your eyes towards something.
2 to seem.
The dog looks friendly.
look for to try to find something.

looking-glass *noun* **looking-glasses**
a mirror.

loop *noun* **loops**
a ring made in rope, wire, thread, or ribbon.

loose *adjective* **looser, loosest**
1 not tight. *My tooth is loose.*
2 free, not fixed or tied up. *The animals were all loose.*

loosen *verb* **loosens, loosening, loosened**
1 to make looser. *He loosened his tie.*
2 to get looser.

lord *noun* **lords**
1 a nobleman.
2 a title. *Lord Nelson.*

lorry *noun* **lorries**
a big, open truck for taking heavy things by road.

lose *verb* **loses, losing, lost**
1 to be without something because you cannot find it. *I've lost my coat.*
2 to be without something you once had. *He's lost one of his front teeth.*
3 to be beaten in a game. *Our team lost the match.*

lost *adjective*
not able to find the right way. *Don't get lost!*

lot *noun* **lots**
a large number, a large amount. *We ate a lot of sweets.*
the lot everything. *We were so hungry that we ate the lot.*

lotion *noun* **lotions**
a liquid that is put on the skin. *sun lotion.*

loud *adjective* **louder, loudest**
easy to hear, making a lot of noise.

loudspeaker *noun* **loudspeakers**
the part of a TV, radio, or music system that the sound comes from.

lounge *noun* **lounges**
a room with comfortable chairs in it.

love *noun*
the strong feeling you have when you like someone very much.

love *verb* **loves, loving, loved**
1 to feel love for someone.
2 to like something. *I love chocolate.*

lovely *adjective* **lovelier, loveliest**
1 beautiful.
2 pleasing. *a lovely idea.*

low *adjective* **lower, lowest**
not high.

loyal *adjective*
always doing your duty.

luck *noun*
things that happen that you have not planned.

lucky *adjective* **luckier, luckiest**
having good luck. *The cat ran across the road and was lucky not to be hit by a car.*
luckily *adverb*

luggage *noun*
bags, boxes, and suitcases taken by someone on a journey.

lukewarm *adjective*
only just warm. *lukewarm water.*

lullaby *noun* **lullabies**
a song that is sung to send a baby to sleep.

lump *noun* **lumps**
1 a solid thing with no clear shape. *a lump of clay.*
2 a swelling. *I've got a lump on my head where I hit it when I fell.*

lunch *noun* **lunches**
a meal eaten in the middle of the day.

lung *noun* **lungs**
one of the two parts inside the body used for breathing.

lurch *verb* **lurches, lurching, lurched**
to lean suddenly to one side. *The train lurched and the passengers were thrown about.*

lure *verb* **lures, luring, lured**
to tempt someone into a trap.

luxury *noun* **luxuries**
something expensive that you like very much but do not really need.

Mm

mac *noun* **macs**
(*informal*) a mackintosh.

a b c d e f g h i j k **l** m n o p q r s t u v w x y z

111

macaroni *noun*
a kind of pasta made into tubes.

machine *noun* **machines**
a thing with several parts that work together to do a job or to make something. *a washing machine.*

machine-gun *noun* **machine-guns**
a gun that can keep firing very quickly for a long time.

machinery *noun*
1 the parts of a machine. *the machinery inside a clock.*
2 a group of machines. *The factory has bought some new machinery.*

mackintosh *noun* **mackintoshes**
a raincoat.

mad *adjective* **madder, maddest**
1 ill in the mind.
2 very silly.
3 very angry.

made *verb* see **make**

magazine *noun* **magazines**
a thin book that comes out every week or month with different stories and pictures in it.

maggot *noun* **maggots**
a tiny worm that comes from an egg laid by a fly.

magic *noun*
the power to do wonderful things or clever tricks that people cannot usually do.
magical *adjective*

magician *noun* **magicians**
1 a person in stories who knows a lot about magic and uses it.
2 a person who does magic tricks to amuse people.

magnet *noun* **magnets**
a piece of metal that can make pieces of iron or steel come and stick to it.

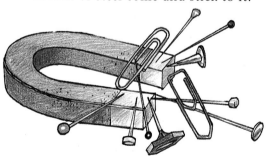

magnificent *adjective*
very good or beautiful. *a magnificent palace.*

magnify *verb* **magnifies, magnifying, magnified**
to make something look bigger. *We magnified the insect under the microscope.*

magpie *noun* **magpies**
a black and white bird.

maid *noun* **maids**
a woman who does cleaning in a hotel or large house.

maiden *noun* **maidens**
an old-fashioned word for a girl.

mail *noun*
letters, cards, and parcels sent through the post.

main *adjective*
the most important. *a main road.*

mainly *adverb*
almost completely, most of all.

majesty *noun*
a word used when speaking to a king or queen. *Your Majesty.*

make *verb* **makes, making, made**
1 to get something new by putting other things together. *Yasmin made a cake.*
2 to cause something to happen. *The balloon made a loud bang when it burst.*
3 to force someone to do something. *Mum made me tidy up my room.*

make-up *noun*
cream, lipstick, and powder that you put on your face to make it look beautiful. *Actors wear make-up to make them look different.*

male *noun* **males**
any person or animal that can become a father.

mammal *noun* **mammals**
any animal that has hair and can feed its babies with its own milk. Whales, lions, and people are all mammals.

man *noun* **men**
a grown-up male human being.

manage *verb* **manages, managing, managed**
1 to be in charge of a shop or factory.
2 to be able to do something although it is difficult.
The box was heavy but she managed to carry it.

mane *noun* **manes**
the long hair along a horse's back or on a lion's head and neck.

manger *noun* **mangers**
a long, narrow container that horses and cattle can eat from.

manner *noun*
the way something happens or is done.

manners *noun*
the way you behave when you are with other people.
It's bad manners to talk with your mouth full.

manor *noun* **manors**
a big house in the country.

mansion *noun* **mansions**
a big house in the country.

mantelpiece *noun* **mantelpieces**
the shelf above a fireplace.

manufacture *verb* **manufactures, manufacturing, manufactured**
to make things in a factory with machines.

manure *noun*
material excreted by animals used to fertilize the ground.

many *adjective, pronoun*
a large number of people or things.

map *noun* **maps**
a drawing of a town, a country, or the world. Maps show you where roads, mountains, and rivers are.

marathon *noun* **marathons**
a running race which goes on for about 26 miles.

marble *noun* **marbles**
1 a small, glass ball used in some games.
2 a kind of smooth stone used for building or making statues.

March *noun*
the third month of the year.

march *verb* **marches, marching, marched**
to walk like soldiers on parade.

margarine *noun*
a food that looks and tastes like butter, but is not made from milk.

margin *noun* **margins**
the empty space between the edge of a page and the writing or pictures.

mark *noun* **marks**
1 a stain, spot, or line that spoils something. *dirty marks on the wall.*
2 a sign or number put on a piece of work to show how good it is.

mark *verb* **marks, marking, marked**
to put marks on something.

market *noun* **markets**
a group of stalls selling food and other things.

marmalade *noun*
jam made from oranges, limes, or lemons.

maroon *verb* **maroons, marooning, marooned**
to leave someone in a wild and lonely place without any way of escaping from it.

marriage *noun* **marriages**
1 a wedding.
2 being married. *They had a long and happy marriage.*

marry *verb* **marries, marrying, married**
to become someone's husband or wife.
Julie and David got married last Saturday.

marsh *noun* **marshes**
a piece of very wet ground.

marvellous *adjective*
wonderful.
marvellously *adverb*

marzipan *noun*
a sweet food made from almonds. *You put marzipan on top of a fruit cake.*

masculine *adjective*
belonging to men, like men, suitable for men.

mash *verb* **mashes, mashing, mashed**
to crush something to make it soft and get rid of the lumps.
mashed potato.

mask *noun* **masks**
a covering worn on the face to protect or hide it.

mass *noun* **masses**
1 a large number or amount. *masses of flowers.*
2 a Roman Catholic church service.

massive *adjective*
very big. *a massive rock.*

mast *noun* **masts**
a tall pole that holds up a ship's sails, a flag, or an aerial.

master *noun* **masters**
a man who is in control of people or animals.
The dog ran to its master.

mat *noun* **mats**
1 a small piece of carpet or other material put on the floor.
2 a piece of material you put on a table to prevent damage from hot dishes.

match *noun* **matches**
1 a small, thin stick that gives a flame when rubbed on something rough.
2 a game played between two sides. *a tennis match.*

match *verb* **matches, matching, matched**
to look the same as something else. *In some card games you have to find the pictures which match.*

mate *noun* **mates**
1 one of a pair of birds or animals that have come together to produce young ones.
2 (*informal*) a friend.

mate *verb* **mates, mating, mated**
to come together as a pair so that the female can produce young ones.

material *noun* **materials**
1 something that you use to make other things. *Wood and stone are building materials.*
2 cloth, anything that is woven and used to make things like clothes or curtains.

maternity *noun*
having a baby.
maternity ward part of a hospital where a woman may go when it is time for her baby to be born.

mathematics, maths *noun*
finding out about numbers, measurement, and shapes.

matter *noun* **matters**
something you need to do or to think about. *There is an important matter we have to talk about.*
What's the matter? What is wrong?

matter *verb* **matters, mattering, mattered**
to be important. *It doesn't matter if you are a bit late.*

mattress *noun* **mattresses**
the thick, soft part of a bed.

mauve *noun, adjective*
a light purple colour.

May *noun*
the fifth month of the year.

may *verb* **might**
1 can. *May I go out to play?*
2 will perhaps. *It might rain later.*

mayor *noun* **mayors**
the person in charge of the council in a town or city.

maze *noun* **mazes**
a set of lines or paths that twist and turn so much that it is very easy to lose the way.
a maze of winding streets.

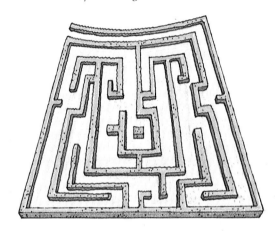

meadow *noun* **meadows**
a field of grass.

meal *noun* **meals**
the food eaten at breakfast, lunch, dinner, tea, or supper.

mean *adjective* **meaner, meanest**
not ready to give or share things.

mean *verb* **means, meaning, meant**
1 to plan in your mind.
I meant to tell him, but I forgot.
2 to have a meaning.
This dictionary tells you what words mean.

meaning *noun* **meanings**
the meaning of the words you use is what you want other people to know when they hear or read those words. *If you don't know the meaning of a word, look it up in the dictionary.*

meanwhile *adverb*
during the time something else is happening. *You set the table. Meanwhile I'll prepare the lunch.*

measles *noun*
an illness that makes red spots come on the skin.

measure *noun* **measures**
a unit used for measuring. Kilograms, grams, pounds, and ounces are measures for weight.

measure *verb* **measures, measuring, measured**
1 to find out the size or amount of something. *I measured the box with a ruler.*
2 to be a certain size or amount. *This room measures 4 metres across.*

measurement *noun* **measurements**
how much something measures. *What are the measurements of this table?*

meat *noun*
the flesh of animals used as food.

mechanic *noun* **mechanics**
a person who works with or repairs machines. *a car mechanic.*

mechanical *adjective*
done or made by machinery. *They used a mechanical digger to make a ditch.*

medal *noun* **medals**
a piece of metal in the shape of a coin, star, or cross given to someone very brave or very good at something. *She won a gold medal in the Olympic Games.*

medallist *noun* **medallists**
someone who has won a medal. *an Olympic gold medallist.*

meddle *verb* **meddles, meddling, meddled**
to take part in something or touch something that has nothing to do with you.
Don't meddle with the papers on my desk.

media *noun*
the media the ways in which news and entertainment are passed on to everyone, such as TV, radio, and newspapers.

medicine *noun* **medicines**
liquid or tablets that a sick person has to swallow in order to get better again.

medium *adjective*
of middle size.

meek *adjective* **meeker, meekest**
gentle and not proud.
meekly *adverb*

meet *verb* **meets, meeting, met**
1 to come together with someone. *Let's meet at the swimming pool at two o'clock.*
2 to see someone for the first time. *Have you met Sally?*
3 to join together with something. *Our house is on the corner where the two roads meet.*

meeting *noun* **meetings**
a group of people who have come together to talk about something or to listen to someone.

melon *noun* **melons**
a large, juicy fruit with a yellow or green skin.

melt *verb* **melts, melting, melted**
to change to a liquid when made warmer. *Ice melts if you take it out of the fridge.*

member *noun* **members**
someone who belongs to a club or group.

memory *noun* **memories**
1 the power to remember things. *Have you got a good memory?*
2 anything that is remembered. *The old man had happy memories of when he was a boy.*
3 the part of a computer that stores information.

mend *verb* **mends, mending, mended**
to make a damaged thing as useful as it was before.

mental *adjective*
in the mind, of the mind. *mental illness.*

mention *verb* **mentions, mentioning, mentioned**
to speak or write a little about something. *She mentioned that she was going on holiday.*

menu *noun* **menus**
a list of the different kinds of food you can choose for your meal.

merchant *noun* **merchants**
a person who buys and sells things, especially from other countries. *a wine merchant.*

merciful *adjective*
showing mercy, not strict.
mercifully *adverb*

mercy *noun*
being kind to someone instead of punishing them. *Show mercy to the prisoners.*

meringue *noun* **meringues**
a crisp cake made from the whites of eggs mixed with sugar.

mermaid *noun* **mermaids**
a creature in stories, that looks like a woman but has a fish's tail instead of legs.

merry *adjective* **merrier, merriest**
happy and lively.
merrily *adverb*

mess *noun*
things that are untidy, dirty, or mixed up. *Don't leave your clothes in a mess.*

message *noun* **messages**
words that you send to a person when you cannot speak to him or her yourself.

messenger *noun* **messengers**
someone who takes a message to someone else.

met *verb* see **meet**

metal *noun* **metals**
something hard that melts when it is very hot. Gold, silver, iron, and tin are kinds of metal.

meteor *noun* **meteors**
a piece of rock or metal that moves through space and burns up when it gets near the earth.

meter *noun* **meters**
a machine that measures how much of something has been used. *a gas meter.*

method *noun* **methods**
the way you choose to do something.

metre *noun* **metres**
a measure for length. *1,000 metres = 1 kilometre.*

metric system *noun*
a decimal system for counting, measuring, and weighing things.

miaow *verb* **miaows, miaowing, miaowed**
to make the cry a cat makes.

mice *noun* see **mouse**

microchip *noun* **microchips**
one of the tiny pieces in a computer that makes it work.

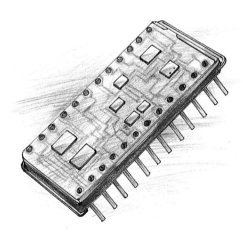

microcomputer *noun* **microcomputers**
the kind of computer people might use in their homes or on their desks at work.

microphone *noun* **microphones**
a machine that changes sound into electricity so that it can be sent along wires.

microscope *noun* **microscopes**
an instrument that makes it possible to see very tiny things by making them look much bigger.

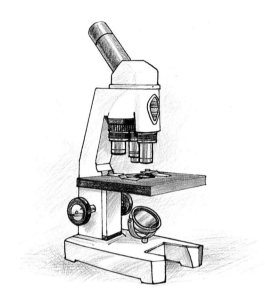

microscopic *adjective*
so small that you can only see it under a microscope.

microwave oven *noun* **microwave ovens**
an electronic oven that cooks food very quickly.

midday *noun*
twelve o'clock in the day.

middle *noun* **middles**
1 the part of something that is the same distance from all its sides or edges or from both its ends.
A peach has a stone in the middle.
2 after the beginning and before the end.
The phone rang in the middle of the night.

midnight *noun*
twelve o'clock at night.

midwife *noun* **midwives**
a person trained to help when a baby is born.

might *verb* see **may** *verb*

mild *adjective* **milder, mildest**
1 gentle.
a mild soap that is kind to your hands.
2 not too bad.
a mild illness.
mildly *adverb*

mile *noun* **miles**
a measure of distance. One mile =
1,760 yards, or roughly 1·6 kilometres.

military *adjective*
of, for, or by soldiers.

milk *noun*
a white liquid that mothers and some
female animals feed their babies with.
People can drink cows' milk.

mill *noun* **mills**
1 a place with machinery for making
corn into flour.
2 a kind of factory.
a paper mill.

millimetre *noun* **millimetres**
a measure of length. There are 10
millimetres in 1 centimetre.

million *noun* **millions**
the number 1,000,000.
millionth *adjective.*

millionaire *noun* **millionaires**
a rich person who has more than a
million pounds.

mime *verb* **mimes, miming, mimed**
to tell someone something by using
actions not words.

mimic *verb* **mimics, mimicking, mimicked**
to copy what someone says or does in
order to make fun of them.

mince *noun*
meat cut into very small pieces.
mince pie a small pie filled with
mincemeat.

mincemeat *noun*
a sweet mixture of chopped fruit and
other things, cooked inside pastry at
Christmas.

mind *noun* **minds**
the power to think, feel, and
understand.

mind *verb* **minds, minding, minded**
to be worried or upset by something.
Do you mind missing the party?

mine *noun* **mines**
1 a place where people work to dig
coal, metal, jewels, or salt out of the
ground.
2 a bomb hidden in the ground or the
sea to blow up things that come close
to it.

miner *noun* **miners**
someone who works down a mine.

mineral *noun* **minerals**
1 any useful or valuable rock that
people get out of the ground.
2 a cold drink with a lot of tiny
bubbles in it. *mineral water.*

miniature *adjective*
tiny, but just like something much
bigger. *a miniature railway.*

minibus *noun* **minibuses**
a van with seats like a small bus.

minister *noun* **ministers**
someone who serves God by being in
charge of a church.

minnow *noun* **minnows**
a tiny fish found in rivers, streams,
lakes, and ponds.

minstrel *noun* **minstrels**
a man who sang or played music to
entertain people long ago.

mint *noun* **mints**
1 a green plant used in cooking to
flavour food.
2 a sweet that tastes of mint.
3 a place where coins are made.

minus *preposition*
take away. *Six minus two is four, 6 − 2
= 4.*

minute *adjective* **minuter, minutest**
very small.

minute *noun* **minutes**
a measure of time. There are 60
minutes in one hour.

miracle *noun* **miracles**
something wonderful that has
happened, although it did not seem
possible. *It's a miracle no one was hurt
in the train crash.*

mirage *noun* **mirages**
a trick of the light that makes people
see things that are not really there,
such as pools of water in deserts.

mirror *noun* **mirrors**
a piece of glass, in which you can see yourself.

misbehave *verb* **misbehaves, misbehaving, misbehaved**
to be naughty.

miscarriage *noun* **miscarriages**
the birth of a baby before it has developed enough to stay alive.

mischief *noun*
silly or bad behaviour that gets you into trouble.

mischievous *adjective*
often getting into mischief, naughty. *The mischievous puppy chewed my shoes.*

miser *noun* **misers**
someone who likes to save money, but hates spending it.

miserable *adjective*
very unhappy. **miserably** *adverb*

misery *noun*
suffering, being miserable.

misfortune *noun* **misfortunes**
bad luck.

mislead *verb* **misleads, misleading, misled**
to give someone an idea that is not true.

miss *verb* **misses, missing, missed**
1 to fail to hit, catch, see, hear, or find something. *I tried to hit the ball but I missed it. I missed the bus again.*
2 to be sad because someone is no longer with you. *I'll miss all my old friends when we move house.*

missile *noun* **missiles**
a weapon or object which is thrown or fired through the air.

missing *adjective*
lost. *We're looking for a missing cat.*

mission *noun* **missions**
an important job that someone is sent away to do.

mist *noun*
damp air that it is difficult to see through.

mistake *noun* **mistakes**
something that you have done or thought that is wrong.

mistake *verb* **mistakes, mistaking, mistook, mistaken**
to get the wrong idea about someone or something. *I mistook her for a friend of mine.*

mistletoe *noun*
a plant with white berries which grows on other trees.

misty *adjective* **mistier, mistiest**
full of mist, covered with mist.

misunderstand *verb* **misunderstands, misunderstanding, misunderstood**
to get the wrong idea about something.

mitten *noun* **mittens**
a kind of glove with two parts, one for the thumb and one for all the fingers.

mix *verb* **mixes, mixing, mixed**
to put different things together to make something new. *Mix yellow and blue paint together to make green.*

mixture *noun* **mixtures**
something made of different things mixed together. *a cake mixture.*

moan *verb* **moans, moaning, moaned**
1 to make a soft sound that shows you are in pain or trouble.
2 to grumble. *The class moaned about missing the swimming lesson.*

moat *noun* **moats**
a ditch dug round a castle and usually filled with water.

mobile *adjective*
that can move or be moved easily. *a mobile phone.*

mobile *noun* **mobiles**
a decoration which you hang up so that it can move about in the air.

mock *adjective*
not real. *a mock battle.*

mock *verb* **mocks, mocking, mocked**
to make fun of someone.

model *noun* **models**
1 a small copy of something. *a model aeroplane.*
2 someone whose job is to wear new clothes to show people what they look like.

moderate *adjective*
not too little and not too much. *Dad drives at moderate speed.*
moderately *adverb*

modern *adjective*
of the kind that is usual now. *a modern house.*

modest *adjective*
1 not boasting. *You didn't tell me you could sing so well – you're very modest!*
2 shy. *He was too modest to undress on the beach.*
modestly *adverb*

moist *adjective* **moister, moistest**
damp, just a little bit wet.

mole *noun* **moles**
a small, grey, furry animal that digs holes under the ground.

molten *adjective*
melted. *molten metal.*

moment *noun* **moments**
a very small amount of time.

monarch *noun* **monarchs**
a ruler who is a king, queen, emperor, or empress.

monastery *noun* **monasteries**
a house where monks live and work.

Monday *noun* **Mondays**
the second day of the week.

money *noun*
the coins and pieces of paper used when people buy and sell things.

mongrel *noun* **mongrels**
a dog that is a mixture of different kinds of dog.

monk *noun* **monks**
a religious man who lives with other men in a **monastery**

monkey *noun* **monkeys**
an animal with hands, feet it can use like hands, long arms, and a tail.

monster *noun* **monsters**
a large, frightening animal in stories.

month *noun* **months**
a measure for time. There are twelve months in a year.

monument *noun* **monuments**
a statue or building made so that people will remember someone or something. *a monument to soldiers who died in the war.*

mood *noun* **moods**
the way you feel.
in a good mood.

moody *adjective* **moodier, moodiest**
often in a bad mood.
moodily *adverb*

moon *noun*
the object that goes round the earth and shines in the sky at night. *There is a full moon tonight.*

moonlight *noun*
the light from the moon.

moor *noun* **moors**
an area of land that has bushes but no trees, because it is too windy. *the Yorkshire moors.*

moor *verb* **moors, mooring, moored**
to tie up a boat so that it will not float away.

mop *noun* **mops**
a bundle of strings or other material on the end of a stick, used to wipe things clean.

moral *noun* **morals**
a lesson about what is right or wrong. *a story with a moral.*

more *adjective, pronoun, adverb*
a bigger number or amount. *You've got more sweets than I have. I like oranges more than apples.*

morning *noun* **mornings**
the time from the beginning of the day until the middle of the day.

mortal *noun* **mortals**
all people are mortals because they cannot live forever.

mortar *noun*
a mixture of sand, cement, and water, used in building to stick bricks together.

mosaic *noun* **mosaics**
a picture made from coloured pieces of paper, glass, stone, or wood.

mosque *noun* **mosques**
a building where Muslims worship.

mosquito *noun* **mosquitoes**
an insect that sucks blood.

moss *noun* **mosses**
a plant that grows in damp places and has no flowers.

most *adjective, pronoun, adverb*
more than any other. *Which story did you like the most?*

moth *noun* **moths**
an insect like a butterfly, that flies usually at night.

mother *noun* **mothers**
a female parent.

motive *noun* **motives**
a reason for doing something.

motor *noun* **motors**
an engine, the part of a toy or machine that makes it go.

motor bike, motor cycle *noun*
motor bikes, motor cycles
a kind of bicycle with an engine.

motor car *noun* see **car**

motorist *noun* **motorists**
a person who drives a car.

motorway *noun* **motorways**
a wide road for fast traffic.

mould *noun* **moulds** (rhymes with *old*)
1 a kind of fungus that sometimes grows on food that has gone bad.
2 a container for making things set in the shape that is wanted. *a jelly mould.*

mound *noun* **mounds**
a pile of earth.

mount *verb* **mounts, mounting, mounted**
to get on to a horse or bicycle so that you can ride it.

mountain *noun* **mountains**
a very high hill.

mouse *noun* **mice**
1 a small, furry animal with a long tail.
2 a small device you move about on your desk to control the cursor on a computer screen.

moustache *noun* **moustaches**
hair that grows above a man's top lip.

mouth *noun* **mouths**
the part of the face that you use for eating and speaking.

move *verb* **moves, moving, moved**
1 to put something in another place. *Let's move the table over there.*
2 to go from one place to another. *We're moving house soon.*

movement *noun* **movements**
moving. *a sudden movement.*

mow *verb* **mows, mowing, mowed, mown**
to cut grass.

mower *noun* **mowers**
a machine that cuts grass.

much *adjective*
a lot. *I haven't got much money. I don't like carrots much.*

muck *noun*
dirt.

mud *noun*
wet soil.
muddy *adjective* a muddy field.

muddle *noun* **muddles**
a mess or something that has been mixed up. *This string has got in a muddle and now I can't undo it.*

muddle *verb* **muddles, muddling, muddled**
to mix things up and make a mess of something.

muesli *noun*
a food made of cereals, nuts, and dried fruit that you eat for breakfast.

muffled *adjective*
hard to hear, not clear. *muffled cries for help.*

mug *noun* **mugs**
a big cup.

mule *noun* **mules**
an animal whose parents were a horse and a donkey.

multiply *verb* **multiplies, multiplying, multiplied**
to make something a number of times bigger. *Two multiplied by four is eight, $2 \times 4 = 8$.*

mum, mummy *noun* **mums, mummies**
(*informal*) mother.

mumble *verb* **mumbles, mumbling, mumbled**
to speak quietly in a way that is not clear so that it is difficult to hear you.

mumps *noun*
an illness that makes the sides of the face swell.

munch *verb* **munches, munching, munched**
to chew noisily. *munching an apple.*

murder *verb* **murders, murdering, murdered**
to kill someone on purpose.

murmur *verb* **murmurs, murmuring, murmured**
to speak in a very soft, low voice.

muscle *noun* **muscles**
one of the parts inside you which you use to make your body move.

museum *noun* **museums**
a place where a lot of interesting things are kept for people to go and see.

mushroom *noun* **mushrooms**
a kind of fungus that you can eat.

music *noun*
the sounds made by someone singing or playing a musical instrument.

musical *adjective*
1 having to do with music. *musical instruments.*
2 good at music.

musician *noun* **musicians**
a person who sings or plays or composes music.

Muslim *noun* **Muslims**
someone who follows the religion of Islam.

mussel *noun* **mussels**
a small sea creature that lives inside a pair of black shells.

must *verb*
have to, be forced to, have a duty to. *You must go to school.*

mustard *noun*
a yellow substance which gives a strong, hot taste to food.
mustard and cress small green plants eaten in salad.

mutiny *noun* **mutinies**
an attack made by soldiers or sailors against the officers in charge of them.

mutter *verb* **mutters, muttering, muttered**
to speak in a low, quiet voice. *People often mutter if they are angry.*

mutton *noun*
meat from a sheep.

muzzle *noun* **muzzles**
1 an animal's nose and mouth.
2 a cover put over an animal's mouth so that it cannot bite.

my *adjective*
belonging to me. *my book.*

myself *pronoun*
I and no one else. *I can do it myself.*
by myself on my own. *I walked home by myself.*

mysterious *adjective*
strange and puzzling.
mysteriously *adverb*

mystery *noun* **mysteries**
something strange and puzzling that has happened.

myth *noun* **myths**
1 an old story, often about gods and goddesses.
2 a story that is not true.

Nn

nag *verb* **nags, nagging, nagged**
to keep telling someone that you are not pleased and that they ought to behave differently. *She nagged him to tidy his room.*

nail *noun* **nails**
1 the hard part at the end of each finger and toe. *fingernails, toenails.*
2 a small thin piece of metal with a sharp point at the end. It is used for fastening pieces of wood together.

nail *verb* **nails, nailing, nailed**
to join things or fix something with nails. *I nailed the two pieces of wood together.*

naked *adjective*
without any clothes on.

name *noun* **names**
the word you use to call or talk about someone or something.

name *verb* **names, naming, named**
to give a name to someone or something. *They named their baby Katie.*

nappy *noun* **nappies**
a piece of cloth or paper put round a baby's bottom.

narrator *noun* **narrators**
the person who tells a story.

narrow *adjective* **narrower, narrowest**
not wide. *a narrow road.*

narrowly *adverb*
only just. *We were narrowly beaten by the other team.*

nasty *adjective* **nastier, nastiest**
bad, not nice. *a nasty person.*

nation *noun* **nations**
a country and the people who live in it.

national *adjective*
belonging to one country. *He's wearing the national costume of Greece.*

native *noun* **natives**
someone born in the place that you are thinking of. *a native of Scotland.*

natural *adjective*
1 made by nature, not by people or machines. *the natural beauty of the Swiss mountains.*
2 normal. *It is natural for birds to fly.*
naturally *adverb*

nature *noun*
1 plants, animals, the sea, and everything else in the world that was not made by people.
2 what a person or animal is really like. *My dog has a gentle nature.*

naughty *adjective* **naughtier, naughtiest**
badly behaved. *the naughtiest boy in the class.*

navigate *verb* **navigates, navigating, navigated**
to make sure that a ship, aeroplane, or car is going in the right direction.

navy *noun* **navies**
a group of ships and the people trained to use them for fighting.

navy *adjective*
dark blue. *a navy blue jumper.*

near *adjective, adverb* **nearer, nearest**
not far away. *We live near the school. Where is the nearest park?*

nearly *adverb*
almost, not quite. *It's nearly 3 o'clock. We're nearly home.*

neat *adjective* **neater, neatest**
clean and tidy.
neatly *adverb Please fold your clothes up neatly.*

necessary *adjective*
having to be done. *It is necessary to water plants in dry weather.*
necessarily *adverb*

neck *noun* **necks**
the part of the body that joins the head to the shoulders.

necklace *noun* **necklaces**
beads, jewels, or a chain worn round the neck.

nectar *noun*
a sweet liquid inside flowers. Bees collect nectar to make honey.

need *verb* **needs, needing, needed**
1 to be without something that you ought to have or that is necessary. *Plants and animals need water.*
2 to have to do something. *I need to go to the dentist.*

needle *noun* **needles**
1 a very thin, pointed piece of metal with a hole at one end. You use needles for sewing. *I can't thread this needle.*
2 one of a pair of long sticks used for knitting. *knitting needles.*
3 a very thin, pointed leaf. Pine trees have needles.

neglect *verb* **neglects, neglecting, neglected**
to leave something alone and not look after it.

neigh *verb* **neighs, neighing, neighed**
to make the noise a horse makes.

neighbour *noun* **neighbours**
someone who lives next door or near to you.

neighbourhood *noun* **neighbourhoods**
the area near where you are. *Is there a shop in the neighbourhood?*

neither *pronoun*
not either. *'I don't like spinach.' 'Neither do I.'*

nephew *noun* **nephews**
the son of a brother or sister.

nerve *noun* **nerves**
1 one of the small parts inside the body that carry messages to and from the brain, so that the body can feel and move.
2 brave or calm behaviour when there is danger. *Don't lose your nerve.*

nervous *adjective*
1 afraid and excited because of something you have to do. *Are you nervous about going to the new school?*
2 easily frightened. *a nervous animal.*

nest *noun* **nests**
a cosy place made by birds, mice, and some other animals for their babies.

nestle *verb* **nestles, nestling, nestled**
to curl up comfortably.

net *noun* **nets**
material made of threads or wires joined together with holes between.

netball *noun*
a game where two teams of players try to throw a ball through a big round net.

nettle *noun* **nettles**
a plant with its stem and leaves covered in hairs that sting.

neutral *adjective*
not taking sides. *The referee has to be neutral.*

never *adverb*
not ever.

new *adjective* **newer, newest**
1 just bought or made. *a new bike.*
2 different. *my new school.*

news *noun*
words that tell you about something that has just happened.

newspaper *noun* **newspapers**
large sheets of paper folded together, with the news printed on them. Most newspapers come out every day.

newt *noun* **newts**
a small creature that lives near water and has four legs and a long tail.

next *adjective*
1 nearest, closest. *My friend lives in the next street.*
2 that comes after this one. *We're going on holiday next week.*

nibble *verb* **nibbles, nibbling, nibbled**
to eat something by biting off a little at a time.

nice *adjective* **nicer, nicest**
pleasant, of the kind you like.
nicely *adverb*

nickname *noun* **nicknames**
a name that your family or friends call you instead of your real name.

niece *noun* **nieces**
the daughter of your brother or sister.

night *noun* **nights**
the time when it is dark.

nightmare *noun* **nightmares**
a frightening dream.

nine *noun* **nines**
the number 9.
ninth *adjective*

nineteen
the number 19.
nineteenth *adjective*

ninety
the number 90.
ninetieth *adjective*

nip *verb* **nips, nipping, nipped**
to bite someone or squeeze their skin between the thumb and forefinger.

noble *adjective* **nobler, noblest**
1 of a rich important family. *a noble prince.*
2 good, honest, and not selfish. *noble thoughts.*

nobody *pronoun*
no person. *There was nobody at home.*

nod *verb* **nods, nodding, nodded**
to move your head up and down, as you do to show you agree with someone.

noise *noun* **noises**
1 a sound. *Did you hear a noise?*
2 a loud and unpleasant sound. *Stop that noise!*

noisy *adjective* **noisier, noisiest**
making an unpleasant noise.
noisily *adverb*

none *pronoun*
not any or not one. *I wanted some cake but there is none left.*

nonsense *noun*
something that does not mean anything.

noodles *noun*
food rather like spaghetti.

noon *noun*
twelve o'clock in the day.

normal *adjective*
usual, ordinary.
normally *adverb I normally get up at 7.30.*

north *noun*
the direction to your left when you face east.

nose *noun* **noses**
the part of the face that is used for breathing and smelling.

nostril *noun* **nostrils**
one of the two holes at the end of the nose for taking in air.

nosy *adjective* **nosier, nosiest**
too interested in what other people are doing. *'Where are you going?' 'Don't be so nosy!'*

note *noun* **notes**
1 a few words written down to remind you of something. *Make a note of the address.*
2 a short letter. *a thank you note.*
3 one sound in music. *I'll play the first few notes, then you join me.*
4 a piece of paper money. *a £5 note.*

nothing *noun*
not anything.

notice *noun* **notices**
a special piece of information, written on a poster or read out at assembly.

notice *verb* **notices, noticing, noticed**
to see something and think about it. *Jo noticed that Mum looked tired.*

nought *noun* **noughts**
the sign for nothing, 0.

noun *noun* **nouns**
a word that is the name of a person, place, thing, or idea. *Ann, England, chair,* and *happiness* are all nouns.

nourishing *adjective*
good for you. *nourishing food.*

novel *noun* **novels**
a long story which fills a book. *'Oliver Twist'* is a novel by Charles Dickens.

novelty *noun* **novelties**
something new or unusual.

November *noun*
the eleventh month of the year.

now *adverb*
at this time.
Do you want to go now?

nowhere *adverb*
not anywhere.

nozzle *noun* **nozzles**
the part at the end of a piece of pipe where a spray of liquid or powder comes out.

nude *adjective*
without any clothes.

nudge *verb* **nudges, nudging, nudged**
to push someone with your elbow to make them notice something.

nugget *noun* **nuggets**
a small piece of something. *gold nuggets.*

nuisance *noun* **nuisances**
someone or something that causes trouble. *It's a nuisance that we missed the bus.*

numb *adjective*
not able to feel anything. *My legs get numb.*

number *noun* **numbers**
the word or sign that tells you how many. 1, 2, and 3 are numbers.

numerous *adjective*
many.

nun *noun* **nuns**
a religious woman who lives with other women in a **nunnery**

nurse *noun* **nurses**
someone whose job is to look after people who are ill, hurt, or old.

nurse *verb* **nurses, nursing, nursed**
1 to look after or feed a baby.
2 to look after someone who is ill, hurt, or old.

nursery *noun* **nurseries**
1 a place where very young children go to play and be looked after.
2 a place where plants are grown from seed.

nut *noun* **nuts**
1 a fruit with a hard shell and a kernel inside that you can eat. *a hazelnut.*
2 a piece of metal with a hole in it which you screw on the end of a long piece of metal called a **bolt**. *You use nuts and bolts to fix things together.*

nuzzle *verb* **nuzzles, nuzzling, nuzzled**
to rub something with the nose.

nylon *noun*
a strong thin material for making clothes and other things.

Oo

oak *noun* **oaks**
a large tree with seeds called acorns.

oar *noun* **oars**
a long pole with a flat part at one end, used for rowing a boat.

oasis *noun* **oases**
a place with water and trees in a desert.

oath *noun* **oaths**
a serious promise.

oats *noun*
a plant grown by farmers. Its seed is used for feeding animals.

obedient *adjective*
willing to do what you are told.
obediently *adverb*

obey *verb* **obeys, obeying, obeyed**
to do what you are told.

object *noun* **objects**
1 anything that you can see or touch. *There were some interesting objects in the museum.*
2 In the sentence *Katie threw the ball*, the object of the verb is *the ball*.

object *verb* **objects, objecting, objected**
to say that you do not like or agree with something. *We objected to their bad language.*
objection *noun* **objections**

oblong *noun* **oblongs**
a rectangle, the shape of a door or the page of a book.

observe *verb* **observes, observing, observed**
to watch carefully. *We observed the robin building her nest.*

obstacle *noun* **obstacles**
something that is in the way and stops you doing what you want to do.

obstinate *adjective*
hard to persuade, sticking to your own ideas even if they might be wrong.
obstinately *adverb*

obtain *verb* **obtains, obtaining, obtained**
to get, to buy, to be given. *Where can I obtain tickets for the play?*

obvious *adjective*
easy to see or understand.
obviously *adverb*

occasion *noun* **occasions**
the time when something happens. *Your birthday is a special occasion.*

occasional *adjective*
happening sometimes, not regular.
occasionally *adverb*

occupation *noun* **occupations**
any job or hobby.

occupy *verb* **occupies, occupying, occupied**
1 to live in or use something. *Is this seat occupied?*
2 to keep someone busy and interested. *Keeping young children occupied is a hard job.*

a b c d e f g h i j k l m **n** **o** p q r s t u v w x y z

occur *verb* **occurs, occurring, occurred**
1 to happen. *When did the accident occur?*
2 to come into your mind. *An idea occurred to me.*

ocean *noun* **oceans**
a big sea. *the Atlantic Ocean.*

o'clock *adverb*
by the clock. *one o'clock.*

octagon *noun* **octagons**
a shape with eight sides.

October *noun*
the tenth month of the year.

octopus *noun* **octopuses**
a sea creature with eight arms.

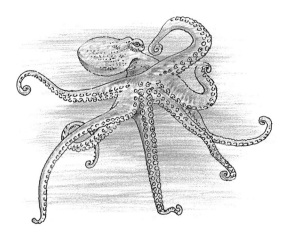

odd *adjective* **odder, oddest**
1 strange. *an odd person.*
2 not even. *Five is an odd number.*
3 not alike. *odd shoes.*

odds and ends *noun*
various things that you do not really want.

of *preposition*
THIS WORD HAS SEVERAL USES. HERE ARE SOME OF THE WAYS YOU CAN USE IT: *a glass of milk, the 1st of June, the front of the book, a box made of wood.*

off *adverb, preposition*
THIS WORD HAS SEVERAL USES. HERE ARE SOME OF THE WAYS YOU CAN USE IT:
1 down from. *He fell off the wall.*
2 not working. *The heating is off.*
3 away. *The thieves ran off.*

offend *verb* **offends, offending, offended**
to hurt someone's feelings.

offensive *adjective*
nasty and very annoying. *an offensive smell.*

offer *verb* **offers, offering, offered**
1 to hold out something so that another person can take it if they want it. *She offered me a piece of cake.*
2 to say that you are willing to do something. *He offered to lay the table.*

office *noun* **offices**
a room with desks and telephones, where people work.

officer *noun* **officers**
1 a person in charge of others in the army, navy, or air force.
2 a policeman or policewoman.

official *adjective*
done or made or said by someone in charge. *Is it official that we've got a holiday next week?*
officially *adverb*

off-licence *noun* **off-licences**
a shop which is allowed to sell alcoholic drinks like beer and wine.

often *adverb*
many times. *We often go swimming on Saturday.*

ogre *noun* **ogres**
a cruel giant in stories.

oil *noun*
a thick, slippery liquid. You can use various kinds of oil as fuel, to make machinery work better, and in cooking.

ointment *noun* **ointments**
a cream for putting on sore skin or cuts.

old *adjective* **older, oldest**
1 born or made a long time ago.
an old man, an old car.
2 known for a long time.
an old friend.

old-fashioned *adjective*
of the kind that was usual a long time ago. *old-fashioned clothes.*

omelette *noun* **omelettes**
eggs that are mixed together and fried.

omit *verb* **omits, omitting, omitted**
to leave out. *Omit verse 2 and sing verses 3 and 4.*

once *adverb*
1 one time. *She only missed school once this term.*
2 at one time. *Once dinosaurs roamed the earth.*
at once immediately, now. *Come here at once!*

one *noun* **ones**
the number 1.

onion *noun* **onions**
a round, white vegetable with a very strong flavour.

only *adjective, adverb*
THIS WORD HAS SEVERAL USES. HERE ARE SOME OF THE WAYS YOU CAN USE IT: *There is only one cake left. It's only 4 o'clock. I only touched it. I didn't break it.*
an only child a child with no brothers or sisters.

onwards *adverb*
forwards. *We walked onwards until we came to the river.*

ooze *verb* **oozes, oozing, oozed**
to come slowly through a hole or small opening. *Blood oozed from the cut.*

open *adjective*
not closed, allowing people or things to go through or in. *an open door.*

open *verb* **opens, opening, opened**
to make something open.

opening *noun* **openings**
a space, a way through. *We crawled through a small opening in the hedge.*

opera *noun* **operas**
a play in which all or most of the words are sung.

operation *noun* **operations**
something done by doctors to a sick person's body to make it healthy again.

opinion *noun* **opinions**
what you think of something. *In your opinion, which colour looks best?*

opponent *noun* **opponents**
a person that you argue or fight with, or play a game against. *We beat our opponents easily.*

opportunity *noun* **opportunities**
a good chance to do something.

oppose *verb* **opposes, opposing, opposed**
to fight or argue or play against someone or something.

opposite *adjective, adverb, preposition*
1 facing. *the opposite side of the road.*
2 completely different. *North is the opposite direction to South.*

opposite *noun* **opposites**
something that is as different as possible from another thing. *Hot and cold are opposites.*

optician *noun* **opticians**
someone who makes or sells glasses to make you see better.

orange *noun* **oranges**
1 a round, juicy fruit with thick peel and white pips.
2 the colour of this fruit.

orbit *noun* **orbits**
the path of something moving round the sun or a planet in space.

orchard *noun* **orchards**
a place where a lot of fruit trees grow. *an apple orchard.*

orchestra *noun* **orchestras**
(*-ch-* in this word sounds like *-k-*) a large group of people playing musical instruments together.

ordeal *noun* **ordeals**
a time when you have to put up with great pain or trouble.

order *noun* **orders**
1 a statement that you must do something. *Soldiers must always obey orders.*
2 the way that you place people or things together. *alphabetical order.*

order *verb* **orders, ordering, ordered**
1 to tell someone to do something. *The officer ordered the soldiers to march.*
2 to ask for something to be brought to you. *He ordered fish and chips.*

orderly *adjective*
properly arranged, well behaved.

ordinary *adjective*
usual, normal, not special.

organ *noun* **organs**
a musical instrument with one or more keyboards like a piano. It sometimes has pedals and pipes.

a
b
c
d
e
f
g
h
i
j
k
l
m
n
o
p
q
r
s
t
u
v
w
x
y
z

organize *verb* **organizes, organizing, organized**
1 to get people working together to do something.
2 to plan and arrange things like parties, concerts, or holidays.

organizer *noun* **organizers**
someone who organizes things.

original *adjective*
1 first, existing from the beginning. *Our car still has the original tyres.*
2 new, not copied. *an original idea.*
originally *adverb*

ornament *noun* **ornaments**
something put in a place to make it look pretty.

orphan *noun* **orphans**
a child whose mother and father are dead.

ostrich *noun* **ostriches**
a very large bird that cannot fly and has long legs.

other *adjective, pronoun*
not the same as this. *I like the other biscuits better. I can't find my other shoe.*

otherwise *adverb, conjunction*
or else.
Hurry up otherwise we'll be late.

otter *noun* **otters**
a furry animal that lives near water. Otters have long tails.

ought *verb*
should. *I ought to go now.*

ounce *noun* **ounces**
a measure for weight. 16 ounces make one pound.

our *adjective*
belonging to us. *Come round to our house.*

ourselves *pronoun*
we and no one else. *We made ourselves some sandwiches.*
by ourselves on our own, without help. *We painted the shed by ourselves.*

out *adjective, adverb*
THIS WORD HAS SEVERAL USES. HERE ARE SOME OF THE WAYS YOU CAN USE IT: *Jo went out today. Put the light out please. The sun has come out again. Fish can't live out of water.*

outfit *noun* **outfits**
a set of clothes you wear together. *Mum bought a new outfit to wear at her sister's wedding.*

outing *noun* **outings**
a day or afternoon out somewhere.

outlaw *noun* **outlaws**
someone long ago who had to hide, because as a punishment they were not protected by the law and anyone could kill them. Robin Hood was a famous outlaw.

outline *noun* **outlines**
a line round the edge of something, that shows its shape.
It was dark but we could still see the outline of the houses.

outside *adjective, adverb, preposition*
not inside. *We went outside to play in the garden.*

outside *noun*
the surface or edge of something, the part farthest from the middle. *The outside of a coconut is brown and hairy and the inside is white.*

outstanding *adjective*
unusually good.

outwards *adverb*
away from the middle. *We stood in a circle facing outwards.*

oval *noun, adjective*
the shape of an egg.

oven *noun* **ovens**
the place inside a cooker, where food can be baked or roasted.

over *adverb, preposition*
THIS WORD HAS SEVERAL USES. HERE ARE SOME OF THE WAYS YOU CAN USE IT: *We climbed over the fence. I won't buy it if it costs over £10. Come straight home when school is over. She put a blanket over the sleeping bag.*

overall *noun* **overalls**
something worn over other clothes to keep them clean.

overboard *adverb*
over the side of a boat into the water. *I nearly fell overboard!*

overcome *verb* **overcomes, overcoming, overcame**
to control or defeat. *She tried to overcome her fear of the dark.*

overflow *verb* **overflows, overflowing, overflowed**
to come over the sides of a container, because there is too much in it. *Turn off the taps. The bath is overflowing!*

overgrown *adjective*
covered with plants you do not want. *an overgrown garden.*

overhead *adjective, adverb*
above the head. *overhead wires, a plane flying overhead.*

oversleep *verb* **oversleeps, oversleeping, overslept**
to go on sleeping too long.

overtake *verb* **overtakes, overtaking, overtook, overtaken**
to catch up and pass someone.

overturn *verb* **overturns, overturning, overturned**
to push or knock something over.

overweight *adjective*
too heavy, too fat.

owe *verb* **owes, owing, owed**
to have to pay money to someone.

owl *noun* **owls**
a bird with large eyes that hunts smaller animals at night.

own *adjective, pronoun*
my own mine and no one else's. *my own room*
on my own by myself. *I played on my own today.*

own *verb* **owns, owning, owned**
to be able to keep something because it belongs to you.
to own up to admit that you have done something wrong.

ox *noun* **oxen**
a large animal kept for its meat or for pulling carts.

oxygen *noun*
the gas in the air that everyone needs to breathe in order to stay alive.

oyster *noun* **oysters**
a sea creature that lives inside a pair of shells.

ozone *noun*
a form of oxygen.
ozone layer a layer of ozone high above the earth which protects us from the dangerous rays of the sun.

Pp

pace *noun* **paces**
1 a step.
2 how quickly something happens or moves. *The horse galloped at a fast pace.*

a b c d e f g h i j k l m n **o** **p** q r s t u v w x y z

131

pack *noun* **packs**
1 a group of dogs or wolves.
2 a group of things that you buy together.
3 a set of cards used in games.

pack *verb* **packs, packing, packed**
to put things into a box, bag, or suitcase.

package *noun* **packages**
something wrapped in paper; a parcel.

packet *noun* **packets**
a small box or bag that you buy things in. *a packet of biscuits.*

pad *noun* **pads**
1 sheets of writing paper joined together along one edge so that you can tear a sheet off when you need it.
2 material used as a kind of cushion to protect something.

pad *verb* **pads, padding, padded**
1 to protect something or make it more comfortable with a pad of soft material.
2 to walk softly.
She padded across the floor with bare feet.

paddle *noun* **paddles**
a length of wood with a flat part at one end, used to make a canoe move.

paddle *verb* **paddles, paddling, paddled**
1 to walk about in shallow water.
We went paddling in the sea.
2 to move a canoe through water.
We paddled down the river.

padlock *noun* **padlocks**
a lock that you use on gates and bicycles.

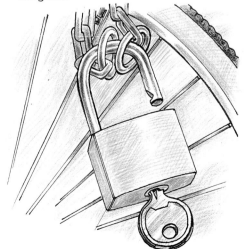

page *noun* **pages**
a piece of paper that is part of a book.

paid *verb* see **pay**

pail *noun* **pails**
a bucket.

pain *noun* **pains**
the feeling you have in your body when you are hurt or ill.

painful *adjective*
giving pain. *a painful cut.*
painfully *adverb*

paint *noun* **paints**
a substance you can use to make coloured pictures or to give things a new colour.

paint *verb* **paints, painting, painted**
to use paint to make a picture or to colour something.
painter *noun* **painters**

painting *noun* **paintings**
a picture that has been painted.

pair *noun* **pairs**
two people, animals, or things that belong together.
a pair of shoes.

palace *noun* **palaces**
a very large house where a king, queen, or some other very important person lives.

pale *adjective* **paler, palest**
1 almost white.
a pale face.
2 light.
a pale blue sky.

palm *noun* **palms**
1 the inside of the hand between the fingers and wrist.
2 a tropical tree with large leaves and no branches.

pamper *verb* **pampers, pampering, pampered**
to treat a person or animal too well.

pan *noun* **pans**
a metal pot that you use for cooking.
a frying pan, a saucepan.

pancake *noun* **pancakes**
flour, milk, and egg mixed together and fried.

panda *noun* **pandas**
an animal found in China. Giant pandas look like large black and white bears.

pane *noun* **panes**
a piece of glass in a window.

panel *noun* **panels**
a long, flat piece of wood or metal that is part of a door, wall, or piece of furniture.

panic *noun*
sudden fear that cannot be controlled. *He felt panic when he saw the fire.*

pansy *noun* **pansies**
a small plant with a brightly coloured flower.

pant *verb* **pants, panting, panted**
to take short, quick breaths, usually after running.

panther *noun* **panthers**
a wild animal like a very big black cat.

pantomime *noun* **pantomimes**
a kind of play, usually done at Christmas.

pantry *noun* **pantries**
a small room where food is kept.

pants *noun*
1 underpants that boys and men wear.
2 knickers that girls and women wear.

paper *noun* **papers**
1 thin material used to write on, to make books with, and to wrap things in. *a sheet of paper, a paper bag.*
2 a newspaper.

parable *noun* **parables**
a story told in order to teach people something.

parachute *noun* **parachutes**
a large piece of cloth that opens up like an umbrella when a cord is pulled. It is tied to someone's back so that they can jump out of an aeroplane and float safely down to the ground.

parade *noun* **parades**
people marching along, while other people watch them.

paradise *noun*
a wonderful place where people are happy; heaven.

paraffin *noun*
a liquid made from oil, that is burnt to make heat.

paragraph *noun* **paragraphs**
a group of lines of writing. You begin each new paragraph on a new line.

parallel lines *noun*
straight lines that are always the same distance from each other.

paralysed *adjective*
someone who is paralysed cannot move or feel anything.

parcel *noun* **parcels**
something wrapped up ready to be carried or posted.

parched *adjective*
very dry or thirsty.

pardon *verb* **pardons, pardoning, pardoned**
to forgive.

parent *noun* **parents**
1 a person who has a child.
2 an animal that has young ones.

parish *noun* **parishes**
an area that has its own church and priest or minister.

park *noun* **parks**
a large space with grass and trees where anyone can walk or play.

park *verb* **parks, parking, parked**
to leave a car somewhere until you need it again.

parliament *noun* **parliaments**
the people who make the laws of a country.

parrot *noun* **parrots**
a brightly coloured bird that can copy things people say.

parsley *noun*
a green plant used in cooking to flavour food.

parsnip *noun* **parsnips**
a pale yellow vegetable with a sweet taste.

part *noun* **parts**
anything that belongs to something bigger. *I've only read part of the story so far.*
part of speech any of the groups into which words are divided in grammar, such as *adjective, adverb, noun,* or *verb.*

particular *adjective*
1 only this one and no other. *I wanted this particular colour.*
2 choosing carefully, fussy. *She's particular about what she eats.*
particularly *adverb*

partly *adverb*
not completely.

partner *noun* **partners**
one of two people who do things together.

party *noun* **parties**
a group of people enjoying themselves together. *a birthday party.*

pass *verb* **passes, passing, passed**
1 to go by. *On my way to school I pass the sweet shop.*
2 to give someone something they want, but cannot reach themselves. *Please pass the salt.*
3 to be successful in a test. *She's passed her driving test.*

passage *noun* **passages**
a corridor.

passenger *noun* **passengers**
a person who is travelling in a bus, train, ship, or aeroplane, but not driving it.

Passover *noun*
a holy time for Jews.

passport *noun* **passports**
a small book with your name and photograph in it. You must take it with you when you go to another country.

past *adjective, adverb, preposition*
THIS WORD HAS SEVERAL USES. HERE ARE SOME OF THE WAYS YOU CAN USE IT: *We watched the cars go past. The bus goes past the school. It's half-past six.*

past *noun*
the time that has gone. *In the past people used candles instead of electric lights.*

pasta *noun*
a food made from flour and water. Spaghetti and macaroni are kinds of pasta.

paste *noun*
a soft wet mixture which is easy to spread.
fish paste, wallpaper paste.

pastime *noun* **pastimes**
something you do or play in your free time.

pastry *noun* **pastries**
1 a mixture of flour, fat, and water rolled flat and used for making pies.
2 a kind of cake made of pastry.

pasture *noun*
land covered in grass that cattle, sheep, or horses can eat.

pat *verb* **pats, patting, patted**
to touch someone or something gently with an open hand. *Tom patted the dog on the head.*

patch *noun* **patches**
1 a small piece of material put over something to mend it or protect it.
2 a small piece of something. *There is a patch of blue in the sky.*

path *noun* **paths**
a narrow way that you can walk along to get somewhere. *a path across the field.*

patience *noun*
if you have patience you can wait a long time or do something difficult without getting angry. *Learning to sew takes a lot of patience.*

patient *adjective*
able to bear pain or able to wait.
patiently *adverb*

patient *noun* **patients**
someone who is ill and being looked after by a doctor.

patio *noun* **patios**
an area by the side of a house covered with paving stones.

patrol *noun* **patrols**
a group of soldiers or policemen who move around a place to guard it.

patter *verb* **patters, pattering, pattered**
to make the light, tapping sound rain makes against a window.

pattern *noun* **patterns**
1 lines, shapes, or colours on something to make it look interesting or attractive. *a dress with a flowery pattern.*
2 anything that people copy in order to make something. *Mum bought some material and a pattern to make me a new skirt.*

pause *verb* **pauses, pausing, paused**
to stop for a very short time.

pavement *noun* **pavements**
the path for people to walk on along the side of a street.

paving stone *noun* **paving stones**
a large, flat stone used to make pavements or patios.

paw *noun* **paws**
an animal's foot.

pawn *noun* **pawns**
one of the small, least important pieces in the game of chess.

pay *verb* **pays, paying, paid**
to give money in return for something.

payment *noun* **payments**
money that you pay for something.

PE
short for physical education.

pea *noun* **peas**
a tiny, round, green vegetable that grows inside a pod.

peace *noun*
1 a time free from war.
2 a time of quiet and rest. *We enjoy the peace and quiet when the baby is asleep.*

peaceful *adjective*
quiet, calm.
peacefully *adverb*

peach *noun* **peaches**
a round, soft, juicy fruit with a large stone and a thin, yellow skin.

peacock *noun* **peacocks**
a large bird with long, brightly coloured tail feathers that it can spread out like a fan.

peak *noun* **peaks**
1 the top of a mountain.
2 the part of a cap that sticks out in front.

peanut *noun* **peanuts**
a tiny, round nut that grows in a pod in the ground.

pear *noun* **pears**
a juicy fruit that is narrow where the stalk is.

pearl *noun* **pearls**
a small, shiny, white ball found inside the shells of some oysters.

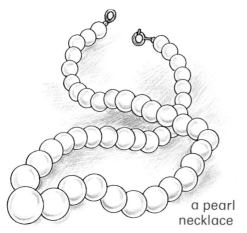

a pearl necklace

peat *noun*
soil that is formed from decaying plants.

pebble *noun* **pebbles**
a small, round stone.

peck *verb* **pecks, pecking, pecked**
to use the beak to pick up food or push at something.

peculiar *adjective*
strange. *This ice cream has a peculiar taste.*
peculiarly *adverb*

pedal *noun* **pedals**
a part of a bicycle or other machine that you press with your foot to make it work.

pedestrian *noun* **pedestrians**
someone who is walking.

peel *noun*
the skin on some fruit and vegetables. *orange peel.*

peel *verb* **peels, peeling, peeled**
to take the skin off something. *Sam peeled the potatoes.*

peep *verb* **peeps, peeping, peeped**
to look quickly or secretly.

peer *verb* **peers, peering, peered**
to get very close to something to look at it.

peg *noun* **pegs**
1 a clip for fixing washing on a line. *a clothes peg.*
2 a short wooden or metal rod to hang things on. *Hang your coats on the pegs.*

pelican *noun* **pelicans**
a bird with a very large beak.

pellet *noun* **pellets**
a tiny ball of wet paper, metal, food, or medicine.

pelt *verb* **pelts, pelting, pelted**
to throw a lot of things at someone. *They pelted the boys with snowballs.*

pen *noun* **pens**
a thing that you use for writing with ink.

penalty *noun* **penalties**
a punishment. *The penalty for travelling without a ticket is £300.*

pencil *noun* **pencils**
a thin stick of wood with black or coloured stuff in the middle, for writing or drawing with.

pendant *noun* **pendants**
something that you hang round your neck on a long chain or string. *a silver pendant.*

pendulum *noun* **pendulums**
a stick with a weight hanging from its end so that it swings backwards and forwards. Some large old-fashioned clocks have pendulums to make them work.

penetrate *verb* **penetrates; penetrating, penetrated**
to make or find a way through something. *The cold wind penetrated even his winter coat.*

penguin *noun* **penguins**
a black and white bird that swims in the sea but cannot fly.

penknife *noun* **penknives**
a small knife that folds up so that you can carry it with you safely.

penny *noun* **pennies** or **pence**
a coin. *100 pence = £1.*

pentagon *noun* **pentagons**
a shape with five sides.

people *noun*
men, women, and children.

pepper *noun*
a spice used to flavour food.

peppermint *noun* **peppermints**
a sweet with a strong mint flavour.

perch *noun* **perches**
anything that a bird rests on when it is not flying.

percussion instrument *noun*
percussion instruments
any musical instrument that is banged, hit, or shaken. Drums, cymbals, and tambourines are percussion instruments.

perfect *adjective*
so good that it cannot be better.
perfectly *adverb*

perform *verb* **performs, performing, performed**
to do something in front of a lot of people.
We performed the school play in front of our parents.
performer *noun* **performers**

performance *noun* **performances**
something done in front of a lot of people.

perfume *noun* **perfumes**
1 a nice smell.
2 a liquid with a nice smell that you put on your body.
a bottle of perfume.

perhaps *adverb*
possibly.
Perhaps it will rain tomorrow.

peril *noun* **perils**
danger.

perimeter *noun*
the distance round the edge of something.
We measured the perimeter of the playground.

period *noun* **periods**
a length of time.
What period of history are you studying?

perish *verb* **perishes, perishing, perished**
1 to die.
The sailors perished in the storm.
2 to become dry and wrinkled and no longer any use. Rubber perishes.

permanent *adjective*
lasting for ever or for a very long time.
permanently *adverb*

permission *noun*
words that say something is allowed.

permit *noun* **permits**
written permission to do something. *a fishing permit.*

permit *verb* **permits, permitting, permitted**
to allow.

persist *verb* **persists, persisting, persisted**
to carry on doing something no matter what happens.

person *noun* **persons**
a man, woman, or child.

a b c d e f g h i j k l m n o **p** q r s t u v w x y z

personal *adjective*
1 by, or for, or belonging to a particular person. *my personal belongings.*
2 about a particular person. *Don't make rude personal remarks.*
personally *adverb*

persuade *verb* **persuades, persuading, persuaded**
to get someone to agree to something. *Jo persuaded her mum to let her go to the cinema.*

pest *noun* **pests**
any person, animal, or plant that causes a lot of trouble.

pester *verb* **pesters, pestering, pestered**
to keep worrying someone by asking questions. *Sam pestered his dad about getting a new bike.*

pet *noun* **pets**
any animal which you keep so that you can enjoy its company.

petal *noun* **petals**
one of the separate, coloured parts of a flower.

petrol *noun*
a liquid that you put in cars to make them work.

pew *noun* **pews**
one of the long wooden seats in a church.

phone *noun* **phones**
a telephone.

phone *verb* **phones, phoning, phoned**
to use a telephone to speak to someone.

photo *noun* **photos**
a photograph.

photocopier *noun* **photocopiers**
a machine which makes copies of things written or printed on paper.

photograph *noun* **photographs**
a picture taken on film with a camera.

photograph *verb* **photographs, photographing, photographed**
to take a photograph of something.

phrase *noun* **phrases**
a group of words that you use together as part of a sentence.

physical *adjective*
having to do with the body. *physical exercise.*
physical education sport that you do at school.

piano *noun* **pianos**
a large musical instrument with white and black keys that you press with your fingers.

pick *verb* **picks, picking, picked**
1 to choose. *We picked Michael for captain of the football team.*
2 to take something up from where it is. *I picked up some shells on the beach.*
3 to take flowers or fruit from plants and trees. *I've picked some flowers for you.*

pickaxe *noun* **pickaxes**
a heavy tool with a long handle, for breaking up very hard ground.

picnic *noun* **picnics**
a meal eaten in the open air away from home. *a picnic lunch.*

picture *noun* **pictures**
a painting, drawing, or photograph.

pie *noun* **pies**
meat, vegetables, or fruit covered with pastry and baked. *an apple pie.*

piece *noun* **pieces**
a part of something. *a piece of cake, pieces of broken glass.*

pier *noun* **piers**
a long structure built out into the sea. Some piers have shops, cafés, and amusements on them.

pierce *verb* **pierces, piercing, pierced**
to make a hole through something.

pig *noun* **pigs**
an animal with short legs and a curly tail kept by farmers. Bacon, ham, and pork come from pigs.

pigeon *noun* **pigeons**
a grey bird that often lives in towns.

piglet *noun* **piglets**
a young pig.

pigtail *noun* **pigtails**
a plait of hair.

pile *noun* **piles**
a number of things put on top of one another. *a pile of books.*

pilgrim *noun* **pilgrims**
someone who makes a journey to a holy place.

pill *noun* **pills**
a small, round tablet that you take if you are ill.

pillar *noun* **pillars**
a wooden or stone post that helps to hold up a building.

pillow *noun* **pillows**
the cushion that you rest your head on in bed.

pilot *noun* **pilots**
1 someone who flies an aeroplane.
2 someone who steers a ship in narrow, difficult places.

pimple *noun* **pimples**
a small, round swelling on the skin.

pin *noun* **pins**
a thin piece of metal, with a sharp point. You use it to hold pieces of material or paper together.

pincers *noun*
a tool for holding something tightly.

pinch *verb* **pinches, pinching, pinched**
1 to squeeze skin between your thumb and finger so that it hurts.
2 (*informal*) to steal. *Who pinched my pencil?*

pine *noun* **pines**
a tree with leaves like needles that do not fall in winter. *pine cones.*

pine *verb* **pines, pining, pined**
to get miserable and ill because you miss someone very much. *Jo's dog pined when she was away.*

pineapple *noun* **pineapples**
a large fruit with a yellow inside that grows in hot countries. It has stiff, pointed leaves and a thick skin covered in lumps.

pink *noun, adjective*
a pale red colour.

pint *noun* **pints**
a measure for liquid.

pip *noun* **pips**
a seed of a fruit such as an apple or orange.

pipe *noun* **pipes**
1 a tube for gas or liquid to go along.
2 a tube with a small bowl at one end, used for smoking tobacco.

pirate *noun* **pirates**
someone on a ship, who attacks and robs other ships.

pistol *noun* **pistols**
a small gun.

pit *noun* **pits**
a deep hole.

pitch *noun* **pitches**
1 ground marked out for cricket, football, or another game.
2 how high or low a sound is.

pitch *verb* **pitches, pitching, pitched**
to put up a tent.

pity *noun*
the feeling you have when you are sorry that someone is in pain or trouble.

pity *verb* **pities, pitying, pitied**
to feel pity for someone.

pizza *noun* **pizzas**
a flat piece of dough covered with tomatoes, cheese, and other things, and baked.

place *noun* **places**
1 a particular building, area, or spot. *We went to our favourite place for a picnic.*
Please put the book back in the right place.
2 where you are in a race or test. *Sam finished in second place.*

place *verb* **places, placing, placed**
to put something somewhere.
Place your rubbish in the bin.
Where have you placed the arrow?

plague *noun* **plagues**
a dangerous illness that spreads very quickly.

plaice *noun* **(the plural is the same)**
a flat sea fish.

plain *adjective* **plainer, plainest**
1 ordinary, not specially attractive. *a plain cake.*
2 easy to understand. *He gave me plain instructions.*

plain *noun* **plains**
a large area of flat ground. *You can see for miles over the plain.*

plait *noun* **plaits**
a long piece of plaited hair.

plait *verb* **plaits, plaiting, plaited**
to twist together three pieces of hair, rope, or wool by crossing them over and under each other.

plan *noun* **plans**
1 a set of ideas about how to do something. *Sam has a plan for making a den in the garden.*
2 a map of a building or a town.

plan *verb* **plans, planning, planned**
to decide what you are going to do and how to do it.
We planned to have a picnic in the holidays.

plane *noun* **planes**
1 an aeroplane.
2 a tool for making wood smooth.

planet *noun* **planets**
any of the worlds in space that move round the sun. The earth is a planet.

plank *noun* **planks**
a long, flat piece of wood.

plant *noun* **plants**
a living thing that is not an animal. Trees, flowers, and mushrooms are all plants.

plant *verb* **plants, planting, planted**
to put something in the ground to grow.

plaster *noun* **plasters**
1 a sticky strip of special material for covering cuts.
2 a soft mixture that goes hard when it dries. Plaster is used for covering walls.

plastic *noun, adjective*
a light, strong material that is made in factories and used for making all kinds of things.
plastic spoons.

plasticine *noun*
a soft, coloured substance you can use to make models.

plate *noun* **plates**
a flat dish for eating from.

platform *noun* **platforms**
1 the place in a station where people wait beside the railway lines for a train.
2 a raised place where people stand so that other people can see them.

play *noun* **plays**
a story acted in a theatre or on television.

play *verb* **plays, playing, played**
1 to have fun. *Jo plays with her friends on Saturdays.*
2 to take part in a game. *Sam likes playing football.*
3 to make music with a musical instrument. *Can you play the piano?*

playful *adjective*
wanting to play, full of fun. *a playful kitten.*

playground *noun* **playgrounds**
a place out of doors where children can play.

playing card *noun* **playing cards**
one of a set of cards used in some games.

playtime *noun* **playtimes**
the time at school when children can go out to play.

plead *verb* **pleads, pleading, pleaded**
to beg for something that you want very much. *She pleaded with her parents to buy a dog.*

pleasant *adjective*
pleasing, nice.
pleasantly *adverb*

please *verb* **pleases, pleasing, pleased**
1 to make someone happy.
2 the polite word you use when you are asking for something. *Please may I have another cake?*

pleasure *noun*
the feeling people have when they are pleased.

pleat *noun* **pleats**
a fold in the material of a dress, skirt, or kilt.

pleated *adjective*
with pleats.

plenty *noun*
a lot of something, as much as you need.

pliers *noun*
a tool for holding something tightly or for bending or breaking wire.

plimsoll *noun* **plimsolls**
a light, canvas shoe with a rubber sole.

plod *verb* **plods, plodding, plodded**
to walk slowly and heavily.

plot *noun* **plots**
a secret plan.

plot *verb* **plots, plotting, plotted**
to plan something secretly.

plough *noun* **ploughs**
(rhymes with *how*)
a machine used on farms for digging and turning over the soil.

plough

pluck *verb* **plucks, plucking, plucked**
1 to pull a feather, flower, or fruit from the place where it is growing.
2 to pull at something and let it go quickly. People play guitars by plucking the strings.

plucky *adjective* **pluckier, pluckiest**
brave.

plug *noun* **plugs**
1 a thing on the end of a wire which fits in an electric socket.
2 a round piece of rubber or plastic which stops water from running out of a bath or sink.
3 anything you use to fill a hole.

plum *noun* **plums**
a juicy fruit with a stone in it.

plumber *noun* **plumbers**
a person whose job is to put in taps, water pipes, and water tanks, or to mend them.

plump *adjective* **plumper, plumpest**
rather fat.

plunge *verb* **plunges, plunging, plunged**
to jump suddenly into water, or to put something suddenly in water.

plural *adjective*
the form of a word you use when you are talking about more than one person or thing. The plural of 'book' is 'books'. The plural of 'child' is 'children'.

plus *preposition*
add. *Three plus three is six, 3 + 3 = 6.*

plywood *noun*
a kind of wood made from thin sheets of wood glued together.

pneumonia *noun*
(*pn-* in this word sounds like *n-*)
a serious illness that makes it painful to breathe.

poach *verb* **poaches, poaching, poached**
1 to cook an egg in boiling water or steam without its shell.
2 to hunt animals that are on someone else's land.

pocket *noun* **pockets**
a small bag in your clothes that you put things in.

pocket money *noun*
money which someone gives you to buy things that you want.

pod *noun* **pods**
a long thin part of some plants that has seeds inside. Peas grow in pods.

poem *noun* **poems**
a piece of writing, often with lines that may rhyme.

poet *noun* **poets**
a person who writes poetry.

poetry *noun*
poems.

point *noun* **points**
1 the sharp end of something. *the point of a needle*
2 a particular place or time. *We should soon reach the point where we can see the sea.*
3 a mark scored in a game. *Our team scored the most points.*
4 the reason for doing something. *The point of going to school is to learn.*

point *verb* **points, pointing, pointed**
1 to show where something is by holding your finger out towards it.
2 to aim a weapon. *He pointed the gun at the target.*

pointed *adjective*
with a point at the end.

poison *noun* **poisons**
any liquid, powder, or plant that will kill or harm you if you swallow it.

poisonous *adjective*
likely to harm you because it contains poison.

poke *verb* **pokes, poking, poked**
to push hard with the end of your finger or a stick.

poker *noun* **pokers**
a metal rod for poking a fire.

polar bear *noun* **polar bears**
a very large, white bear that lives in the Arctic.

pole *noun* **poles**
a long, round stick, a tall post.
North Pole the cold place that is the farthest north in the world.
South Pole the cold place that is the farthest south in the world.

police *noun*
the people whose job is to catch criminals and make sure that the law is kept.

policeman *noun* **policemen**
a man who is in the police.

policewoman *noun* **policewomen**
a woman who is in the police.

polish *noun* **polishes**
a substance which helps to make something shine. *furniture polish.*

polish *verb* **polishes, polishing, polished**
to rub the surface of something to make it shine.

polite *adjective* **politer, politest**
having good manners. *a polite boy.*
politely *adverb*

politician *noun* **politicians**
a person who works in the government.

politics *noun*
the work of government.

pollen *noun*
yellow powder in a flower which wind or insects take to other flowers so that they can produce seeds.

pollute *verb* **pollutes, polluting, polluted**
to make air, water, and other things dirty and dangerous.
Many rivers are polluted with chemicals from factories.

pollution *noun*
dirty and unhealthy air or water.
Smoke and waste from factories cause pollution.

pond *noun* **ponds**
a very small lake.

pony *noun* **ponies**
a small horse.

ponytail *noun* **ponytails**
a bunch of long hair tied together at the back of your head.

poodle *noun* **poodles**
a kind of dog with curly hair often cut very short on some parts of its body.

pool *noun* **pools**
a small area of water.

poor *adjective* **poorer, poorest**
1 having very little money.
2 bad. *poor work, poor light.*

poorly *adjective*
rather ill.
Jo didn't go to school today because she was poorly.

pop *noun*
a kind of popular music.

pop *verb* **pops, popping, popped**
to make a sound like a small explosion.

poppy *noun* **poppies**
a bright red flower often found growing near corn.

popular *adjective*
liked by a lot of people. *Katie is the most popular girl in the class.*

population *noun*
the number of people who live in a place.

porch *noun* **porches**
a small place with a roof, in front of the door of a building.

pork *noun*
meat from a pig.

porpoise *noun* **porpoises**
a sea animal like a small whale.

porridge *noun*
a hot food made from oats boiled in water or milk, that you get for breakfast.

port *noun* **ports**
a large place where ships can stay safely in the water when they are not at sea.

portable *adjective*
that you can move or carry about easily. *a portable television.*

a b c d e f g h i j k l m n o **p** q r s t u v w x y z

143

porter *noun* **porters**
someone whose job is to carry other people's luggage at hotels and railway stations.

portion *noun* **portions**
the part or amount given to you. *Get a small portion of chips.*

portrait *noun* **portraits**
a picture of a person.

posh *adjective* **posher, poshest**
very smart and expensive. *a posh restaurant.*

position *noun* **positions**
1 the place where something is or should be. *This is a good position to pitch the tent.*
2 how the body and its parts are arranged. *a sitting position.*

positive *adjective*
completely sure. *I am positive I gave you the book.*

possess *verb* **possesses, possessing, possessed**
to own. *They lost everything they possessed in the fire.*

possession *noun* **possessions**
something that you own. *Be careful with other people's possessions.*

possibility *noun* **possibilities**
something that might happen. *There is a possibility that it will snow tomorrow.*

possible *adjective*
if something is possible, it can happen or you can do it. *Is it possible to mend my bicycle?*
possibly *adverb*

post *noun* **posts**
an upright pole fixed in the ground. *goal posts.*

post *verb* **posts, posting, posted**
to send a letter, parcel, or postcard.

postcard *noun* **postcards**
a piece of card that you can write a message on and post.

postcode *noun* **postcodes**
a group of letters and numbers that show the district a person lives in, so that the post office can deliver the mail more quickly.

poster *noun* **posters**
a large notice for everyone to read.

postman, postwoman *noun* **postmen, postwomen**
someone who collects and delivers letters and parcels.

post office *noun* **post offices**
a place that sells stamps and deals with letters and parcels.

postpone *verb* **postpones, postponing, postponed**
to put off until later.
They postponed the race until the rain had stopped.

pot *noun* **pots**
a deep round container, such as a teapot or a plant pot.

potato *noun* **potatoes**
a round white vegetable that you dig out of the ground.

potion *noun* **potions**
a drink with medicine or poison in it.

pottery *noun*
cups, plates, and other things made out of baked clay.

pouch *noun* **pouches**
1 a small bag.
2 a pocket of skin that some animals, such as kangaroos, have to carry their babies in.

poultry *noun*
birds kept for their meat and eggs.
Hens and turkeys are poultry.

pounce *verb* **pounces, pouncing, pounced**
to attack something by jumping on it suddenly.
The cat pounced on the mouse.

pound *noun* **pounds**
1 a measure for weight. *five pounds of potatoes.*
2 a measure for money, also written £.
£1 = 100 pence.

pour *verb* **pours, pouring, poured**
to make liquid go into or out of a container. *Dad poured me a glass of milk.*

powder *noun*
anything that is very dry and made up of many separate tiny bits, like flour or dust.

power *noun* **powers**
1 if you have power, you can do what you want, or make other people do what you want. *the power of the government.*
2 strength. *the power of the storm.*

powerful *adjective*
strong, having a lot of power. *a powerful engine, a powerful leader.*
powerfully *adverb*

practical *adjective*
1 useful or easy to do. *a practical idea.*
2 if you are a practical person, you can do useful things.

practically *adverb*
nearly, almost. *I've practically finished.*

practice *noun*
something you keep doing in order to get better at it. *piano practice.*

practise *verb* **practises, practising, practised**
to do something over and over again in order to get better at doing it. *If you keep practising you will soon improve.*

praise *verb* **praises, praising, praised**
to say that someone or something is very good.

pram *noun* **prams**
a kind of cot on wheels for a baby.

prawn *noun* **prawns**
a sea creature with a shell, like a large shrimp.

pray *verb* **prays, praying, prayed**
to talk to God.

prayer *noun* **prayers**
talking to God.

preach *verb* **preaches, preaching, preached**
to give a religious talk, as a minister does in church.
preacher *noun* **preachers**

precious *adjective*
very valuable.
precious jewels.

precipice *noun* **precipices**
a cliff, a very steep rock, or a very steep part of a mountain.

precise *adjective*
exact, correct.
precisely *adverb*

prefer *verb* **prefers, preferring, preferred**
to like one person or thing more than another person or thing. *She preferred singing to dancing.*

pregnant *adjective*
expecting a baby.

prehistoric *adjective*
belonging to a time very long ago.
prehistoric animals.

premature *adjective*
happening or being born early. *a premature baby.*
prematurely *adverb*

preparations *noun*
things that you do to get ready for something. *preparations for a birthday party.*

prepare *verb* **prepares, preparing, prepared**
to get something ready. *We prepared lunch.*

prescription *noun* **prescriptions**
a note from a doctor to a chemist saying what medicine you need.

present *adjective*
1 happening now, or existing now. *the present queen.*
2 here.
All the children are present.
at present now.

present *noun* **presents**
something you give to or get from someone.
a wedding present.

a b c d e f g h i j k l m n o **p** q r s t u v w x y z

145

present *verb* **presents, presenting, presented**
1 to give something to someone on a special occasion. *The head presented the prizes.*
2 to introduce someone or something. *to present a television programme or a concert.*
presenter *noun* **presenters** *a television presenter.*

presently *adverb*
soon.

preserve *verb* **preserves, preserving, preserved**
1 to keep safe, not destroy. *Many very old buildings in the town have been preserved.*
2 to do things to food so that it will not go bad. *You can preserve vegetables by freezing them.*

president *noun* **presidents**
someone chosen to rule a country that does not have a king or queen.

press *verb* **presses, pressing, pressed**
1 to push hard on something. *Press the doorbell.*
2 to make clothes smooth and flat with an iron.

pressure *noun*
a force which presses or pushes. *the air pressure in a bicycle tyre.*

pretend *verb* **pretends, pretending, pretended**
to try to make someone believe something that is not true. *Sam pretended he was ill.*

pretty *adjective* **prettier, prettiest**
pleasant to look at, attractive.
prettily *adverb*

prevent *verb* **prevents, preventing, prevented**
to stop something from happening. *Close the door to prevent the room getting cold.*

previous *adjective*
coming just before. *We got things ready on the previous day.*
previously *adverb*

prey *noun*
any animal hunted and eaten by other animals.
birds of prey birds that hunt and eat other animals.

price *noun* **prices**
the amount of money you have to pay for something.

priceless *adjective*
very valuable.

prick *verb* **pricks, pricking, pricked**
to make a tiny hole with something sharp.

prickle *noun* **prickles**
a sharp part like a thorn.

prickly *adjective*
giving you a pricking feeling.

pride *noun*
the feeling people have when they are proud.

priest *noun* **priests**
a person who leads people in religious ceremonies.

primary school *noun* **primary schools**
a school for children from about five up to about eleven years old.

prime minister *noun* **prime ministers**
the leader of a government.

primrose *noun* **primroses**
a small, pale yellow flower that comes out early in the spring.

prince *noun* **princes**
the son of a king or queen.

princess *noun* **princesses**
1 the daughter of a king or queen.
2 the wife of a prince.

principal *adjective*
most important, chief. *This map only shows the principal towns.*
principally *adverb*

principle *noun* **principles**
an important rule.

print *verb* **prints, printing, printed**
1 to write with letters that are not joined together.
2 to use a machine that puts words or pictures onto paper.
printer *noun* **printers**

prison *noun* **prisons**
a place where criminals are kept as a punishment.

prisoner *noun* **prisoners**
1 someone who has been captured.
2 someone in prison.

private *adjective*
1 not open to everyone. *a private road.*
2 not known by other people. *private thoughts.*

prize *noun* **prizes**
something that you give to a person who wins a game or competition.

probable *adjective*
likely to be true or to happen.
probably *adverb* *I'll probably go swimming tomorrow.*

problem *noun* **problems**
something that is difficult to understand or answer.

proceed *verb* **proceeds, proceeding, proceeded**
to go on. *The carnival parade proceeded slowly along the street.*

process *noun* **processes**
a series of actions for doing or making something. *the process of making cheese from milk.*

procession *noun* **processions**
a group of people moving along in a long line.

prod *verb* **prods, prodding, prodded**
to push something with the end of a finger or stick.

produce *verb* **produces, producing, produced**
1 to make. *Cows produce milk.*
2 to bring something out so that it can be seen. *The magician produced a rabbit from his hat.*
3 to organize people in a play, film, or television programme.

profit *noun* **profits**
the extra money got by selling something for more than it cost to buy or make. *If you buy a bike for £40 and sell it for £50, you have made £10 profit.*

program *noun* **programs**
a list of instructions for a computer.

```
10  CLS
20  LET X = 10: Let Y = 10
30  Let A$ = INKEY$
40  IF A$ = "" THEN GOTO 30
50  IF A$ = "A" THEN LET Y = Y-1
60  IF A$ = "Z" THEN LET Y = Y+1
70  IF A$ = "N" THEN LET X = X-1
```

programme *noun* **programmes**
1 a talk, play, or show on the radio or television.
2 a list for people at a play or concert telling them about what they will see or hear.

progress *noun*
moving forward, or getting better.
to make progress to move forward, or to get better.

prohibit *verb* **prohibit, prohibiting, prohibited**
to say that people must not do something.
Smoking prohibited.

project *noun* **projects**
1 a piece of work where you find out as much as you can about something interesting and write about it. *I'm doing a project on India.*
2 a plan. *a project to build a new swimming pool.*

promenade *noun* **promenades**
a kind of road or wide path where people can walk by the sea.

promise *verb* **promises, promising, promised**
to say that you will certainly do or not do something.
Don't forget – you promised to help me wash the car.

prompt *adjective* **prompter, promptest**
without delay. *a prompt reply.*
promptly *adverb*

a
b
c
d
e
f
g
h
i
j
k
l
m
n
o
p
q
r
s
t
u
v
w
x
y
z

prong *noun* **prongs**
one of the thin, pointed parts on the end of a fork.

pronounce *verb* **pronounces, pronouncing, pronounced**
to say a sound or word in a certain way.
How do you pronounce your name?

pronunciation *noun*
the way you pronounce something.

proof *noun*
something that proves that an idea is true.

prop *verb* **props, propping, propped**
to support something so that it does not fall or sag.

propel *verb* **propels, propelling, propelled**
to drive forward.

propeller *noun* **propellers**
a set of blades that spin round. Propellers are fixed to aeroplanes, helicopters, and ships to make them move.

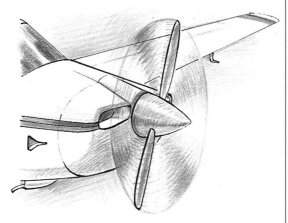

proper *adjective*
correct, suitable.
Put the books back in their proper places.
properly *adverb*

property *noun* **properties**
1 a house or other building with land around it.
2 things that belong to you.

prophet *noun* **prophets**
1 a great religious teacher.
2 someone who tells you what he or she thinks is going to happen.

prosecute *verb* **prosecutes, prosecuting, prosecuted**
to make someone go to court so that they can be punished if they have done wrong. *Trespassers will be prosecuted.*

prosperous *adjective*
rich and successful.

protect *verb* **protects, protecting, protected**
to keep safe from danger. *The cyclist wore a helmet to protect his head.*
protection *noun*

protest *verb* **protests, protesting, protested**
to say or show that you think what someone else is saying or doing is wrong.

proud *adjective* **prouder, proudest**
very pleased with yourself or with someone else who has done well. *Jo was proud when her brother won a prize.*

prove *verb* **proves, proving, proved**
to show that an idea is true.

proverb *noun* **proverbs**
a short, well-known saying which gives advice, such as 'Many hands make light work'.

provide *verb* **provides, providing, provided**
to give something that someone needs. *Cows provide us with milk.*

provoke *verb* **provokes, provoking, provoked**
to make someone angry. *If you provoke the dog, he may bite you.*

prowl *verb* **prowls, prowling, prowled**
to move about like an animal looking for something to kill and eat.

prune *noun* **prunes**
a dried plum.

pry *verb* **pries, prying, pried**
to try to find out about something that has nothing to do with you. *He liked to pry into other people's business.*

psalm *noun* **psalms**
(*ps–* in this word sounds like *s–*)
one of the hymns in the Bible.

pub *noun* **pubs**
a place where people go to have a drink and meet friends.

public *adjective*
open to everyone.
in public where anyone can see or hear, not in private.

publish *verb* **publishes, publishing, published**
to have something printed so that a lot of people can get a copy. *This dictionary was published by Oxford University Press.*
publisher *noun* **publishers**

pudding *noun* **puddings**
any sweet food which you eat after the main part of your dinner.

a Christmas pudding

puddle *noun* **puddles**
a small pool of water.

puff *verb* **puffs, puffing, puffed**
to blow out a small amount of smoke or air at a time.
puffed out out of breath.

puffin *noun* **puffins**
a sea bird with a large orange and blue beak.

pull *verb* **pulls, pulling, pulled**
to get hold of something and make it come towards you.

pullover *noun* **pullovers**
a jersey or jumper.

pulpit *noun* **pulpits**
the high wooden desk in a church, where the priest stands to talk to the people.

pulse *noun*
the throbbing you can feel in a vein as the blood is pumped around your body.

pump *noun* **pumps**
a machine for pumping air or liquid in or out of something, or along pipes. *a bicycle pump.*

pump *verb* **pumps, pumping, pumped**
to force air or liquid in or out of something, or along pipes. *I've got to pump up my bicycle tyre.*

pumpkin *noun* **pumpkins**
a very large, round fruit with a hard yellow skin.

punch *noun* **punches**
a tool for making holes in paper or other materials.

punch *verb* **punches, punching, punched**
1 to hit someone with your fist.
2 to make a hole with a punch.

punctual *adjective*
exactly on time.
punctually *adverb*

punctuation *noun*
marks such as commas and full stops put into a piece of writing to make it easier to read.

puncture *noun* **punctures**
a hole in a tyre.

punish *verb* **punishes, punishing, punished**
to make somebody suffer because they have done wrong.

punishment *noun* **punishments**
something you have to suffer if you have done wrong.

pupil *noun* **pupils**
1 someone who has a teacher.
2 the black spot at the centre of the eye.

puppet *noun* **puppets**
a kind of doll, with a head and limbs that you can move by pulling strings or wires, or by fitting it over your hand like a glove.

puppy *noun* **puppies**
a very young dog.

pure *adjective* **purer, purest**
with nothing else mixed with it. *pure water.*

purple *noun, adjective*
a colour, between red and blue.

a b c d e f g h i j k l m n o **p** q r s t u v w x y z

purpose *noun* **purposes**
what someone means to do.
on purpose deliberately, not by
accident.
I didn't push you on purpose.

purposely *adverb*
on purpose.

purr *verb* **purrs, purring, purred**
to make the sound a cat makes when it
is very pleased.

purse *noun* **purses**
a small bag for holding money.

pursue *verb* **pursues, pursuing, pursued**
to go after someone and try to catch
them.

push *verb* **pushes, pushing, pushed**
to use your hands to move something
away from you.

pussy *noun* **pussies**
(*informal*) a cat or kitten.

put *verb* **puts, putting, put**
to move something to a place, to leave
something in a place.
Please put the book back on the shelf.
to put something off to decide to do it
later instead of now.
*I decided to put off doing my homework
till later.*
to put up with something to let it
happen without complaining even if
you don't like it.
*We had to put up with the noise until the
police came.*

puzzle *noun* **puzzles**
a problem or question that is hard to
solve.
a jigsaw puzzle.

puzzle *verb* **puzzles, puzzling, puzzled**
to make you think hard to find the
answer.
The riddle puzzled me.

pyjamas *noun*
trousers and a jacket worn in bed.

pylon *noun* **pylons**
a metal tower that holds up high
electric cables.

pyramid *noun* **pyramids**
1 a large, stone building made by the
ancient Egyptians to hold the body of
a dead king or queen.
2 the shape of a pyramid.

Qq

quack *verb* **quacks, quacking, quacked**
to make the sound a duck makes.

quaint *adjective* **quainter, quaintest**
unusual but pleasant. *a quaint cottage.*

quake *verb* **quakes, quaking, quaked**
to shake because you are very
frightened. *She was quaking with fear.*

qualify *verb* **qualifies, qualifying, qualified**
1 to pass a test or exam so that you are
allowed to do something. *Jane has
qualified as a doctor.*
2 to get enough points to go on to the
next part of a competition.

quality *noun* **qualities**
how good or bad something is. *You
need best quality paper for model-
making.*

quantity *noun* **quantities**
an amount. *Add a small quantity of
salt.*

quarrel *verb* **quarrels, quarrelling,
quarreled**
to talk angrily with someone because
you do not agree.

quarry *noun* **quarries**
a place where people cut stone out of
the ground so that it can be used for
building. *a chalk quarry.*

quarter *noun* **quarters**
one of the four equal parts something
can be divided into. It can also be
written as $\frac{1}{4}$.

quay *noun* **quays** (rhymes with *key*)
a place where ships can be loaded and
unloaded.

queen *noun* **queens**
1 a woman who has been crowned as
ruler of a country.
2 a king's wife.

queer *adjective* **queerer, queerest**
very strange. *queer shapes.*

quench *verb* **quenches, quenching,
quenched**
1 to put an end to someone's thirst.
Water quenches your thirst.
2 to use water to put out a fire. *The
firemen soon quenched the flames.*

quest *noun* **quests**
a long search.

question *noun* **questions**
something that you ask when you want to find out or get something.
question mark the mark ? that you write at the end of a question.

queue *noun* **queues**
(rhymes with *due*)
a line of people waiting for something.

quiche *noun* **quiches**
a kind of tart with a filling made from eggs, cheese, and other things.

quick *adjective* **quicker, quickest**
1 done in less time than usual.
a quick snack.
2 fast.
It's often quicker by train than by car.
quickly *adverb* Come as quickly as you can!

quiet *adjective* **quieter, quietest**
1 without any noise. *The night was still and quiet.*
2 not loud, not making a lot of noise. *quiet music.*
quietly *adverb* Please close the door quietly.

quilt *noun* **quilts**
a bed cover like an eiderdown. It has lines of stitching across it to keep the filling in place.

quite *adverb*
1 completely.
I'm not quite sure.
2 not very but fairly.
I'm quite cold.

quiver *verb* **quivers, quivering, quivered**
to shake because you are very cold or frightened.

quiz *noun* **quizzes**
a game in which people try to answer a lot of questions.

quote *verb* **quotes, quoting, quoted**
to repeat words which were first said or written by someone else.
The teacher quoted some lines from a play.
quotation *noun* **quotations**
a quotation from a poem.

Rr

rabbi *noun* **rabbis**
a teacher or leader of the Jewish religion.

rabbit *noun* **rabbits**
a furry animal with long ears. Rabbits live in holes they have dug in the ground.

race *noun* **races**
1 a competition to find who is fastest.
2 a group of people who come from the same part of the world and have the same colour skin, the same type of hair, and so on.

race *verb* **races, racing, raced**
to have a race against someone.

racial *adjective*
connected with the race a person belongs to.

racist *noun* **racists**
a person who treats other people unfairly because they belong to a different race.

rack *noun* **racks**
a kind of shelf made of bars that you can put things on or in.
a luggage rack.

racket *noun* **rackets**
1 a bat for hitting a ball in tennis, squash, and badminton. It has a frame with strings stretched across it.
2 (*informal*) a lot of loud noise.

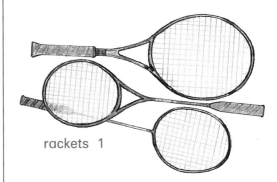

rackets 1

radar *noun*
a way of finding where a ship or aeroplane is and how fast it is travelling using radio waves.

a
b
c
d
e
f
g
h
i
j
k
l
m
n
o
p
q
r
s
t
u
v
w
x
y
z

a b c d e f g h i j k l m n o p q r s t u v w x y z

radiator *noun* **radiators**
1 a metal container filled with hot water that you use to make a room warm.
2 a part of a car that has water in it to keep the engine cool.

radio *noun* **radios**
a machine that picks up signals sent through the air and changes them into programmes or messages that you can listen to.

radish *noun* **radishes**
a small, hard, round, red vegetable that you eat raw in salads.

radius *noun* **radii**
the distance from the centre of a circle to the edge.

raffle *noun* **raffles**
a way of getting money by selling tickets with numbers on them. People who buy tickets with lucky numbers on them win prizes.

raft *noun* **rafts**
a flat boat made of pieces of wood joined together and used instead of a boat.

rafter *noun* **rafters**
one of the long, sloping pieces of wood that hold up a roof.

rag *noun* **rags**
a small piece of cloth that you use for cleaning.
rags clothes that are very old and torn.
She was dressed in rags.

rage *noun* **rages**
great anger.

raid *noun* **raids**
a sudden attack on a place.
a bank raid.

rail *noun* **rails**
1 a bar or rod.
2 a long metal bar that is part of a railway line.

railings *noun*
a fence made of metal bars.

railway *noun* **railways**
1 the set of metal bars that trains travel on.
2 a train service that carries people and things.

rain *noun*
drops of water that fall from the sky.
rainy *adjective* a rainy day.

rain *verb* **rains, raining, rained**
when it rains, drops of water fall from the sky. *We'll go out when it stops raining.*

rainbow *noun* **rainbows**
the curved band of different colours you see in the sky when the sun shines through rain.

rainforest *noun* **rainforests**
a large forest in a tropical part of the world.

raise *verb* **raises, raising, raised**
1 to lift up or make something higher.
2 to gather together the money or people needed for something. *We need to raise money for the school trip.*

raisin *noun* **raisins**
a dried grape used in cooking.

rake *noun* **rakes**
a tool used in the garden. It has a long handle and a row of short spikes.

rake *verb* **rakes, raking, raked**
to move or smooth something with a rake. *He raked up the dead leaves.*

rally *noun* **rallies**
1 a lot of people who have come together for a big meeting.
2 a race for cars or motorcycles.

ram *noun* **rams**
a male sheep.

ram *verb* **rams, ramming, rammed**
to push something very hard into something else.

Ramadan *noun*
a holy time for Muslims when they fast during the day.

ramble *verb* **rambles, rambling, rambled**
to wander, to go for a long walk in the country.

ran *verb* see **run**

ranch *noun* **ranches**
a large American farm with a lot of cattle or horses.

rang *verb* see **ring**

rank *noun* **ranks**
1 a title or job that shows how important someone is. The rank of general is higher than the rank of captain.
2 a row of people. *The soldiers stood in neat ranks.*

ransack *verb* **ransacks, ransacking, ransacked**
to search for something and leave things very untidy.

rap *noun* **raps**
the sound you make when·you knock on a door quickly.

rapid *adjective*
very quick. **rapidly** *adverb*

rare *adjective* **rarer, rarest**
not often found. *Pandas are rare animals.*
rarely *adverb*

rascal *noun* **rascals**
someone who is naughty.

rash *noun* **rashes**
red spots or patches that suddenly come on the skin. *a measles rash.*

raspberry *noun* **raspberries**
a soft, sweet, red berry.

rat *noun* **rats**
an animal like a large mouse.

rather *adverb*
1 fairly, quite.
It's rather cold.
2 more willingly.
I'd rather have an orange than an apple.

ration *noun* **rations**
the amount you are allowed to have when food is shared out between people. *You can't have any more, because you've had your ration.*

rattle *verb* **rattles, rattling, rattled**
to make quick, hard noises by shaking something.
The windows rattle when a lorry goes past.

rave *verb* **raves, raving, raved**
to talk in a very excited or enthusiastic way.

raven *noun* **ravens**
a large, black bird.

ravenous *adjective*
very hungry.

raw *adjective*
not cooked. *a raw tomato.*

ray *noun* **rays**
a thin line of light. *the sun's rays.*

razor *noun* **razors**
a thin, sharp blade used for shaving.

a b c d e f g h i j k l m n o p q **r** s t u v w x y z

153

reach *verb* **reaches, reaching, reached**
1 to stretch out the hand in order to touch something. *He reached for a cake.*
2 to arrive at a place. *We reached home by 6 o'clock.*

reaction *noun* **reactions**
what you say or do because of something that has happened. *What was Dad's reaction to the broken window?*

read *verb* **reads, reading, read**
to look at and understand words that are written down.
reader *noun* **readers**

ready *adjective*
1 prepared and willing to do something. *Are you ready to go?*
2 fit to be used or eaten at once. *Is dinner ready?*

real *adjective*
1 true. *John is not his real name.*
2 not a copy. *real gold.*
really *adverb I'm really hungry.*

realistic *adjective*
like the real thing. *The acting in the film was very realistic.*

realize *verb* **realizes, realizing, realized**
to know or understand something. *I suddenly realized that everyone was waiting for me.*

reap *verb* **reaps, reaping, reaped**
to cut down and gather in the corn when it is ready.

rear *noun*
the back part of something. *Sit at the rear of the bus.*

rear *verb* **rears, rearing, reared**
1 to look after children or young animals until they are big. *She reared the puppies.*
2 to stand on the back legs and lift the front legs into the air. *The horse reared in fright and the rider fell off.*

reason *noun* **reasons**
anything that explains why something has happened. *Is there any reason why you are late?*

reasonable *adjective*
1 fair or right. *a reasonable price.*
2 willing to listen to others. *Be reasonable! I can't do all the work.*
reasonably *adverb*

rebel *verb* **rebels, rebelling, rebelled**
to decide not to obey the people in charge.

recall *verb* **recalls, recalling, recalled**
to remember.

receipt *noun* **receipts**
a piece of paper which proves that you have paid for something.

receive *verb* **receives, receiving, received**
to get something that has been given or sent to you. *Did you receive a letter this morning?*

recent *adjective*
done or made a short time ago. *Is this a recent photo of your brother?*
recently *adverb*

reception *noun* **receptions**
1 a welcome.
We gave the visitors a warm reception.
2 the place where someone welcomes visitors or customers.

recipe *noun* **recipes**
instructions that tell you how to cook something.

recite *verb* **recites, reciting, recited**
to say a poem or something else that you have learnt by heart.

reckless *adjective*
likely to do silly or dangerous things. *a reckless driver.*
recklessly *adverb*

reckon *verb* **reckons, reckoning, reckoned**
1 to count or add up.
Jo reckoned how much pocket money she had left.
2 to feel sure.
I reckon our side will win on Saturday.

recognize *verb* **recognizes, recognizing, recognized**
to know who someone is because you have seen them before.

recommend *verb* **recommends, recommending, recommended**
1 to tell someone that another person or thing is useful.
Can you recommend a good sports shop?
2 to tell someone in a helpful way what you think they should do.
I recommend that you see a doctor.

record *noun* **records**
1 a round piece of black plastic that you play on a record player.
2 a written list of things you have done, seen, or found out. *We keep a record of the birds we see.*
3 the best that has been done so far. *Jo's time for the race was a record.*

record *verb* **records, recording, recorded**
1 to put music or other sounds onto a tape or disc.
2 to write down things you have done, seen, or found out.

recorder *noun* **recorders**
a wooden or plastic musical instrument that you play by blowing into one end.

record player *noun* **record players**
a machine that makes sounds come out of records.

recover *verb* **recovers, recovering, recovered**
1 to get better after being ill.
2 to get something back that you have lost. *The police recovered the stolen car.*

recreation *noun*
hobbies or games people like playing in their spare time.

rectangle *noun* **rectangles**
the shape of a postcard.
rectangular *adjective*

recycle *verb* **recycles, recycling, recycled**
to use paper, glass, or other things again instead of throwing them away.

red *noun, adjective*
the colour of blood.

reduce *verb* **reduces, reducing, reduced**
to make smaller or less. *Reduce speed when you approach a bend.*

redundant *adjective*
without a job because you are no longer needed.

reed *noun* **reeds**
a plant like tall grass with a strong stem that grows near water.

reef *noun* **reefs**
a line of rocks just below or just above the surface of the sea. *a coral reef.*

reel *noun* **reels**
a round piece of wood, metal, or plastic on which you wind things like cotton or film.
Put a new reel of film in the camera.

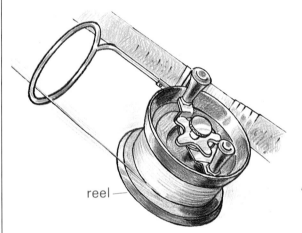

reel—

refer *verb* **refers, referring, referred**
1 to talk about someone or something. *When I said some people are stupid, I wasn't referring to you!*
2 to look in a book for information. *If you don't know how to spell a word, you can refer to the dictionary.*

referee *noun* **referees**
someone who makes sure that the players in a game keep to the rules.

reference book *noun* **reference books**
a book that gives you information. Dictionaries are reference books.

reflect *verb* **reflects, reflecting, reflected**
1 to send back light from a shiny surface.
2 to show a picture of something, as a mirror does. *The trees were reflected in the still water.*
reflection *noun* **reflections**

refrain *noun* **refrains**
the chorus of a song.

refresh *verb* **refreshes, refreshing, refreshed**
to make a tired person feel fresh and strong again.
a refreshing drink.

refreshments *noun*
drinks and snacks.

refrigerator *noun* **refrigerators**
a kind of metal cupboard that keeps food and drink cold and fresh, often called a fridge.

refugee *noun* **refugees**
a person who had to leave his or her country because of a war.

refuse *noun*
rubbish.

refuse *verb* **refuses, refusing, refused**
to say you will not do something you have been asked to do. *She refused to tidy her room.*

regard *verb* **regards, regarding, regarded**
to think of someone or something in a certain way. *He regarded me as a friend.*

regiment *noun* **regiments**
a large, organized group of soldiers.

region *noun* **regions**
a part of a country or the world. *the desert regions of Africa.*

register *noun* **registers**
a book in which people record important information. *a school register.*

regret *verb* **regrets, regretting, regretted**
to be sad or sorry about something you have done or something that has happened.

regular *adjective*
1 always happening at certain times. *regular meals.*
2 usual, normal. *Who is your regular teacher?*
regularly *adverb*

rehearsal *noun* **rehearsals**
a practice for a concert or play.

rehearse *verb* **rehearses, rehearsing, rehearsed**
to practise something before you do it in front of an audience.

reign *noun* **reigns**
the time when someone is king or queen. *the reign of Elizabeth I.*

reign *verb* **reigns, reigning, reigned**
to be king or queen. *Elizabeth I reigned 400 years ago.*

reindeer *noun* **(the plural is the same)**
a deer that lives in very cold countries.

reins *noun*
the two long straps used for guiding a horse.

reject *verb* **rejects, rejecting, rejected**
to refuse to accept someone or something. *The calf was rejected by its mother.*

rejoice *verb* **rejoices, rejoicing, rejoiced**
to be very happy about something.

related *adjective*
belonging to the same family.

relation *noun* **relations**
a relative.

relative *noun* **relatives**
someone who is related to you.

relax *verb* **relaxes, relaxing, relaxed**
to rest and let your body become less stiff.
to relax in a hot bath.

release *verb* **releases, releasing, released**
to set someone free.

relent *verb* **relents, relenting, relented**
to become less angry or less strict than you were at first. *Mum relented and let us watch TV.*

reliable *adjective*
if you are reliable, people trust you. *a reliable friend.*

relic *noun* **relics**
something very old that was left by people who lived long ago.

relief *noun*
the feeling you have when you are no longer in trouble, pain, or danger.

relieved *adjective*
happy because you are no longer in trouble, pain, or danger.

religion *noun* **religions**
what people believe about God or gods, and how they worship.
religious *adjective*

reluctant *adjective*
if you are reluctant to do something you do not want to do it.
reluctantly *adverb*

rely *verb* **relies, relying, relied**
to trust someone or something to help you. *The blind man relied on his dog.*

remain *verb* **remains, remaining, remained**
to stay after other people or things have gone. *Remain where you are!*

remainder *noun*
what is left over.

remains *noun*
1 ruins. *the remains of a castle.*
2 a dead body. *His remains are buried near the church.*

remark *verb* **remarks, remarking, remarked**
to say something that you have thought or noticed. *'It's very hot today,' she remarked.*

remarkable *adjective*
so unusual that you remember it.
remarkably *adverb*

remedy *noun* **remedies**
a way of making something better. *Hot lemon is a good remedy for colds.*

remember *verb* **remembers, remembering, remembered**
to bring something into your mind when you want to. *I can't remember his name.*

remind *verb* **reminds, reminding, reminded**
to make or help someone remember something.

remote *adjective* **remoter, remotest**
far away.

remove *verb* **removes, removing, removed**
to take something off or away. *Please remove your muddy boots before you come in.*

rent *noun*
the money that you pay every week or month to live in a place or use something that belongs to another person.

rent *verb* **rents, renting, rented**
to pay to live in a place or use something that belongs to another person. *to rent a flat.*

repair *verb* **repairs, repairing, repaired**
to mend something that is broken or doesn't work anymore. *Can you repair my bike?*

repay *verb* **repays, repaying, repaid**
to pay back what you owe.

repeat *verb* **repeat, repeating, repeated**
to say or do the same thing again.
repeatedly *adverb* **repetition** *noun*

repent *verb* **repents, repenting, repented**
to be very sorry about something you have said or done. *She repented after she had been so unkind.*

replace *verb* **replaces, replacing, replaced**
1 to put something back. *He replaced the book on the shelf.*
2 to take the place of another person or thing. *We have a new car to replace the old one.*

reply *noun* **replies**
an answer.

reply *verb* **replies, replying, replied**
to answer.

report *noun* **reports**
1 something that someone says or writes about something that has happened. *a news report.*
2 something that teachers write about your work. *a school report.*

report *verb* **reports, reporting, reported**
to tell or write about something that has happened. *We reported the accident to the police.* **reporter** *noun* **reporters**

represent *verb* **represents, representing, represented**
to be a picture or model of something. *These red lines on the map represent roads.*

a
b
c
d
e
f
g
h
i
j
k
l
m
n
o
p
q
r
s
t
u
v
w
x
y
z

reproduce *verb* **reproduces, reproducing, reproduced**
1 to make a copy of something.
2 to produce babies.
reproduction *noun* **reproductions**

reptile *noun* **reptiles**
an animal with cold blood that lays eggs. Snakes, crocodiles, lizards, chameleons, and tortoises are reptiles.

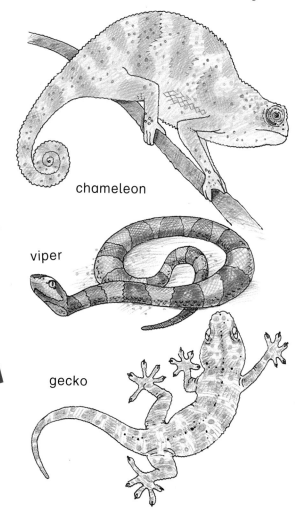

chameleon

viper

gecko

reputation *noun* **reputations**
the things everyone says or thinks about a person. *She has a reputation for being noisy.*

request *verb* **requests, requesting, requested**
to ask politely for something.

require *verb* **requires, requiring, required**
to need.

rescue *verb* **rescues, rescuing, rescued**
to save from danger.

research *noun*
studying something carefully to find out more about it.

resemble *verb* **resemble, resembling, resembled**
to look or sound like another person or thing. *Sam resembles his father.*

reserve *noun* **reserves**
a person who will play in a game if another person cannot play.

reserve *verb* **reserves, reserving, reserved**
1 to ask someone to keep a place or a seat for you. *Reserve a seat on the train.*
2 to keep something for later. *Reserve some sweets for tomorrow.*

reservoir *noun* **reservoirs**
a lake with a dam at one end where water is stored.

resign *verb* **resigns, resigning, resigned**
to give up your job.

resist *verb* **resists, resisting, resisted**
to fight against something and not give way.

resources *noun*
things which are useful for making things or for making our lives better. *Oil is one of our most important natural resources.*

respect *noun*
the feeling you have for someone you like and admire.

respectable *adjective*
if you are respectable, people think you behave in the right way.

respond *verb* **responds, responding, responded**
to answer.

responsible *adjective*
in charge and likely to take the blame if anything goes wrong.

rest *noun* **rests**
a time which you spend sleeping or being still and quiet. *We climbed the hill and had a rest at the top.*
the rest the people or things that are left. *If you don't want the rest, I'll eat it.*

rest *verb* **rests, resting, rested**
to stop doing things for a time so that you can get your strength back. *Half way up the hill we sat down to rest.*

restaurant *noun* **restaurants**
a place where you can buy a meal and eat it.

restore *verb* **restores, restoring, restored**
to make something as good as it was before.

result *noun* **results**
1 anything that happens because of other things. *I got up late and as a result I missed the bus.*
2 the score or marks at the end of a game, competition, or test.

retire *verb* **retires, retiring, retired**
to stop working because you are too old or ill.

retreat *verb* **retreats, retreating, retreated**
to go back because it is too dangerous to carry on. *The soldiers retreated.*

return *verb* **returns, returning, returned**
1 to go back to a place. *We returned home at tea time.*
2 to give something back. *Jo returned the book to the library.*

reveal *verb* **reveals, revealing, revealed**
to let something be seen or known.

revenge *noun*
a wish to hurt someone because they have hurt you or one of your friends.

reverse *verb* **reverses, reversing, reversed**
to go backwards in a car.

revolt *verb* **revolts, revolting, revolted**
to say that you will not obey the people in charge.

revolting *adjective*
horrible, disgusting.

revolution *noun* **revolutions**
a fight to get rid of the government and put a new kind of government in its place.

revolve *verb* **revolves, revolving, revolved**
to turn round like a wheel.

revolver *noun* **revolvers**
a small gun that can be fired several times without having to be loaded again.

reward *noun* **rewards**
a present given to someone because of something good they have done.

rhinoceros *noun* **rhinoceroses**
a big, wild animal with a horn on its nose, found in Africa and Asia. It is often called a rhino for short.

rhubarb *noun*
a plant with pink stalks that are cooked and eaten with sugar.

rhyme *noun* **rhymes**
A word that has the same sound at the end as another word. *Bat* and *mat* are rhymes.

rhythm *noun* **rhythms**
the pattern made in music or poetry by the strong and weak sounds.

rib *noun* **ribs**
one of the curved bones above the waist.

ribbon *noun* **ribbons**
a strip of nylon, silk, or some other material.

rice *noun*
white or brown grains that you cook and eat.

rice plants

rich *adjective* **richer, richest**
having a lot of money.

rick *noun* **ricks**
a neat pile of straw or hay.

rid *verb*
to get rid of to make someone or something go away.

riddle *noun* **riddles**
a question or puzzle that is a joke.

a b c d e f g h i j k l m n o p q **r** s t u v w x y z

159

ride *noun* **rides**
a journey on a horse or bicycle, or in a bus, train, or car.

ride *verb* **rides, riding, rode, ridden**
1 to sit on something and be carried along on it. *to ride a horse.*
2 to travel in a car, bus, or train.
rider *noun* **riders**

ridge *noun* **ridges**
a long, narrow part higher than the rest, like the line along the top of a roof.

ridiculous *adjective*
so silly that people laugh.
ridiculously *adverb*

rifle *noun* **rifles**
a long gun that is held against the shoulder when it is fired.

right *adjective*
1 on the side opposite the left. Most people hold a knife in their right hand and a fork in their left.
2 correct. *the right answer.*
3 fair. *It is not right to cheat.*

right *adverb*
correctly.
Have I spelt your name right?

right-handed *adjective*
if you are right-handed you use the right hand to write and do other important things.

rim *noun* **rims**
the edge round the top of a round container or round the outside of a wheel. *the rim of a cup.*

rind *noun*
the skin on bacon, cheese, or fruit.

ring *noun* **rings**
1 a circle.
2 a circle of metal worn on a finger. *a wedding ring.*

ring *verb* **rings, ringing, rang, rung**
1 to make a sound like a bell.
2 to make a telephone call to someone. *We ring Granny every Sunday.*

rink *noun* **rinks**
an area of ice for skating on.

rinse *verb* **rinses, rinsing, rinsed**
to wash something in clean water after using soap.

riot *noun* **riots**
violent, noisy behaviour by a crowd of people.

rip *verb* **rips, ripping, ripped**
to tear.

ripe *adjective* **riper, ripest**
fruit that is ripe is ready to eat.

ripple *noun* **ripples**
a tiny wave on the surface of water.

rise *verb* **rises, rising, rose, risen**
1 to go upwards. *The sun rises in the east.*
2 to get up. *They all rose as she came in.*

risk *noun* **risks**
the chance that something bad or dangerous might happen.

risky *adjective* **riskier, riskiest**
dangerous.

rival *noun* **rivals**
someone trying to win the same prize as you are.

river *noun* **rivers**
a large amount of water that flows into the sea.

road *noun* **roads**
a way that cars, buses, and lorries go along.

roam *verb* **roams, roaming, roamed**
to move around without trying to get anywhere. *They roamed all over the hills.*

roar *verb* **roars, roaring, roared**
to make the loud, deep sound a lion makes.

roast *verb* **roasts, roasting, roasted**
to cook meat or vegetables inside the oven with fat.

rob *verb* **robs, robbing, robbed**
to steal something from someone.
robber *noun* **robbers**

robbery *noun* **robberies**
robbing other people. *a bank robbery.*

robe *noun* **robes**
a long, loose garment. *a bath robe.*

robin *noun* **robins**
a small, brown bird with a red patch on its front.

robot *noun* **robots**
a machine in a factory controlled by a computer. *Robots can work like a person.*

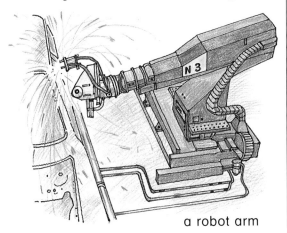

a robot arm

rock *noun* **rocks**
1 something hard and heavy that is part of mountains, hills, and the ground.
2 a sort of music.
3 a hard sweet shaped like a stick and sold at the seaside.

rock *verb* **rocks, rocking, rocked**
to move gently backwards and forwards or from side to side.

rocket *noun* **rockets**
1 a tall metal tube that is used to launch a spacecraft.
2 a firework joined to a stick. Rockets shoot high into the air when they are lit.

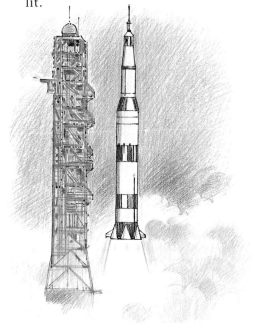

rocket 1

rod *noun* **rods**
a long, thin, round piece of wood or metal.

rodent *noun* **rodents**
an animal that gnaws things. Rats, mice, and squirrels are rodents.

roll *noun* **rolls**
1 a long round shape made by rolling something up.
a roll of carpet.
2 a very small loaf of bread.

roll *verb* **rolls, rolling, rolled**
to turn over and over like a ball moving along the ground.

roller *noun* **rollers**
a heavy cylinder you roll over things to make them flat or smooth. *a road roller.*

roller skate *noun* **roller skates**
a shoe with wheels on the bottom, for moving quickly over smooth ground.

romp *verb* **romps, romping, romped**
to play roughly and noisily.

roof *noun* **roofs**
the part that covers the top of a building.

room *noun* **rooms**
1 one of the spaces with walls round it inside a building. Bathrooms, kitchens, and lounges are rooms.
2 enough space for something.

roost *noun* **roosts**
the place where a bird rests at night.

root *noun* **roots**
the part of a plant that grows under the ground.

a b c d e f g h i j k l m n o p q **r** s t u v w x y z

161

rope *noun* **ropes**
a lot of strong threads twisted together.

rose *noun* **roses**
a flower with a sweet smell and thorns on its stem.

rose *verb* see **rise**

rosy *adjective* **rosier, rosiest**
coloured like a pink or red rose.

rot *verb* **rots, rotting, rotted**
to go soft or bad so that it cannot be used. Fruit and wood rot.

rotten *adjective*
1 so soft or bad that it cannot be used. *rotten wood, a rotten apple.*
2 (*informal*) very bad. *a rotten joke.*

rough *adjective* **rougher, roughest**
1 not smooth or flat. *rough wood.*
2 not gentle. *rough seas.*
3 not exact. *a rough guess.*

round *adjective*
shaped like a circle or ball. *a round mirror.*

round *adverb, preposition*
THIS WORD HAS SEVERAL USES. HERE ARE SOME OF THE WAYS YOU CAN USE IT: *The wheels spun round. Please turn round.*

roundabout *noun* **roundabouts**
1 a moving machine at a fair that you can ride on as it goes round and round.
2 a place where roads meet, where cars must drive round in a circle.

— roundabout 1

rounders *noun*
a game played outside between two teams with a small ball and a bat like a heavy stick.

rouse *verb* **rouses, rousing, roused**
to wake someone up.

route *noun* **routes**
the way you go to get to a place.

row *noun* **rows**
(rhymes with *how*)
1 a quarrel.
2 a lot of noise.

row *noun* **rows**
(rhymes with *toe*)
people or things arranged in a straight line.

row *verb* **rows, rowing, rowed**
(rhymes with *toe*)
to use oars to make a boat move.

royal *adjective*
belonging to a king or queen.

royalty *noun*
kings, queens, and their families.

rub *verb* **rubs, rubbing, rubbed**
to move something backwards and forwards against another thing. *I rubbed my hands together to keep warm.*
rub out to take writing or marks off something.

rubber *noun* **rubbers**
1 a strong material that stretches, bends, and bounces. *Rubber is used for making car tyres.*
2 a piece of rubber for rubbing out pencil marks.

rubbish *noun*
1 things that are not wanted or needed.
2 nonsense. *You're talking rubbish!*

ruby *noun* **rubies**
a red jewel.

rudder *noun* **rudders**
a flat part at the end of a boat or aeroplane. It moves to make the boat or aeroplane go left or right.

rude *adjective* **ruder, rudest**
not polite.

rug *noun* **rugs**
a thick blanket or a mat.

ruin *noun* **ruins**
a building that has fallen down. *castle ruins.*

ruin *verb* **ruins, ruining, ruined**
to spoil something completely. *The rain ruined our picnic.*

rule *noun* **rules**
something that everyone ought to obey. *When you play a game, you must obey the rules.*

rule *verb* **rules, ruling, ruled**
1 to be in charge of a country and the people who live there.
2 to draw a straight line with a ruler.

ruler *noun* **rulers**
1 someone who rules a country.
2 a strip of wood, metal, or plastic with straight edges, used for measuring and drawing lines.

rumble *verb* **rumbles, rumbling, rumbled**
to make the deep, heavy sound thunder makes.

rumour *noun* **rumours**
something that a lot of people are saying, although it might not be true.

run *verb* **runs, running, ran**
1 to use your legs to move quickly.
2 to flow. *The river runs into the sea.*
3 to control something. *Who runs this factory?*
runner *noun* **runners**

rung *noun* **rungs**
one of the short bars on a ladder.

rung *verb* see **ring**

runny *adjective* **runnier, runniest**
flowing like water. *The jelly hasn't set yet – it's still runny.*

rush *verb* **rushes, rushing, rushed**
to move very quickly.

rusk *noun* **rusks**
a kind of biscuit for babies to chew.

rust *noun*
a rough, red surface that covers iron that has got wet.
rusty *adjective*

rustle *verb* **rustles, rustling, rustled**
to make the light sounds dry leaves make when they are blown by the wind.

rut *noun* **ruts**
a deep line made in the ground by wheels going over it many times.

Ss

sack *noun* **sacks**
a large bag made of strong material. *a sack of potatoes.*
to get the sack to lose your job.

sacred *adjective*
with a special religious meaning. *A church is a sacred building.*

sacrifice *noun* **sacrifices**
1 something you like which you give up in order to help someone.
2 a gift offered to a god.

sad *adjective* **sadder, saddest**
not happy.
sadly *adverb*

saddle *noun* **saddles**
the seat on a bicycle, or the seat you put on a horse.

safari *noun* **safaris**
a journey you make in order to see lions and other wild animals.
safari park a park where you can see wild animals roaming about.

safe *adjective* **safer, safest**
if you are safe, you are not in any danger.
safely *adverb*

safe *noun* **safes**
a strong metal box with a lock where you can keep money or things like jewellery.

safety *noun*
a time or place without danger. *The fireman carried her to safety.*

sag *verb* **sags, sagging, sagged**
to go down in the middle. *The bed sagged under his weight.*

said *verb* see **say**

sail *noun* **sails**
a large piece of strong cloth which makes a boat move along when the wind blows into it.

a b c d e f g h i j k l m n o p q r s t u v w x y z

163

sail *verb* **sails, sailing, sailed**
to travel in a boat.

sailor *noun* **sailors**
a person who works on a ship.

saint *noun* **saints**
a very good and holy person.

sake *noun*
for the sake of to help or please someone or something. *Will you do it for my sake?*

salad *noun* **salads**
a mixture of vegetables eaten raw or cold.

salary *noun* **salaries**
money paid to someone each month for the work they do.

sale *noun* **sales**
1 the selling of things. *These toys are not for sale.*
2 a time when things in a shop are sold at lower prices than usual.

saliva *noun*
a liquid in your mouth that helps you to eat your food.

salmon *noun* **(the plural is the same)**
a large fish with pink flesh that you can eat.

salt *noun*
a white powder put on food to give it flavour.

salty *adjective* **saltier, saltiest**
tasting of salt.

salute *verb* **salutes, saluting, saluted**
to touch your forehead with your hand, as soldiers do to show respect.

same *adjective*
not different in any way. *Yasmin goes to the same school as me.*

sample *noun* **samples**
a small amount that shows what something is like. *free samples of shampoo.*

sand *noun* **sands**
powder made of tiny bits of rock that you find in deserts and next to the sea.

sandal *noun* **sandals**
a light shoe with straps that you wear in warm weather.

sandwich *noun* **sandwiches**
two slices of bread and butter with a different food between them. *a cheese sandwich.*

sandy *adjective*
covered with sand, full of sand. *sandy beaches.*

sang *verb* see **sing**

sank *verb* see **sink**

sap *noun*
the sticky liquid that carries food through plants and trees.

sarcastic *adjective*
if you are sarcastic, you say something funny in an unkind way. *Jo hates it when her brother makes sarcastic remarks.*

sardine *noun* **sardines**
a small sea fish you can eat.

sari *noun* **saris**
a long piece of cloth worn as a dress by Indian women and girls.

sat *verb* see **sit**

satellite *noun* **satellites**
a planet or spacecraft that moves in space round another planet. *The moon is a satellite of the earth.*
satellite television a television channel which comes to you by using a satellite.

satin *noun*
smooth cloth that is very shiny on one side.

satisfactory *adjective*
good enough but not very good. *Her work is satisfactory.*

satisfy *verb* **satisfies, satisfying, satisfied**
to be good enough to please someone, to give someone what they want or need.

Saturday *noun* **Saturdays**
the seventh day of the week.

sauce *noun* **sauces**
a thick liquid put on food. *tomato sauce.*

saucepan *noun* **saucepans**
a metal pan with a long handle used for cooking.

saucer *noun* **saucers**
a small plate for putting a cup on.

sausage *noun* **sausages**
a skin tube stuffed with tiny pieces of meat and bread.

savage *adjective*
wild and fierce. *a savage attack by a large dog.*
savagely *adverb*

save *verb* **saves, saving, saved**
1 to take someone or something away from danger. *The doctor saved her life.*
2 to keep something, especially money, to use later.

savings *noun*
money that you put in a bank so that you can use it later.

saw *noun* **saws**
a tool with a wide, thin blade with sharp teeth. You move a saw backwards and forwards across a piece of wood to cut it.

saw *verb* **saws, sawing, sawed, sawn**
to use a saw to cut wood.

saw *verb* see **see**

sawdust *noun*
a powder that comes from wood when it is cut with a saw.

say *verb* **says, saying, said**
to use the voice to make words. *'Hello,' he said.*

saying *noun* **sayings**
a sentence or phrase which people often use.
'Many hands make light work' is an old saying.

scab *noun* **scabs**
a piece of hard skin that covers a cut or graze while it is getting better.

scabbard *noun* **scabbards**
a cover for the blade of a sword.

scaffolding *noun*
planks fixed to poles and put round a building so that builders and painters can stand on them.

scald *verb* **scalds, scalding, scalded**
to burn yourself with very hot liquid.

scales *noun*
1 a machine for weighing things.
2 thin pieces of skin or bone that cover the outside of animals such as fish and snakes.

scalp *noun* **scalps**
the skin covering the top of the head where the hair grows.

scamper *verb* **scampers, scampering, scampered**
to run about quickly.

scampi *noun*
sea creatures like large prawns.

scandal *noun*
unkind talk about someone who is supposed to have done something wrong.

scar *noun* **scars**
a mark left on your skin by a cut or burn after it has healed.

scarce *adjective* **scarcer, scarcest**
not enough, not often found, rare.
Water is scarce in the desert.

scarcely *adverb*
only just, hardly. *He was so frightened he could scarcely speak.*

scare *verb* **scares, scaring, scared**
to frighten. *Are you scared of the dark?*

scarecrow *noun* **scarecrows**
something that looks like a person and is put in a field to frighten away birds.

scarf *noun* **scarves**
a piece of material that you wear round the neck or head.

scarlet *noun, adjective*
bright red.

scatter *verb* **scatters, scattering, scattered**
to throw small things so that they fall in many different places. *She scattered some crumbs for the birds.*

scene *noun* **scenes**
1 the place where something happens. *the scene of the crime.*
2 part of a play.

scenery *noun*
1 things that you can see around you when you are out in the country. *beautiful mountain scenery.*
2 things on a stage of a theatre to make it look like a real place.

scent *noun* **scents**
1 a liquid with a sweet smell.
2 a pleasant smell. *the scent of roses.*
3 an animal's smell. *a fox's scent.*

scheme *noun* **schemes**
(*sch-* in this word sounds like *sk-*)
a plan.

scholar *noun* **scholars**
(*sch-* in this word sounds like *sk-*)
1 a pupil.
2 a person who likes to study.

scholarship *noun* **scholarships**
(*sch-* in this word sounds like *sk-*)
money given to someone in order to help them to go on studying.

school *noun* **schools**
(*sch-* in this word sounds like *sk-*)
the place where children go to learn.

science *noun* **sciences**
knowledge about the world that people get by studying things and testing ideas about the way they work.

scientific *adjective*
having to do with science.

scientist *noun* **scientists**
someone who studies science.

scissors *noun*
a tool for cutting that has two sharp blades joined together.

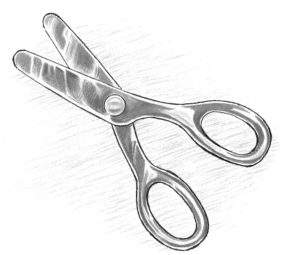

scold *verb* **scolds, scolding, scolded**
to tell someone you are angry with them because of what they have done. *Jo scolded the dog for eating her chocolate.*

scoop *noun* **scoops**
a deep spoon for lifting up and measuring out things such as ice cream.

scoop *verb* **scoops, scooping, scooped**
to use a tool or your arms or hands to gather things together and lift them up.

scooter *noun* **scooters**
1 a motorbike with a small engine.
2 a toy with two wheels that you ride by standing on it with one foot and pushing with the other.

scooter 1

scorch *verb* **scorches, scorching, scorched**
to make something so hot that it goes brown.

score *noun* **scores**
1 the number of points or goals scored by each side in a game.
2 twenty.

score *verb* **scores, scoring, scored**
to get a goal or point in a game.

scorn *noun*
the feeling that you have when you think someone or something is not good enough.
She looked at him with scorn and hatred.

scornful *adjective*
showing that you think someone or something is not worth bothering about.
scornfully *adverb*

scowl *verb* **scowls, scowling, scowled**
to have a cross look on your face.

scramble *verb* **scrambles, scrambling, scrambled**
to use your hands and feet to climb up or down something. *We scrambled over the rocks.*
scrambled eggs eggs mixed up with milk and cooked in butter.

scrap *noun* **scraps**
1 a small piece. *a scrap of material.*
2 something that you do not want anymore but that is made of material that can be used again. *scrap paper.*

scrape *verb* **scrapes, scraping, scraped**
to move a rough or sharp thing across something. *Scrape the mud off your shoes.*

scratch *verb* **scratches, scratching, scratched**
1 to cut or make a mark on something with a sharp thing.
2 to rub your skin to stop it itching.

scream *verb* **screams, screaming, screamed**
to make a loud cry that shows you are hurt or afraid.

screech *verb* **screeches, screeching, screeched**
to make a loud, high sound. *An owl screeched in the night.*

screen *noun* **screens**
1 the flat glass part of a television or computer where words or pictures appear.
2 the flat surface where films are shown at the cinema.
3 a kind of thin wall or a set of curtains on rails, that can be moved about. Screens are used to divide a room or to hide things.

screw *noun* **screws**
a kind of nail with a slot on the top and ridges round the sharp end. You put it in a hole and twist it round to fix things together.

screw *verb* **screws, screwing, screwed**
1 to fix something with a screw.
2 to turn or twist something to make it tighter.

screwdriver *noun* **screwdrivers**
a tool for turning a screw until it fits tightly into something.

scribble *verb* **scribbles, scribbling, scribbled**
to write or draw quickly and untidily.

scripture *noun* **scriptures**
the Bible.

scroll *noun* **scrolls**
a book written on a long sheet of paper that is rolled up.

a
b
c
d
e
f
g
h
i
j
k
l
m
n
o
p
q
r
s
t
u
v
w
x
y
z

167

scrub *verb* **scrubs, scrubbing, scrubbed**
to rub something hard with a brush to clean it.

scruffy *adjective* **scruffier, scruffiest**
dirty and untidy.

sculptor *noun* **sculptors**
an artist who makes things in stone, wood, clay, or metal.

sculpture *noun* **sculptures**
a statue or something else made by a sculptor.

scuttle *verb* **scuttles, scuttling, scuttled**
to move quickly like a frightened mouse.

sea *noun* **seas**
the large area of salty water that covers large parts of the earth.

seagull *noun* **seagulls**
a white or grey sea bird with a loud cry.

seal *noun* **seals**
a furry animal that lives in the sea and on land.

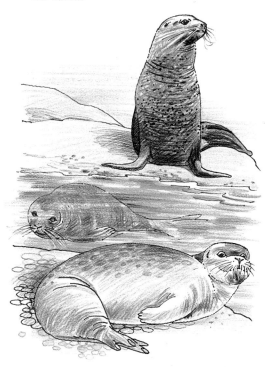

seal *verb* **seals, sealing, sealed**
to close something by sticking two parts together. *Did you seal the envelope?*

seam *noun* **seams**
the line where two pieces of material are sewn together.

search *verb* **searches, searching, searched**
to look carefully for something.

searchlight *noun* **searchlights**
a strong light that can be pointed in any direction.

seaside *noun*
a place by the sea where people go to enjoy themselves.

season *noun* **seasons**
one of the four parts of the year. Spring, summer, autumn, and winter are the seasons.

seat *noun* **seats**
a chair or stool or anything else that people sit on.

seaweed *noun*
a plant that grows in the sea.

second *adjective, adverb*
coming after the first. *February is the second month of the year.*

second *noun* **seconds**
a measure of time. There are 60 seconds in one minute.

secondary school *noun* **secondary schools**
a school for children from the age of about eleven to sixteen or eighteen.

second-hand *adjective*
not new, already owned by someone else.

168

secret *adjective*
not known by everybody, not to be told or shown to other people.
secretly *adverb*

secret *noun* **secrets**
something which is not to be told or shown to other people.

secretary *noun* **secretaries**
someone whose job is to type letters, answer the telephone, and arrange things in an office.

section *noun* **sections**
a part of something.

secure *adjective* **securer, securest**
safe or firm. *Make sure the ladder is secure before you climb it.*
securely *adverb*

security *noun*
trying to make sure that people and their property are safe.

see *verb* **sees, seeing, saw, seen**
1 to use your eyes to look at something.
2 to understand. *Do you see what I mean?*

seed *noun* **seeds**
a tiny thing that a plant can grow from.

seedling *noun* **seedlings**
a young plant.

seek *verb* **seeks, seeking, sought**
to try to find.

seem *verb* **seems, seeming, seemed**
to make you think something is true. *Jo seems sad today.*

see-saw *noun* **see-saws**
a piece of wood or metal that is balanced in the middle and can go up and down.

seize *verb* **seizes, seizing, seized**
(rhymes with *sneeze*)
to take hold of something suddenly. *The thief seized the bag and ran.*

seldom *adverb*
not often.

select *verb* **selects, selecting, selected**
to choose.

self *noun* **selves**
everything in a person that makes them different from anyone else.

selfish *adjective*
If you are selfish you only think about yourself and don't care what other people want. **selfishly** *adverb*

sell *verb* **sells, selling, sold**
to give in return for money. *I sold my bike yesterday.*

semicircle *noun* **semicircles**
half of a circle.

semi-colon *noun* **semi-colons**
a mark like this ; that you use in writing.

semi-final *noun* **semi-finals**
a match played to decide who plays in the final.

send *verb* **sends, sending, sent**
to make a person or thing go somewhere. *Send for an ambulance!*

senior *adjective*
older or more important.

sensation *noun* **sensations**
1 anything that you can feel happening to yourself. *The cold water gave me a tingling sensation.*
2 something exciting that happens.

sense *noun* **senses**
1 the power to see, hear, smell, feel, or taste. *Dogs have a good sense of smell.*
2 knowing what is the right thing to do. *She had the sense to call an ambulance.*

sensible *adjective*
If you are sensible, you think carefully about something and do the right thing.
sensibly *adverb*

sensitive *adjective*
easily hurt.

a
b
c
d
e
f
g
h
i
j
k
l
m
n
o
p
q
r
s
t
u
v
w
x
y
z

169

sent *verb* see **send**

sentence *noun* **sentences**
a group of words that belong together. A written sentence begins with a capital letter and ends with a full stop like this.

sentry *noun* **sentries**
a soldier who is guarding a building.

separate *adjective*
not joined to anything.
separately *adverb*

September *noun*
the ninth month of the year.

sequel *noun* **sequels**
a book or film which continues the story of an earlier book or film.

sergeant *noun* **sergeants**
a policeman or soldier in charge of other policemen or soldiers.

serial *noun* **serials**
a story told in parts.
a television serial.

series *noun* **(the plural is the same)**
1 a number of things that come one after another.
We had a series of accidents.
2 a number of television programmes about the same people or subject.
What's your favourite comedy series?

serious *adjective*
1 careful and thoughtful.
a serious boy.
2 important.
a serious decision.
3 very bad.
a serious accident.
seriously *adverb*

sermon *noun* **sermons**
a talk given in church.

serpent *noun* **serpents**
a large snake.

servant *noun* **servants**
someone whose job is to work in someone else's house.

serve *verb* **serves, serving, served**
1 to sell things in a shop.
Are you being served madam?
2 to give food out at a meal.
Breakfast is served from 7.00 to 9.00 am.

service *noun* **services**
1 a business that does useful work for people. *a bus service, the postal service.*
2 serving people in a shop, hotel, or restaurant.
3 work that must be done regularly to keep a car or machine in good condition.
4 a meeting in church with prayers and singing.

serviette *noun* **serviettes**
a square of cloth or paper for keeping you clean while you eat.

session *noun* **sessions**
a time spent doing one thing.

set *noun* **sets**
a group of people or things that belong together.

set *verb* **sets, setting, set**
1 to become solid or hard. *Has the jelly set yet?*
2 to put things ready to use. *Set the table for dinner.*
3 to give someone work to do. *Our teacher set us a lot of homework.*
to set off to start.

settee *noun* **settees**
a long, comfortable seat with a back, for more than one person.

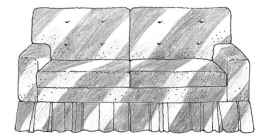

settle *verb* **settles, settling, settled**
1 to get comfortable in a place and stay there. *The cat settled on my lap.*
2 to decide. *We've settled who goes first by tossing a coin.*

seven *noun* **sevens**
the number 7.
seventh *adjective*

seventeen *noun*
the number 17.
seventeenth *adjective*

seventy *noun*
the number 70.
seventieth *adjective*

several *adjective*
more than a few but not a lot. *I've read this story several times.*

severe *adjective* **severer, severest**
1 not gentle or kind. *a severe punishment.*
2 very bad. *a severe illness.*
severely *adverb*

sew *verb* **sews, sewing, sewed, sewn**
to use a needle and cotton to join pieces of cloth together.
sewing machine *noun* **sewing machines**

sex *noun* **sexes**
one of the two groups, either male or female, that all people and animals belong to.

shabby *adjective* **shabbier, shabbiest**
looking old and nearly worn out. *shabby clothes.*

shade *noun* **shades**
1 a place that is darker than other places, because the light of the sun cannot get to it. *We sat under the shade of the tree.*
2 how light or dark a colour is. *Do you like this shade of pink?*

shade *verb* **shades, shading, shaded**
1 to keep strong light away from something.
2 to make part of a drawing darker than the rest.

shadow *noun* **shadows**
the dark shape that you see near someone or something that is in front of the light.

shady *adjective* **shadier, shadiest**
out of the strong light of the sun. *We sat in a shady part of the garden.*

shaft *noun* **shafts**
1 a long, thin pole.
2 a deep, narrow hole. *a mine shaft.*

shake *verb* **shakes, shaking, shook, shaken**
to move or make something move quickly up and down or from side to side. *Shake the bottle before opening it.*

shaky *adjective*
shaking, weak.

shall *verb*
THIS WORD IS USED IN SENTENCES ABOUT THE FUTURE: *We shall go home soon. I shall see you tomorrow.*

shallow *adjective*
not deep. *shallow water.*

shame *noun*
the feeling you have when you are unhappy because you have done wrong.

shameful *adjective*
so bad that it brings you shame. *It's shameful to lose 12-0!*
shamefully *adverb*

shampoo *noun* **shampoos**
liquid soap that you use to wash your hair.

shape *noun* **shapes**
the pattern that a line drawn round the outside of something makes. *A ball has a round shape.*

share *verb* **shares, sharing, shared**
1 to divide something into parts and give them out to other people.
Mum shared out the cake.
2 to use something that someone else is also using.
Can I share your book?

shark *noun* **sharks**
a large sea fish with sharp teeth.

sharp *adjective* **sharper, sharpest**
1 with an edge or point that can cut or make holes. *a sharp knife.*
2 sudden. *a sharp bend in the road.*
3 quick to see or hear things. *sharp eyes, sharp ears.*
sharply *adverb*

sharpen *verb* **sharpens, sharpening, sharpened**
to make something sharp. *sharpen a pencil.*

a b c d e f g h i j k l m n o p q r **s** t u v w x y z

171

shatter *verb* **shatters, shattering, shattered**
to break or make something break into tiny pieces. *A stone hit the window and shattered the glass.*

shave *verb* **shaves, shaving, shaved**
to cut hair from the skin to make it smooth.

shawl *noun* **shawls**
a piece of cloth or knitting worn round the shoulders or wrapped round a baby.

sheaf *noun* **sheaves**
a bundle of corn stalks tied together at harvest time.

shears *noun*
a tool like a very large pair of scissors for cutting plants or for clipping wool from sheep.

garden shears

sheath *noun* **sheathes**
a cover for the blade of a sword or knife.

shed *noun* **sheds**
a small wooden building. *a garden shed.*

shed *verb* **sheds, shedding, shed**
to let something fall. *A lorry shed its load on the motorway.*

sheep *noun* **(the plural is the same)**
an animal kept by farmers for its wool and meat.

sheet *noun* **sheets**
1 one of the two large pieces of smooth cloth you sleep between in bed.
2 a thin, flat piece of something. *a sheet of ice, a sheet of plastic, a sheet of paper.*

shelf *noun* **shelves**
a long piece of wood fastened to a wall, for putting things on. *a book shelf.*

shell *noun* **shells**
1 the thin, hard part round an egg, a nut, and some kinds of animals, such as snails.
2 a large bullet that explodes when it hits something.

shelter *noun* **shelters**
a place that protects people from wind, rain, heat, cold, or danger. *a bus shelter. Your plants need shelter from very hot sun.*

shelter *verb* **shelters, sheltering, sheltered**
to make someone or something safe from bad weather or danger. *The tree sheltered us from the rain.*

shepherd *noun* **shepherds**
someone whose job is to look after sheep.

sheriff *noun* **sheriffs**
a man in charge of the law in a county or district.

shield *noun* **shields**
a flat or curved sheet of metal, wood, plastic, or leather used to protect a person in a battle or in a riot.

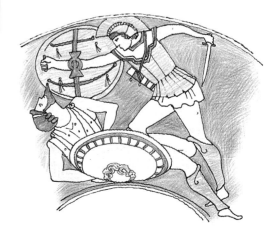

shift *verb* **shift, shifting, shifted**
to move something. *Help me shift the table.*

shin *noun* **shins**
the front of the leg between the knee and ankle.

shine *verb* **shines, shining, shone**
1 to give out light. *The sun shone all day.*
2 to look very bright. *He polished the table until it shone.*

shingle *noun*
a lot of small stones by the edge of the sea.

shiny *adjective* **shinier, shiniest**
with a surface that shines. *a shiny new bike.*

ship *noun* **ships**
a large boat that takes people or things on the sea.

shipwreck *noun* **shipwrecks**
a bad accident that destroys or sinks a ship while it is at sea.

shirt *noun* **shirts**
a piece of clothing for the top half of the body with sleeves, a collar, and buttons down the front.

shiver *verb* **shivers, shivering, shivered**
to shake because you are cold or frightened.

shoal *noun* **shoals**
a large number of fish swimming together.

shock *noun* **shocks**
a big surprise that is not pleasant.

shock *verb* **shocks, shocking, shocked**
to give someone a nasty surprise, or to upset them.

shoe *noun* **shoes**
a leather or plastic thing that you wear on your foot with a sole and heel.

shoot *noun* **shoots**
a part of a plant that has just grown.

shoot *verb* **shoots, shooting, shot**
1 to use a gun or a bow and arrow.
2 to hurt or kill by shooting.
3 to kick, hit, or throw a ball at the goal.

shop *noun* **shops**
a place that people go into to buy things.

shop *verb* **shops, shopping, shopped**
to go to a shop to buy something.
shopper *noun* **shoppers**

shopkeeper *noun* **shopkeepers**
a person who looks after a shop.

shore *noun* **shores**
the land along the edge of the sea.

short *adjective* **shorter, shortest**
1 not long.
a short visit.
2 not tall.
a short person.
for short a short way of saying or writing something.
Her name is Katherine, but we call her Katie for short.

shortly *adverb*
soon, in a little while.

shorts *noun*
trousers that only cover the top part of the legs.

shot *noun* **shots**
1 the firing of a gun.
2 a photograph. *That's a good shot of you.*
3 kicking or hitting a ball in games like football or tennis.

shot *verb* see **shoot**

should *verb*
ought to. *I should go home now.*

shoulder *noun* **shoulders**
the part of the body between the neck and arm.

shout *verb* **shouts, shouting, shouted**
to speak very loudly.

shove *verb* **shoves, shoving, shoved**
to push hard.

shovel *noun* **shovels**
a kind of curved spade for lifting things such as coal or sand.

show *noun* **shows**
1 something that you watch at the theatre or on television.
2 things arranged for people to look at.
a flower show.

show *verb* **shows, showing, showed, shown**
1 to let people see something. *Show me your new bike.*
2 to make something clear to someone. *He's shown me how to switch on the computer.*

a b c d e f g h i j k l m n o p q r **s** t u v w x y z

173

shower *noun* **showers**
1 a short fall of rain or snow.
2 a piece of equipment that gives out water. You stand under it and wash yourself.
to have a shower to stand under a spray of water and wash yourself.

shrank *verb* see **shrink**

shred *noun* **shreds**
a tiny strip or piece that has been cut, broken, or torn off something. *She tore the paper into shreds.*

shriek *noun* **shrieks**
a short scream.

shrill *adjective* **shriller, shrillest**
sounding very high and loud.

shrimp *noun* **shrimps**
a small sea animal that you can eat.

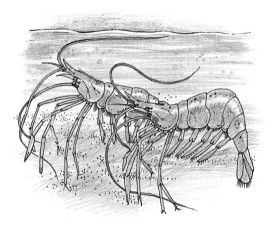

shrink *verb* **shrinks, shrinking, shrank, shrunk**
to become smaller. *These jeans have shrunk.*

shrivel *verb* **shrivels, shrivelling, shrivelled**
to get very dry and curl up at the edges like a dead leaf.

shrub *noun* **shrubs**
a bush.

shrug *verb* **shrugs, shrugging, shrugged**
to lift your shoulders to show that you do not know something or care about it.

shudder *verb* **shudders, shuddering, shuddered**
to shake because you are cold or frightened.

shuffle *verb* **shuffles, shuffling, shuffled**
to drag your feet along the ground as you walk. *He shuffled round the room in his slippers.*

shut *verb* **shuts, shutting, shut**
to move a cover, lid, or door to close an opening.
to shut up to stop talking.

shutter *noun* **shutters**
1 a wooden cover that fits over a window.
2 the part inside a camera that opens to let in light as you take a photograph.

shutters 1

shuttle *noun* **shuttles**
1 a train, bus, or plane which goes quickly between two places.
2 see **space shuttle**

shy *adjective* **shyer, shyest**
1 if you are shy, you do not like meeting people you do not know.
2 easily frightened. *Otters are very shy animals.*
shyly *adverb*

sick *adjective* **sicker, sickest**
ill.
to be sick to bring food back up from the stomach through the mouth.
to be sick of to be tired of.

side *noun* **sides**
1 one of the outer parts between the front and back of a person, animal, or thing.
2 a flat surface. *A cube has six sides.*
3 an edge. *A triangle has three sides.*
4 a group playing or fighting against another group. *Whose side are you on?*

sideboard *noun* **sideboards**
  a long, heavy piece of furniture with drawers, cupboards, and a flat top.

sideways *adverb*
  1 with the side first.
  The piano will fit through the door if you carry it sideways.
  2 to one side.
  He moved sideways to avoid the puddle.

siege *noun* **sieges**
  a time when an army surrounds a town or castle so that people and things cannot get in or out.

sigh *verb* **sighs, sighing, sighed**
  to breathe out heavily to show you are feeling sad, tired, or happy.

sight *noun*
  1 the power to see.
  You are lucky to have good sight.
  2 something that you see.
  He was a funny sight in that hat.

sign *noun* **signs**
  anything written, drawn, or done to tell or show people something. *road signs.*

sign *verb* **signs, signing, signed**
  to write your name in your own writing.

signal *noun* **signals**
  a light, sound, or movement that tells people something.
  A red light is a signal for cars to stop.

signal *verb* **signals, signalling, signalled**
  to give a signal.
  The cyclist put out his right arm to signal he was turning right.

signature *noun* **signatures**
  your name written by yourself in your own writing.

Sikh *noun* **Sikhs**
  a person who follows one of the religions of India, called **Sikhism**

silence *noun*
  a time when there is no sound at all.

silent *adjective*
  without any sound.
  silently *adverb*

silk *noun*
  fine, shiny cloth made from threads spun by insects called **silkworms**

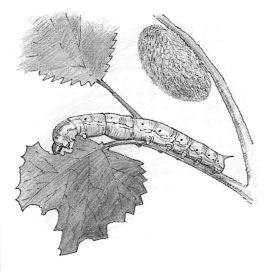

silky *adjective* **silkier, silkiest**
  smooth like silk.

sill *noun* **sills**
  a ledge underneath a window.

silly *adjective* **sillier, silliest**
  stupid, not clever

silver *noun*
  a valuable, shiny white metal.

similar *adjective*
  of the same kind, like another person or thing. *The bridesmaids wore similar dresses.*
  similarly *adverb*

simple *adjective* **simpler, simplest**
  1 easy. *a simple question.*
  2 plain. *a simple dress.*
  simply *adverb*

sin *noun* **sins**
  something that your religion says you should not do because it is very bad.

since *adverb, conjunction, preposition*
  1 from that time. *We have been friends since last summer. The cat jumped out of the window and I haven't seen it since.*
  2 because. *We couldn't play outside since it was raining.*

sincere *adjective*
  truly meant. *sincere good wishes.*
  sincerely *adverb*

a b c d e f g h i j k l m n o p q r **s** t u v w x y z

175

sing *verb* **sings, singing, sang, sung**
to use your voice to make music.
singer *noun* **singers**

singe *verb* **singes, singeing, singed**
to burn something slightly.

single *adjective*
1 only one. *The tree has a single apple.*
2 not married.

singular *adjective*
the form of a word you use when you are talking about only one person or thing. The word *child* is singular, but *children* is plural.

sink *noun* **sinks**
a place with taps where you do the washing-up.

sink *verb* **sinks, sinking, sank, sunk**
1 to go under water. *The ship sank in the storm.*
2 to go down. *The sun sank behind the mountains.*

sip *verb* **sips, sipping, sipped**
to drink a very small amount at a time.

sir *noun*
a word used when speaking politely to a man, instead of his name.

siren *noun* **sirens**
a machine that makes a loud sound to warn people about something. *Police cars and fire engines have sirens.*

sister *noun* **sisters**
a girl or woman who has the same parents as another person.

sit *verb* **sits, sitting, sat**
to rest on your bottom, as you do when you are on a chair.

site *noun* **sites**
the ground that is or was used for something. *a camping site.*

sitting room *noun* **sitting rooms**
a room with comfortable chairs.

situation *noun* **situations**
1 the place where something is. *Jo's house is in a nice situation near the park.*
2 the things that are happening to you. *I was in a difficult situation when I lost my money.*

six *noun* **sixes**
the number 6.
sixth *adjective*

sixteen *noun*
the number 16.
sixteenth *adjective*

sixty *noun*
the number 60.
sixtieth *adjective*

size *noun* **sizes**
1 how big or small something is. *My room is the same size as yours.*
2 the measurement something is made in. *size ten shoes.*

sizzle *verb* **sizzles, sizzling, sizzled**
to make a hissing and crackling sound. *food sizzling in the frying pan.*

skate *noun* **skates**
1 an ice-skate, a boot with a steel blade under it that you wear for moving on ice.
2 a roller skate, a boot with wheels on the bottom that you wear for moving quickly over smooth ground.

skate *verb* **skates, skating, skated**
to move smoothly over ice or the ground on skates or roller skates.
skater *noun* **skaters**

skeleton *noun* **skeletons**
all the bones inside the body of a person or animal.

sketch *verb* **sketches, sketching, sketched**
to draw quickly.

ski *noun* **skis**
a long piece of wood, metal, or plastic strapped to the foot for moving over snow.

a skier

ski

ski *verb* **skis, skiing, skied**
to move along on skis.

skid *verb* **skids, skidding, skidded**
to slide without meaning to. *The car skidded on the wet road.*

skill *noun* **skills**
the power to do something well.
skilful *adjective*
skilfully *adverb*

skim *verb* **skims, skimming, skimmed**
1 to take the cream off the top of the milk.
2 to move quickly over the surface of something and only just touch it.

skin *noun* **skins**
1 the outer covering of your body.
2 the outer covering of some fruits and vegetables. *banana skin.*

skinny *adjective* **skinnier, skinniest**
very thin.

skip *verb* **skips, skipping, skipped**
1 to move lightly and quickly by jumping from one foot to the other.
2 to jump over a rope that is turning.
3 to miss out. *Skip the next page.*

skirt *noun* **skirts**
a piece of clothing for women and girls that hangs down from the waist.

skittle *noun* **skittles**
one of a set of pieces of wood or plastic shaped like bottles that you try to knock down with a ball.

skull *noun* **skulls**
the bones in the head of a person or animal.

sky *noun* **skies**
the space above the earth where you can see the sun, moon, and stars.

skyscraper *noun* **skyscrapers**
a very tall building.

slab *noun* **slabs**
a flat, thick piece. *a slab of toffee.*

slack *adjective* **slacker, slackest**
1 not tight.
a slack rope.
2 careless.
slack work.
3 not busy.
a slack day.

slam *verb* **slams, slamming, slammed**
to close something loudly. *She slammed the door.*

slang *noun*
words you sometimes use in talking but which you don't normally use in writing or on important occasions.

slant *verb* **slants, slanting, slanted**
to have one put higher than the other; to be not straight. *My writing slants backwards.*

slap *verb* **slaps, slapping, slapped**
to hit with the flat part of your hand.

slash *verb* **slashes, slashing, slashed**
to make long cuts in something.

slate *noun* **slates**
smooth, grey rock. Pieces of slate are used to cover a roof.

slaughter *verb* **slaughters, slaughtering, slaughtered**
1 to kill an animal for food.
2 to kill many people or animals.

slave *noun* **slaves**
someone who belongs to another person and has to work without wages.

slay *verb* **slays, slaying, slew, slain**
to kill.

a b c d e f g h i j k l m n o p q r **s** t u v w x y z

177

sledge *noun* **sledges**
something used for travelling over snow with strips of metal or wood instead of wheels.

sleek *adjective* **sleeker, sleekest**
neat, smooth, and shiny. *sleek fur.*

sleep *verb* **sleeps, sleeping, slept**
to close your eyes and rest completely, as you do every night.

sleepy *adjective* **sleepier, sleepiest**
ready to go to sleep.

sleet *noun*
a mixture of rain and snow.

sleeve *noun* **sleeves**
the part of a coat, shirt, blouse, or jumper, that covers your arm.

sleigh *noun* **sleighs** (rhymes with *say*)
a large sledge pulled by animals.

slender *adjective*
thin, graceful. *a slender girl.*

slice *noun* **slices**
a thin piece cut off something. *a slice of bread.*

slide *noun* **slides**
1 a long, sloping piece of shiny metal that people can slide on.
2 something that girls put in their hair to keep it tidy.
3 a small photograph that you show on a screen using a **projector.**

slide *verb* **slides, sliding, slid**
to move smoothly and quickly over something. *We slid on the ice.*

slight *adjective* **slighter, slightest**
small, not important. *a slight cold.*

slim *adjective* **slimmer, slimmest**
thin, but not too thin.

slime *noun*
nasty wet, slippery stuff.

slimy *adjective* **slimier, slimiest**
covered with slime.

sling *noun* **slings**
1 a piece of cloth that goes round your arm and is tied round your neck. You wear a sling to support your arm if you have broken or hurt it.
2 a short leather strap used for throwing stones.

slink *verb* **slinks, slinking, slunk**
to move in a secret way because you are afraid or feel guilty about something. *The dog saw me and slunk away.*

slip *verb* **slips, slipping, slipped**
1 to slide accidentally. *Sam slipped and fell over.*
2 to go away quickly and quietly. *She slipped out of the room.*

slipper *noun* **slippers**
a soft, comfortable kind of shoe that you wear indoors.

slippery *adjective*
with a smooth surface so that it is difficult to get hold of or walk on.

slit *noun* **slits**
a long cut or a narrow opening in something.

a
b
c
d
e
f
g
h
i
j
k
l
m
n
o
p
q
r
s
t
u
v
w
x
y
z

slop *verb* **slops, slopping, slopped**
to make a mess by letting liquid run over the edge of a container.
The bucket was so full that some water slopped out.

slope *noun* **slopes**
ground that is like the side of a hill.

slope *verb* **slopes, sloping, sloped**
to be not level, to have one part higher than the other.
a sloping roof.

slot *noun* **slots**
a narrow opening for something like a coin to fit into.
Put a coin in the slot and you'll get a ticket.

slow *adjective* **slower, slowest**
1 a person or thing that is slow does not move or do something quickly. *You are slow this morning!*
2 showing a time that is earlier than the right time. *I'm sorry I'm late, but my watch is slow.*
slowly *adverb*

slug *noun* **slugs**
a small creature like a snail without its shell.

slumber *verb* **slumbers, slumbering, slumbered**
to sleep.

slunk *verb* see **slink**

slush *noun*
melting snow.

sly *adjective* **slyer, slyest**
clever at tricking people secretly.
slyly *adverb*

smack *verb* **smacks, smacking, smacked**
to hit with the flat part of the hand.

small *adjective* **smaller, smallest**
not big or as big as usual. *The dress is too small for me. A mouse is much smaller than an elephant.*

smart *adjective* **smarter, smartest**
1 neat and tidy. *You look very smart in your new jacket.*
2 clever. *What a smart dog!*
smartly *adverb*

smart *verb* **smarts, smarting, smarted**
to feel a stinging pain. *The smoke made my eyes smart.*

smash *verb* **smashes, smashing, smashed**
to break into pieces with a loud noise.
The firemen had to smash the windows to get into the house.

smear *verb* **smears, smearing, smeared**
to spread a sticky or dirty substance over something.

smell *noun* **smells**
something that you find out about with your nose. *Roses have a nice smell.*

smell *verb* **smells, smelling, smelled** or **smelt**
to use your nose to find out about something. *Can you smell something burning?*

smelly *adjective* **smellier, smelliest**
having a bad smell. *smelly socks.*

smile *verb* **smiles, smiling, smiled**
to move your mouth to show that you are happy.

smith *noun* **smiths**
someone who makes things out of metal. *a silversmith.*

smoke *noun*
blue or grey gas that floats up from a fire and looks like a cloud.

smoke *verb* **smokes, smoking, smoked**
1 to give off smoke. *smoking chimneys.*
2 to breathe in smoke from cigarettes or tobacco.

smooth *adjective* **smoother, smoothest**
1 without any lumps or rough parts. *a smooth surface.*
2 without any bumps or jerks. *a smooth ride.*

smother *verb* **smothers, smothering, smothered**
to cover someone's mouth and nose so that they cannot breathe.

smoulder *verb* **smoulders, smouldering, smouldered**
to burn slowly with a lot of smoke.

smudge *noun* **smudges**
a mark made by rubbing against something wet or dirty.

smudge *verb* **smudges, smudging, smudged**
to make something dirty by touching it. *Leave the painting to dry or you'll smudge it.*

smuggle *verb* **smuggles, smuggling, smuggled**
to take something into or out of a country secretly when it is against the law.
smuggler *noun* **smugglers**

snack *noun* **snacks**
something you can eat quickly instead of a meal.

snail *noun* **snails**
a small animal that lives inside a shell. Snails are found on land and in water.

snake *noun* **snakes**
an animal with a long body and no legs. Some snakes can give poisonous bites.

snap *verb* **snaps, snapping, snapped**
1 to break suddenly.
The rope snapped.
2 to try to bite.
The dog snapped at the stranger.

snare *noun* **snares**
a trap for catching animals.

snarl *verb* **snarls, snarling, snarled**
to make the sound a dog makes when it is angry.

snatch *verb* **snatches, snatching, snatched**
to take something quickly.

sneak *verb* **sneaks, sneaking, sneaked**
to move trying not to be seen or heard.
She sneaked up behind me and made me jump.

sneer *verb* **sneers, sneering, sneered**
to speak or smile in an unkind way.

sneeze *verb* **sneezes, sneezing, sneezed**
to make a sudden noise as air rushes out of the nose.
I can't stop sneezing.

sniff *verb* **sniffs, sniffing, sniffed**
to make a noise by suddenly taking in air through the nose. *People sniff when they have a cold.*

snip *verb* **snips, snipping, snipped**
to cut a little bit off something.

snooker *noun*
a game you play on a special table with coloured balls that you hit with rods called cues.

snooze *verb* **snoozes, snoozing, snoozed**
to have a short sleep.

snore *verb* **snores, snoring, snored**
to breathe very noisily while sleeping.

snorkel *noun* **snorkels**
a tube for someone to breathe through while they are swimming under water.

snorkel

snort *verb* **snorts, snorting, snorted**
to make a short, loud noise by forcing air through the nose.

snout *noun* **snouts**
an animal's nose and mouth sticking out from the rest of its face. Pigs have snouts.

snow *noun*
small, thin, white pieces of frozen water. Snow floats down from the sky when the weather is very cold.

snowball *noun* **snowballs**
a ball made of snow pressed together.

snowdrop *noun* **snowdrops**
a small, white flower that grows in January and February.

snowflake *noun* **snowflakes**
one piece of falling snow.

snowman *noun* **snowmen**
a person made out of snow.

snug *adjective* **snugger, snuggest**
cosy, warm, and comfortable.
snugly *adverb*

snuggle *verb* **snuggles, snuggling, snuggled**
to curl up in a warm, comfortable place.

so *adverb, conjunction*
THIS WORD HAS SEVERAL USES. HERE ARE SOME OF THE WAYS YOU CAN USE IT: *Why are you so late? 'I like this colour.' 'So do I.' Speak up so we can all hear you.*

soak *verb* **soaks, soaking, soaked**
to make something very wet.

soap *noun* **soaps**
1 stuff you use with water for washing.
2 a television series which is supposed to be about the lives of ordinary people.

soar *verb* **soars, soaring, soared**
to move high into the air.

sob *verb* **sobs, sobbing, sobbed**
to cry noisily, making gasping sounds.

soccer *noun*
the game of football.

sock *noun* **socks**
a covering for the foot and part of the leg.

socket *noun* **sockets**
the part that an electric light bulb or plug fits into.

sofa *noun* **sofas**
a long, comfortable seat with a back.

soft *adjective* **softer, softest**
1 not hard, easy to cut or change into another shape.
soft butter, a soft bed.
2 not loud.
soft music.
softly *adverb*

software *noun*
the programs that are put into a computer to make it work.

soggy *adjective* **soggier, soggiest**
very wet.
soggy grass.

soil *noun*
earth, the brown stuff on the ground that plants grow in.

solar *adjective*
anything to do with the sun. *solar energy, the solar system.*

sold *verb* see **sell**

soldier *noun* **soldiers**
a person in an army.

sole *noun* **soles**
1 the flat part underneath a foot or shoe.
2 a sea fish that you can eat.

solemn *adjective*
serious.
solemnly *adverb*

solid *adjective*
1 without a space inside. *Tennis balls are hollow but cricket balls are solid.*
2 hard, not like a liquid or gas. *Water becomes solid when it freezes.*

solitary *adjective*
alone or lonely.

solo *noun* **solos**
something sung, played, danced, or done by one person.

solution *noun* **solutions**
the answer to a puzzle or problem.

solve *verb* **solves, solving, solved**
to find the answer to a puzzle.

a b c d e f g h i j k l m n o p q r **s** t u v w x y z

a b c d e f g h i j k l m n o p q r **s** t u v w x y z

some *adjective, pronoun*
1 a few but not all. *Some of us can swim, but the others can't.*
2 a number or amount of something. *Would you like some cake?*
3 a, an, or one. *Some insect has just bitten me.*

somebody *pronoun*
a person.

somehow *adverb*
in some way that you do not know. *We must find him somehow.*

someone *pronoun*
a person.

somersault *noun* **somersaults**
a movement in which you turn head over heels and finish on your feet.

something *pronoun*
a thing that you do not know or do not say what it is. *I have forgotten something.*

sometimes *pronoun*
at some times. *Sometimes I cycle to school, sometimes I walk.*

somewhere *adverb*
in some place or to some place. *I put the book somewhere but I've forgotten where.*

son *noun* **sons**
someone's male child. *Sam is Mr and Mrs Smith's son.*

song *noun* **songs**
a short piece of music with words for singing.

soon *adverb*
in a very short time from now. *Jo will be home soon.*

soot *noun*
the black powder left behind by smoke.

soothe *verb* **soothes, soothing, soothed**
to make someone who is upset feel calm.
soothing words.

sore *adjective* **sorer, sorest**
painful when it is touched.

sorrow *noun* **sorrows**
a very sad feeling.

sorry *adjective* **sorrier, sorriest**
1 sad about something that you wish you had not done.
2 sad because of something that has happened to another person.
3 a word you use when you feel bad about something. *Sorry I'm late!*

sort *noun* **sorts**
a kind. *Which sorts of ice cream do you like?*

sort *verb* **sorts, sorting, sorted**
to put things into different groups. *The apples are sorted into different sizes.*
sort out to make things tidy.

sought *verb* see **seek**

soul *noun* **souls**
the part of a person that cannot be seen but is believed to go on living after they have died.

sound *adjective* **sounder, soundest**
1 healthy, strong, in good condition. *a sound building.*
2 right and good. *sound work.*
soundly *adverb*

sound *noun* **sounds**
anything that you can hear.

sound *verb* **sounds, sounding, sounded**
to make a certain kind of sound.

soup *noun* **soups**
a hot liquid made from meat or vegetables.

sour *adjective* **sourer, sourest**
1 with the kind of taste lemons have, not sweet.
2 not fresh. *sour milk.*

source *noun* **sources**
the place something has come from. *The source of the river is up in the hills.*

south *noun, adjective*
the direction to your right when you face east.

souvenir *noun* **souvenirs**
something that you keep because it makes you think about a person or place. *He brought back souvenirs from his holiday.*

sovereign *noun* **sovereigns**
a ruler who is a king, queen, emperor, or empress.

sow *noun* **sows**
(rhymes with *cow*)
a female pig.

sow *verb* **sows, sowing, sowed, sown**
(rhymes with *low*)
to put seeds in the ground so that they will grow into plants.

space *noun* **spaces**
1 the area or distance between things.
2 a place with nothing in it. *There is a space here for you to write your name.*
3 all the places beyond the earth, where the stars and planets are.

spacecraft *noun* **(the plural is the same)**
any kind of vehicle that can travel in space.

spaceship *noun* **spaceships**
a machine that can travel in space.

space shuttle *noun* **space shuttles**
a spaceship that can carry people and things from earth to a satellite and back.

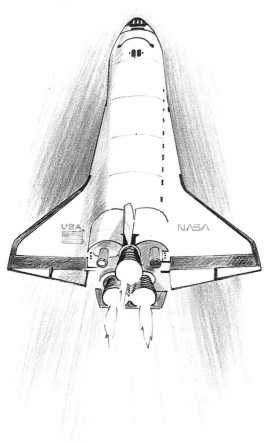

spacious *adjective*
with plenty of space.
a spacious room.

spade *noun* **spades**
1 a tool with a long handle and a wide blade that you use for digging.
2 a small, black spade printed on some playing cards.

spaghetti *noun*
a thin, long kind of pasta.

span *verb* see **spin**

spaniel *noun* **spaniels**
a dog with silky fur and long ears.

spank *verb* **spanks, spanking, spanked**
to smack someone on the bottom.

spanner *noun* **spanners**
a tool that fits round a **nut** so that you can turn it.

spare *adjective*
not used but kept in case it is needed. *a spare tyre.*

spare *verb* **spares, sparing, spared**
to give up something so that someone else can have it. *Could you spare one of your pencils?*

spark *noun* **sparks**
1 a tiny piece of burning material that shoots out from a fire.
2 a tiny flash. *There was a spark as the wires touched.*

sparkle *verb* **sparkles, sparkling, sparkled**
to shine with a lot of tiny flashes of bright light. *The sea sparkled in the sunlight.*

sparrow *noun* **sparrows**
a small, brown bird that you often see in gardens.

spat *verb* see **spit**

spawn *noun*
the eggs of frogs, fish, and some other water creatures.

speak *verb* **speaks, speaking, spoke, spoken**
to say something.
speaker *noun* **speakers**

spear *noun* **spears**
a long pole or stick with a sharp point, used as a weapon.

a
b
c
d
e
f
g
h
i
j
k
l
m
n
o
p
q
r
s
t
u
v
w
x
y
z

special *adjective*
1 different from any other kind. *Your birthday is a special day.*
2 for one person or thing. *Jo has her tea in her own special mug.*
specially *adverb I bought this book specially for you.*

specialist *noun* **specialists**
a person who is an expert in something, such as a doctor who is an expert in certain illnesses.

specimen *noun* **specimens**
1 a small amount of something that shows what the rest is like. *a specimen of rock.*
2 an example of one kind of plant or animal. *She showed them a specimen of an oak leaf.*

speck *noun* **specks**
a tiny bit. *a speck of dust.*

speckled *adjective*
covered with small spots.

spectacles *noun*
a pair of glasses.

spectacular *adjective*
very exciting or impressive to watch. *a spectacular fireworks display.*

spectator *noun* **spectators**
someone watching a game or show. *football spectators.*

speech *noun* **speeches**
1 the power of speaking.
2 a talk given to a group of people.

speed *noun*
how quickly something moves or happens.

speed *verb* **speeds, speeding, sped**
to go or move very fast. *He sped past me on his bike.*

spell *noun* **spells**
magic words that are supposed to make things happen.

spell *verb* **spells, spelling, spelled** or **spelt**
to put the right letters in the right order to make a word.

spend *verb* **spends, spending, spent**
1 to use money to pay for things. *How much have you spent so far?*
2 to pass time. *I spent all morning tidying my room.*

sphere *noun* **spheres**
the shape of a ball or the earth.

spice *noun* **spices**
part of a plant that is dried and used to flavour food. Ginger and pepper are spices.
spicy *adjective spicy food.*

spider *noun* **spiders**
a small creature with eight legs that spins webs.

spike *noun* **spikes**
a thin piece of metal with a sharp point. *The fence has spikes along the top.*

spill *verb* **spills, spilling, spilled** or **spilt**
to let something fall out of a container. *Who spilt their tea on the carpet?*

spin *verb* **spins, spinning, spun**
1 to turn round and round quickly, to make something turn round quickly. *I spun round until I was dizzy.*
2 to make thread by twisting long, thin pieces of wool or cotton together.
3 to make a web. *The spider spun a web.*

spinach *noun*
a vegetable with a lot of green leaves, which you cook to eat.

spine *noun* **spines**
1 the long bone down the centre of your back.
2 one of the long sharp points on some plants and animals. *Hedgehogs have spines.*

spinning wheel *noun* **spinning wheels**
a machine for spinning thread.

spiral *noun* **spirals**
the shape of a line that keeps going round the same point in smaller and smaller or bigger and bigger curves, like the jam in a slice of Swiss roll.

spire *noun* **spires**
a tall, pointed part on top of a church tower.

spirit *noun* **spirits**
1 the part of a person that you cannot see but is believed to go on living after they have died.
2 a ghost.
3 something that makes a person very brave and lively.

spit *verb* **spits, spitting, spat**
to send drops of liquid out of the mouth. *The baby spat out the nasty medicine.*

spiteful *adjective*
wanting to hurt someone by what you say or do.
spitefully *adverb*

splash *verb* **splashes, splashing, splashed**
to make water fly about noisily.

splendid *adjective*
very good. *We had a splendid holiday.*

splint *noun* **splints**
a straight piece of wood or metal that is tied to a broken arm or leg to hold it firm.

splinter *noun* **splinters**
a sharp bit of wood, glass, or metal.

split *verb* **splits, splitting, split**
1 to break or make something break into parts. *He split the log with an axe.*
2 to share something. *We split the money between us.*

spoil *verb* **spoils, spoiling, spoiled** or **spoilt**
1 to make something less good than it was. *The mud spoilt my shoes.*
2 to be too kind to someone so that they think they can always have what they want.

spoke *noun* **spokes**
one of the wires or rods that go from the centre of a wheel to the edge.

spoke, spoken *verb* see **speak**

sponge *noun* **sponges**
1 a light, soft cake.
2 something thick and soft with a lot of holes in it. Sponges soak up water and are used for washing.

sponsor *verb* **sponsors, sponsoring, sponsored**
to support a person or a group of people by giving them money. *a sponsored swim.*

spool *noun* **spools**
a round piece of wood or metal that cotton, string, or film is wound round.

spoon *noun* **spoons**
what you use for eating soup and ice cream.
spoonful *noun* **spoonfuls**

sport *noun* **sports**
a game that you do that is usually done outside and exercises your body. Swimming, football, and tennis are sports.

spot *noun* **spots**
1 a round mark.
2 a small red swelling on the skin.
3 a place.
This is a good spot for a picnic.

spot *verb* **spots, spotting, spotted**
to notice something. *Jo spotted Sam's mistake at once.*

spotless *adjective*
perfectly clean.

spotlight *noun* **spotlights**
a strong light that can shine on one small area.

spotty *adjective* **spottier, spottiest**
covered with spots.

spout *noun* **spouts**
the part of a container that is made like a pipe so that you can pour liquid out of it easily. *the spout of a teapot.*

spout

sprain *verb* **sprains, spraining, sprained**
to twist your wrist or ankle so that it swells and is painful.

sprawl *verb* **sprawls, sprawling, sprawled**
to sit or lie with your arms and legs spread out.

spray *verb* **sprays, spraying, sprayed**
to make tiny drops of liquid fall all over something.

spread *verb* **spreads, spreading, spread**
1 to stretch something out to its full size. *The bird spread its wings.*
2 to make something cover a surface. *She spread the cloth on the table.*

spring *noun* **springs**
1 the part of the year when plants start to grow and the days are getting lighter and warmer.
2 a place where water comes out of the ground.
3 a piece of metal wound into rings so that it jumps back into shape after it has been pressed or stretched.

spring *verb* **springs, springing, sprang, sprung**
1 to jump suddenly. *Jo sprang up to catch the ball.*
2 to grow quickly. *Weeds had sprung up all over the garden.*

sprinkle *verb* **sprinkles, sprinkling, sprinkled**
to make a few tiny pieces or drops fall on something. *to sprinkle sugar on top of a cake.*

sprout *noun* **sprouts**
a green vegetable like tiny hard cabbages, also called Brussels sprouts.

sprout *verb* **sprouts, sprouting, sprouted**
to start to grow, to send out shoots.

sprung *verb* see **spring** *verb*

spun *verb* see **spin**

spurt *verb* **spurts, spurting, spurted**
to shoot out or upwards quickly. *Blood spurted out of the wound.*

spy *noun* **spies**
someone who works secretly to find out things about another person or country.

spy *verb* **spies, spying, spied**
to see, to notice.

squabble *verb* **squabbles, squabbling, squabbled**
to quarrel about something that is not important.

square *noun* **squares**
1 a flat shape with four straight sides that are all the same length.
2 an open space in a town with buildings round it.

squash *noun*
1 a drink made from fruit. *orange squash.*
2 a game played indoors with rackets and a small rubber ball.

squash *verb* **squashes, squashing, squashed**
1 to press something hard so that it goes out of shape. *One of the sandwiches got squashed.*
2 to push a lot of things or people into a small space.

squat *verb* **squats, squatting, squatted**
to sit on the ground with your knees bent and your bottom resting on your heels.

squeak *verb* **squeaks, squeaking, squeaked**
to make the tiny, high sound a mouse makes.

squeaky *adjective*
making a squeaking sound. *a squeaky voice.*

squeal *verb* **squeals, squealing, squealed**
to make a long, loud sound that a pig makes.

a b c d e f g h i j k l m n o p q r **s** t u v w x y z

squeeze *verb* **squeezes, squeezing, squeezed**
1 to press something between your hands or two other things.
2 to go or push too much into a small space. *squeeze another person in.*

squirrel *noun* **squirrels**
a small animal with a thick tail that lives in trees.

squirt *verb* **squirts, squirting, squirted**
to come or squeeze suddenly out of something.

stab *verb* **stabs, stabbing, stabbed**
to push a knife or other sharp thing into a person or thing.

stable *noun* **stables**
a building in which horses are kept.

stack *noun* **stacks**
a neat pile. *a stack of books.*

stadium *noun* **stadiums**
a large place where people can watch sports and games. *a football stadium.*

staff *noun*
a group of people who work together in an office, shop, or school.

stag *noun* **stags**
a male deer.

stage *noun* **stages**
1 a raised floor in a hall or theatre, on which people act, sing, or dance to entertain other people.
2 the point someone has reached in doing something. *The baby is at the crawling stage.*

stagger *verb* **staggers, staggering, staggered**
to try to stand or walk but find it difficult to stay upright.

stagnant *adjective*
not flowing or fresh. *a pool of stagnant water.*

stain *noun* **stains**
a dirty mark made on something by liquid.

stair *noun* **stairs**
one of a set of steps for going up or down inside a building.

staircase *noun* **staircases**
a set of stairs with a rail to hold on to.

stake *noun* **stakes**
a thick, pointed stick. *Stakes are often used to support young trees.*

stale *adjective* **staler, stalest**
not fresh. *stale bread.*

stalk *noun* **stalks**
a thin stem that flowers and fruit grow on.

stall *noun* **stalls**
1 a small shop or a table that things are sold on. Markets have stalls.
2 a place for one animal in a stable or shed.

stallion *noun* **stallions**
a male horse.

stammer *verb* **stammers, stammering, stammered**
to keep repeating the sounds at the beginning of words when you speak.

stamp *noun* **stamps**
a piece of sticky paper with a picture on it. People put stamps on letters and parcels to show that they have paid to post them.

stamp *verb* **stamps, stamping, stamped**
to bang your foot heavily on the ground.

stand *noun* **stands**
something to put things on. *a music stand.*

stand *verb* **stands, standing, stood**
to get on your feet, or to be on your feet without moving. *He stood by the door. The teacher asked us all to stand.*

a
b
c
d
e
f
g
h
i
j
k
l
m
n
o
p
q
r
s
t
u
v
w
x
y
z

standard *noun* **standards**
1 how good something is. *a high standard of work.*
2 a flag.

stank *verb* see **stink**

stapler *noun* **staplers**
a small machine that fixes papers together by pressing little pieces of wire into them.

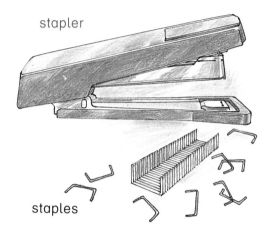

stapler

staples

star *noun* **stars**
1 one of the tiny, bright lights you see in the sky at night.
2 a famous singer or actor. *a film star.*

starch *noun*
a substance which is in many foods, such as potatoes and rice.

stare *verb* **stares, staring, stared**
to look at someone or something for a long time, without moving your eyes.

starling *noun* **starlings**
a dark brown bird that you often see in large flocks.

starry *adjective*
full of stars. *a starry night.*

start *verb* **starts, starting, started**
1 to begin to do something. *We started to tidy the room.*
2 to get something going. *Mum started the car.*

startle *verb* **startles, startling, startled**
to make someone surprised or frightened suddenly. *You startled me when you shouted.*

starve *verb* **starves, starving, starved**
to be ill or to die because you have not got enough food.
starvation *noun*

state *noun* **states**
1 how someone or something is. *Your room is in a very untidy state.*
2 a country or part of a country with its own government. *The United States of America.*

state *verb* **states, stating, stated**
to say or write something clearly. *Please state your name and address.*
statement *noun* **statements**

station *noun* **stations**
1 a place where people get on or off trains or buses. *a railway station.*
2 a building for policemen or firemen.

statue *noun* **statues**
a model of a person made in stone or metal.

stay *verb* **stays, staying, stayed**
1 to be in the same place.
2 to live somewhere as a visitor.

steady *adjective* **steadier, steadiest**
firm, not shaking.
steadily *adverb*

steak *noun* **steaks**
a thick slice of meat or fish.

steal *verb* **steals, stealing, stole, stolen**
to take something that does not belong to you and keep it.

steam *noun*
the gas that water turns into when it gets very hot.

steel *noun*
a strong, shiny metal made from iron. *Knives and forks are made of steel.*

steep *adjective* **steeper, steepest**
sloping sharply.
a steep hill.

steeple *noun* **steeples**
a tall, pointed tower on top of a church.

steer *verb* **steers, steering, steered**
to make a ship, car, or bicycle go in the direction you want.

steering wheel *noun* **steering wheels**
the wheel you use to steer a car.

stem *noun* **stems**
1 the main part of a plant above the ground.
2 the thin part that joins a leaf, flower, or fruit to the rest of the plant.

step *noun* **steps**
1 the movement you make with your foot when you are walking, running, or dancing.
2 a flat place where you can put your foot when you are going up or down something.

stepfather *noun* **stepfathers**
a man who is married to your mother but is not your real father.

stepmother *noun* **stepmothers**
a woman who is married to your father but is not your real mother.

stereo *noun* **stereos**
a machine for playing music.

stereo *adjective*
with the sound coming from two loudspeakers.
a stereo cassette player.

stern *adjective* **sterner, sternest**
serious, strict.
The teacher had a stern expression on her face.
sternly *adverb*

stew *noun* **stews**
meat or vegetables cooked in gravy or sauce.

stew *verb* **stews, stewing, stewed**
to cook food slowly in liquid.

stick *noun* **sticks**
1 a long, thin piece of wood.
2 a long, thin piece of anything. *a stick of rock.*

stick *verb* **sticks, sticking, stuck**
1 to become fixed. *The door has stuck.*
2 to fasten one thing to another. *He stuck a stamp on the envelope.*
3 to press a sharp point into something. *She stuck a pin in me!*
4 (*informal*) to put. *Stick out your hand to stop the bus.*

sticky *adjective* **stickier, stickiest**
able to stick to things. Glue, jam, and honey are all sticky.

stiff *adjective* **stiffer, stiffest**
not easily bent. *stiff card.*
stiffly *adverb*

stile *noun* **stiles**
a set of steps made to help people to get over a fence.

stile

still *adjective* **stiller, stillest**
without moving. *The injured man lay still.*

still *adverb*
1 not moving. *Stand still!*
2 the same now as before. *He's still asleep.*

stilts *noun*
a pair of poles with which you can walk high above the ground.

sting *noun* **stings**
a sharp part with poison on it that some animals and plants have. *a bee sting.*

sting *verb* **stings, stinging, stung**
to hurt someone with a sting. *A bee stung me yesterday.*

stink *verb* **stinks, stinking, stank** or **stunk**
to have a strong smell.

stir *verb* **stirs, stirring, stirred**
1 to move a liquid or a soft mixture round with a spoon.
2 to start to move. *After a long sleep the baby stirred.*

stirrup *noun* **stirrups**
the metal loop that hangs down each side of a horse's saddle for you to put your foot in.

stitch *noun* **stitches**
1 a loop of thread made by the needle in sewing or knitting.
2 a sudden pain in your side.

stoat *noun* **stoats**
a small, brown, furry animal with a long body.

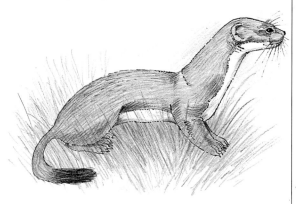

stock *noun* **stocks**
a lot of things kept ready to be sold or used.

stocking *noun* **stockings**
a covering for the foot and leg worn next to the skin.

stole, stolen *verb* see **steal**

stomach *noun* **stomachs**
the part in the middle of the body, where food goes when it is eaten.

stone *noun* **stones**
1 rock. *The castle was built of stone.*
2 a small piece of rock. *He threw a stone into the water.*
3 the hard seed in the middle of a cherry, plum, peach, or apricot.
4 a measure for weight. *She weighs 4 stones.*

stool *noun* **stools**
a small seat without a back.

stoop *verb* **stoops, stooping, stooped**
to bend the body forwards.

stop *verb* **stops, stopping, stopped**
1 to make someone or something stay still. *The policeman stopped the traffic.*
2 to become still. *The bus stopped.*
3 to finish. *The baby stopped crying.*

store *noun* **stores**
a large shop.

store *verb* **stores, storing, stored**
to keep things until you need them.

storey *noun* **storeys**
all the rooms on the same floor in a building.

stork *noun* **storks**
a large bird with very long legs and a long beak.

storm *noun* **storms**
a very strong wind with a lot of rain or snow.

stormy *adjective* **stormier, stormiest**
very windy, with bad storms.

story *noun* **stories**
words that tell you about something that has happened or about something that someone has made up. *adventure stories.*

stout *adjective* **stouter, stoutest**
1 rather fat. *a stout person.*
2 thick and strong. *a stout stick.*

stove *noun* **stoves**
something that gives out heat for warming a room or for cooking.

straight *adjective* **straighter, straightest**
not bending, going the shortest way from one place to another. *a straight road, straight hair.*
straight away now, immediately.

straighten *verb* **straightens, straightening, straightened**
1 to make something straight. *Straighten your tie.*
2 to become straight. *The road bends then straightens out again.*

strain *verb* **strains, straining, strained**
1 to stretch, push, or try too hard.
2 to hurt part of yourself by stretching or pushing too hard.
3 to separate a liquid from lumps or other things floating in it.

strange *adjective* **stranger, strangest**
1 not known or seen before. *a strange place.*
2 unusual and surprising. *a strange story.*
strangely *adverb*

stranger *noun* **strangers**
1 a person you do not know.
2 a person in a place he or she does not know. *Please show me the way, because I am a stranger here.*

strangle *verb* **strangles, strangling, strangled**
to kill someone by pressing their throat until they cannot breathe.

strap *noun* **straps**
a flat strip of leather or another strong material. *a watch strap.*

straw *noun* **straws**
1 dry stalks of corn.
2 a very thin tube for drinking through.

strawberry *noun* **strawberries**
a small, red, juicy fruit.

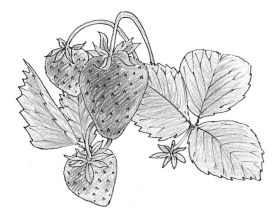

stray *verb* **strays, straying, strayed**
to wander, to get lost. *The sheep had strayed onto the road.*

streak *noun* **streaks**
a long, narrow line. *a streak of lightning.*

streak *verb* **streaks, streaking, streaked**
1 to mark something with streaks.
2 (*informal*) to move very quickly. *The car streaked past.*

stream *noun* **streams**
1 a small river.
2 anything else which moves in a line like a stream of water. *a stream of cars.*

streamer *noun* **streamers**
a long strip of paper or ribbon used to decorate something.

street *noun* **streets**
a road with houses along each side.

strength *noun*
how strong someone or something is.

strengthen *verb* **strengthens, strengthening, strengthened**
to make something stronger.

stretch *verb* **stretches, stretching, stretched**
1 to pull something to make it longer, wider, or tighter. *You can stretch a piece of elastic.*
2 to push your arms and legs as far as you can. *Sam got out of bed and stretched.*

stretcher *noun* **stretchers**
a pair of poles with canvas stretched across them for carrying a person who is hurt or ill.

strict *adjective* **stricter, strictest**
someone who is strict does not allow you to behave badly. *The new teacher is very strict.*

stride *verb* **strides, striding, strode**
to walk with long steps.

a b c d e f g h i j k l m n o p q r **s** t u v w x y z

191

strike *verb* **strikes, striking, struck**
1 to hit. *The tree was struck by lightning.*
2 to stop working because you want more money or are angry about something.
to strike a match to rub it along something rough until it bursts into flame.

string *noun* **strings**
very thin rope.

strip *noun* **strips**
a long, narrow piece of something.

strip *verb* **strips, stripping, stripped**
to take off clothes or a covering.

stripe *noun* **stripes**
a coloured band across or down something. *a shirt with blue and white stripes.*
striped *adjective a striped dress.*

strode *verb* see **stride**

stroke *verb* **strokes, stroking, stroked**
to move the hand gently along something. *Cats like being stroked.*

stroll *verb* **strolls, strolling, strolled**
to walk slowly.

strong *adjective* **stronger, strongest**
1 healthy and able to do things that need a lot of energy. *a strong horse.*
2 not easily broken. *strong rope.*
3 with a lot of flavour. *strong tea.*
strongly *adverb*

struck *verb* see **strike**

structure *noun* **structures**
1 anything that has been built. *Schools, houses, and fences are structures.*
2 the way something has been made or built. *We are studying the structure of a leaf.*

struggle *verb* **struggles, struggling, struggled**
1 to use your arms and legs in fighting or trying to get free.
2 to try hard to do something you find difficult. *Sam struggled with his homework.*

stubborn *adjective*
not wanting to change your ideas even though they might be wrong.

stuck *verb* see **stick** *verb*

stud *noun* **studs**
a small knob like the ones on the sole of a football boot.

student *noun* **students**
someone who studies at college or university.

studio *noun* **studios**
a place where an artist works, or where people make films or radio or television programmes.

study *noun* **studies**
a room where someone studies.

study *verb* **studies, studying, studied**
1 to spend time learning about something. *We are studying rivers in geography.*
2 to look at something very carefully. *He studied the map looking for the place.*

stuff *noun*
any kind of substance or material. *What's that stuff in the attic?*

stuff *verb* **stuffs, stuffing, stuffed**
1 to fill something tightly.
2 to put soft material into such things as cushions and soft toys.

stuffy *adjective* **stuffier, stuffiest**
without fresh air.
a stuffy room.

stumble *verb* **stumbles, stumbling, stumbled**
to fall over something.

stump *noun* **stumps**
1 the part of a broken tree, tooth, or pencil that is left.
2 one of the set of three upright sticks put at each end of the pitch in cricket.

stump 1

stun *verb* **stuns, stunning, stunned**
1 to hit or hurt someone so much that they cannot think properly.
2 to make someone very surprised. *She was stunned to receive so many presents.*

stung *verb* see **sting**

stunk *verb* see **stink**

stunt *noun* **stunts**
something difficult or dangerous done as part of a film or to attract people's attention.

stupid *adjective*
1 very silly. *a stupid idea.*
2 slow to learn and understand. *a stupid person.*
stupidly *adverb*

sturdy *adjective* **sturdier, sturdiest**
strong; not easily broken.
sturdy shoes.

stutter *verb* **stutters, stuttering, stuttered**
to keep repeating the sounds at the beginning of words when you speak.

sty *noun* **sties**
1 a sore swelling on the edge of an eyelid.
2 a place where pigs are kept.

style *noun* **styles**
the way something is done or made. *a neat style of writing, a hairstyle.*

subject *noun* **subjects**
1 the person or thing that you are writing about or learning about.
2 the subject of a sentence is the person or thing that does the action of the verb. In the sentence *Sam threw the ball*, *Sam* is the subject.
3 someone who is ruled by a king, queen, or government.

submarine *noun* **submarines**
a ship that can travel under water.

submit *verb* **submits, submitting, submitted**
1 to surrender.
2 to give something in to someone. *We must submit our work tomorrow.*

subscription *noun* **subscriptions**
money you pay regularly – for example, to belong to a club, or to get the same magazine each month.

substance *noun* **substances**
anything that you can see, touch, or use for making things. *Glue is a sticky substance.*

substitute *noun* **substitutes**
a person or thing used instead of the proper person or thing. *Our goalkeeper was ill, so we found a substitute.*

subtract *verb* **subtracts, subtracting, subtracted**
to take away. If you subtract 6 from 9 you get 3.
subtraction *noun* **subtractions**

subway *noun* **subways**
a tunnel made under the ground so that people can get to the other side of a road safely.

a b c d e f g h i j k l m n o p q r **s** t u v w x y z

succeed *verb* **succeeds, succeeding, succeeded**
to do or get what you wanted to do or get. *Jo succeeded in winning the race.*

success *noun* **successes**
a person or thing that does well or that people like a lot. *The party was a great success.*

successful *adjective*
able to do or get what you wanted to do or get.
successfully *adverb*

such *adjective*
1 of the same kind. *I like sweet things such as ice cream and chocolate.*
2 so great. *It was such a surprise!*

suck *verb* **sucks, sucking, sucked**
1 to take in air or liquid from something. *I sucked milk through a straw.*
2 to keep moving something around inside your mouth without chewing it. *He was sucking a sweet.*

sudden *adjective*
happening quickly without any warning. *a sudden scream.*
suddenly *adverb*

suede *noun*
a kind of soft leather that is not shiny.

suffer *verb* **suffers, suffering, suffered**
to have to put up with pain or something else that is not pleasant.

sufficient *adjective*
enough. *Have you got sufficient money for your journey?* **sufficiently** *adverb*

sugar *noun*
a sweet food that is put in drinks and other foods to make them taste sweet.

suggest *verb* **suggests, suggesting, suggested**
to give someone an idea that you think is useful.
suggestion *noun* **suggestions**

suit *noun* **suits**
a jacket and trousers or skirt that are meant to be worn together.

suit *verb* **suits, suiting, suited**
1 to fit in with someone's plans. *Does it suit you if we start at once?*
2 to look good on someone. *That colour suits you.*

suitable *adjective*
just right for something. *suitable shoes for a long walk.*

suitcase *noun* **suitcases**
a kind of box with a lid and a handle for carrying clothes and other things on journeys.

suite *noun* **suites**
a set of furniture such as two armchairs and a sofa.

sulk *verb* **sulks, sulking, sulked**
to stop speaking to your friends, because you are angry about something.

sulky *adjective* **sulkier, sulkiest**
silent and bad tempered, sulking.

sum *noun* **sums**
1 a problem to be solved in arithmetic.
2 an amount. *a sum of money.*

summer *noun* **summers**
the hottest part of the year.

summit *noun* **summits**
the top of a mountain.

sun *noun*
the star that shines in the sky and gives the earth heat and light.

Sunday *noun* **Sundays**
the first day of the week.

sundial *noun* **sundials**
a kind of clock that uses a shadow made by the sun to show what time it is.

194

sung *verb* see **sing**

sunk *verb* see **sink** *verb*

sunny *adjective* **sunnier, sunniest**
with the sun shining.
a sunny day.

sunrise *noun*
the time when the sun rises.

sunset *noun*
the time when the sun goes down.

sunshine *noun*
the light and heat that come from the sun when it is shining.

supermarket *noun* **supermarkets**
a large shop where people help themselves to things as they go round and pay for them all on the way out.

supernatural *adjective*
not natural, to do with gods, ghosts, fairies, or other strange beings.

superstitious *adjective*
believing that certain things will bring you good luck, and other things will bring you bad luck.

supper *noun* **suppers**
a meal or snack that you eat in the evening.

supply *noun* **supplies**
things kept ready to be used when you need them. *supplies of food.*

supply *verb* **supplies, supplying, supplied**
to give or sell you what you need. *The school supplies me with paper to write on.*

support *verb* **supports, supporting, supported**
1 to hold up something so that it does not fall. *These pieces of wood support the roof.*
2 to help or encourage someone. *Which team do you support?*
supporter *noun* **supporters**

suppose *verb* **supposes, supposing, supposed**
to think something is true although it might not be.

sure *adjective*
knowing something is true or right. *I'm sure her name is Mary.*

surf *noun*
big, white, foaming waves.

surface *noun* **surfaces**
the outside or top of something. *This leaf has a shiny surface. She dived below the surface.*

surgeon *noun* **surgeons**
a doctor who is trained to do operations.

surgery *noun* **surgeries**
the room you go in to see a doctor or dentist.

surname *noun* **surnames**
your last name that is the same as your family's name.

surprise *noun* **surprises**
1 the feeling you have when something suddenly happens that you were not expecting. *She looked at me in surprise when I said I don't like ice cream.*
2 something that happens and was not expected. *We arranged the party as a surprise.*

surprise *verb* **surprises, surprising, surprised**
to give someone a surprise. *I came early to surprise you.*
surprised *adjective*
surprising *adjective*

surrender *verb* **surrenders, surrendering, surrendered**
to stop fighting and agree to obey the enemy.

surround *verb* **surrounds, surrounding, surrounded**
to be all round someone or something. *The lake is surrounded by trees.*

surroundings *noun*
the things and places that surround you.

survey *noun* **surveys**
1 a careful look at something.
2 a set of questions to find out what people think about something.

survive *verb* **survives, surviving, survived**
to carry on living after an accident or some other event.
survivor *noun* **survivors**

suspect *verb* **suspects, suspecting, suspected**
to have a feeling that there might be something wrong. *We suspect he has stolen some money.*

a b c d e f g h i j k l m n o p q r **s** t u v w x y z

195

suspicious *adjective*
feeling that there might be something wrong.
suspiciously *adverb*

swallow *noun* **swallows**
a bird with a dark blue body, a long tail, and pointed wings.

swallow *verb* **swallows, swallowing, swallowed**
to let something go down your throat.

swam *verb* see **swim**

swamp *noun* **swamps**
an area of very wet ground.

swan *noun* **swans**
a big white bird with a long neck that lives on water or near to it.

swap *verb* **swaps, swapping, swapped**
to change one thing for another.

swarm *noun* **swarms**
a large number of insects together. *a swarm of bees.*

sway *verb* **sways, swaying, swayed**
to move from side to side. *The trees were swaying in the wind.*

swear *verb* **swears, swearing, swore, sworn**
1 to make a serious promise. *He swore to tell the truth.*
2 to use bad words. *He swore when he hit his finger.*

sweat *verb* **sweats, sweating, sweated**
to lose liquid through your skin, because you are ill or very hot.

sweater *noun* **sweaters**
a warm piece of clothing that you wear on the top part of your body, a jumper.

sweatshirt *noun* **sweatshirts**
a kind of cotton sweater.

sweep *verb* **sweeps, sweeping, swept**
to use a brush to clear away dust and litter from something.

sweet *adjective* **sweeter, sweetest**
1 with the taste of sugar or honey.
2 very pleasant. *a sweet smell.*

sweet *noun* **sweets**
1 a small piece of sweet food made of sugar or chocolate.
2 a pudding.

swell *verb* **swells, swelling, swelled, swollen**
to get bigger than it usually is. *I twisted my ankle and now it's swollen.*

swelling *noun* **swellings**
a lump on the body that is bigger than it usually is.

swerve *verb* **swerves, swerving, swerved**
to move suddenly to one side. *The driver swerved when she saw the child run onto the road.*

swift *adjective* **swifter, swiftest**
quick.
swiftly *adverb*

swim *verb* **swims, swimming, swam, swum**
to move yourself through water without touching the bottom.
swimmer *noun* **swimmers**

swimming pool *noun* **swimming pools**
a place built for people to swim in.

swindle *verb* **swindles, swindling, swindled**
to cheat someone.
swindler *noun* **swindlers**

swing *noun* **swings**
a seat hung from a tree or metal frame so that you can move backwards and forwards on it.

swing *verb* **swings, swinging, swung**
to move or make something move backwards and forwards, from side to side, or in a curve. *The monkey was swinging from a tree.*

swipe *verb* **swipes, swiping, swiped**
to hit hard.

swirl *verb* **swirls, swirling, swirled**
to move around quickly in circles.

switch *noun* **switches**
anything that is turned or pressed to make something work or stop working. *an electric light switch.*

switch *verb* **switches, switching, switched**
to change from one thing to another.
to switch on to switch off to use a switch to make something work or stop working. *Sam switched on the television.*

swollen *verb* see **swell**

swoop *verb* **swoops, swooping, swooped**
to fly down suddenly to attack something. *The bird swooped down on the house.*

sword *noun* **swords**
a weapon like a knife with a long blade.

swore, sworn *verb* see **swear**

swum *verb* see **swim**

swung *verb* see **swing** *verb*

sycamore *noun* **sycamores**
a kind of large tree. Its seeds have wings, so they can be carried a long way by the wind.

syllable *noun* **syllables**
any word or part of a word that has one separate sound when you say it. *Bi-cy-cle* has three syllables and *bike* has one syllable.

syllabus *noun* **syllabuses**
a list of the things pupils have to study.

symbol *noun* **symbols**
a sign which shows or means something. The + symbol means you add numbers together.

symmetrical *adjective*
with two halves that are exactly alike but the opposite way round.

sympathy *noun*
the feeling you have when you are sorry for someone who is sad, ill, or in trouble.
sympathetic *adjective* Everyone was *very sympathetic when I hurt myself.*

symphony *noun* **symphonies**
a long piece of music for an orchestra.

symptom *noun* **symptoms**
one of the things you notice is wrong with you when you are ill. *A sore throat is a symptom of a cold.*

synagogue *noun* **synagogues**
a building where Jews worship.

synonym *noun* **synonyms**
a word which has nearly the same meaning as another word. *Beautiful* and *lovely* are synonyms.

syrup *noun* **syrups**
a very sweet, sticky, liquid.

system *noun* **systems**
a set of parts, things, or ideas that work together. *a railway system, a computer system.*

Tt

table *noun* **tables**
1 a piece of furniture with a flat top and legs.
2 a list of facts or numbers arranged in order.

tablet *noun* **tablets**
a small, hard piece of medicine.

tack *verb* **tacks, tacking, tacked**
to sew two pieces of material together with long stitches.

tackle *noun*
all the things you need for doing something. *fishing tackle.*

tackle *verb* **tackles, tackling, tackled**
1 to start to do a difficult job.
2 to try to get the ball from someone else in a game like football.
3 to try to catch and hold someone. *The policeman tackled the thief.*

tactful *adjective*
careful not to upset people.
tactfully *adverb*

tadpole *noun* **tadpoles**
a tiny animal that lives in water and will turn into a frog, toad, or newt. Tadpoles have long tails.

a b c d e f g h i j k l m n o p q r **s t** u v w x y z

197

tail *noun* **tails**
1 the part at the end of the body of an animal, bird, or fish. *The dog wagged its tail.*
2 the part at the back of something. *the tail of an aeroplane.*

tailback *noun* **tailbacks**
a long queue of traffic.

tailor *noun* **tailors**
someone whose job is to make suits and coats.

take *verb* **takes, taking, took, taken**
1 to get hold of something. *He took his prize and smiled.*
2 to move something or go with someone to another place. *Dad took us to the cinema.*

talc, talcum powder *noun*
a fine powder you put on your skin to make it feel smooth and give it a nice smell.

tale *noun* **tales**
a story. *a fairy tale.*

talent *noun* **talents**
if you have a talent for something, you can do it very well. *Jo has a talent for singing.*

talented *adjective*
very good at something.

talk *verb* **talks, talking, talked**
to use words to speak to other people.

talkative *adjective*
a person who is talkative talks a lot.

tall *adjective* **taller, tallest**
1 measuring more than usual from top to bottom. *a tall person, a tall tree.*
2 how high a person or thing is. *She's 1·42 metres tall.*

tambourine *noun* **tambourines**
a musical instrument that you shake or hit with your fingers.

tame *adjective* **tamer, tamest**
if a bird or animal is tame it is not wild or afraid of people.

tamper *verb* **tampers, tampering, tampered**
to make changes in something so that it will not work properly. *Who's been tampering with the computer?*

tan *noun*
When you have a tan, your skin is darker than usual because you have been in the hot sun.
tanned *adjective*

tan *verb* **tans, tanning, tanned**
1 to lie in the sun and get a tan.
2 to make the skin of an animal into leather.

tangle *noun* **tangles**
a mass of things like hair, string, or branches that are twisted together in an untidy way so that it is difficult to separate them.

tangled *adjective*
twisted up in knots. *tangled hair.*

tank *noun* **tanks**
1 a large container for liquid. *an oil tank, a fish tank.*
2 a strong, heavy car used in war. It has a big gun on top and can move over very rough ground.

tanker *noun* **tankers**
1 a large ship for carrying oil.
2 a large lorry for carrying milk or petrol.

tanker 1

tanker 2

tantrum *noun* **tantrums**
a sudden bad temper. *My little brother is having a tantrum because he doesn't want to go to bed.*

tap *noun* **taps**
a thing you can turn on and off to control water or gas in a pipe.

tap *verb* **taps, tapping, tapped**
to hit or touch someone or something quickly and lightly. *She tapped me on the shoulder.*

tape *noun* **tapes**
1 a narrow strip of special material that you can record sound or pictures on.
2 a narrow strip of cotton used in tying things and making loops or labels for clothes.

tape *verb* **tapes, taping, taped**
to record sound or pictures. *I taped the film that was on TV last night.*

tape recorder *noun* **tape recorders**
a machine for recording music on tape and playing it back.

tapestry *noun* **tapestries**
a piece of strong cloth covered with stitches that make a picture.

tar *noun*
a thick, black, sticky liquid made from coal or wood and used for making roads.

target *noun* **targets**
something that people aim at and try to hit. *The bullet hit the target.*

tart *noun* **tarts**
pastry with jam or fruit on it. *apple tart.*

tartan *noun*
woollen material with a special check pattern that comes from Scotland.

task *noun* **tasks**
a piece of work that must be done. *I had the task of washing-up.*

tassel *noun* **tassels**
a bundle of threads tied together at the top and used to decorate things.

taste *noun*
the feeling you get through your tongue when you eat something. Sugar has a sweet taste. Lemons have a sour taste.

taste *verb* **tastes, tasting, tasted**
to eat a little bit of food or sip a drink to see what it is like.

tasty *adjective* **tastier, tastiest**
with a strong, pleasant taste.

tattered *adjective*
badly torn.

taught *verb* see **teach**

tax *noun* **taxes**
money that people have to give to the government.

taxi *noun* **taxis**
a car that you can travel in if you pay the driver.

tea *noun*
1 a hot drink made with boiling water and the dried leaves of a **tea plant.**
2 a meal eaten in the afternoon.

teach *verb* **teaches, teaching, taught**
to tell or show someone how to do something. *She taught me to swim last year.*
teacher *noun* **teachers**

team *noun* **teams**
a group of people who work together or play together on the same side in a game. *a football team.*

teapot *noun* **teapots**
a container with a spout and a lid, used for making tea.

tear *noun* **tears** (rhymes with *fear*)
a small drop of water that comes out of the eye when you cry.

tear *verb* **tears, tearing, tore, torn** (rhymes with *fair*)
to pull something apart so that you damage it. *I tore the letter up and threw it away. Paper tears easily.*

tease *verb* **teases, teasing, teased**
to make fun of someone for fun. *People often tease me because I'm short.*

technical *adjective*
concerned with machines and how things work.

technology *noun*
studying machines and how things work.

teddy bear *noun* **teddy bears**
a stuffed toy bear.

teenager *noun* **teenagers**
someone who is between thirteen and nineteen years old.

teeth *noun* see **tooth**

teething *adjective*
beginning to grow teeth. *The baby is crying because she's teething.*

telegraph pole *noun* **telegraph poles**
a tall pole that holds up telephone wires.

telephone *noun* **telephones**
an instrument which you use to speak to another person a long way away.

telephone *verb* **telephones, telephoning, telephoned**
to speak to someone on a telephone. *I telephoned Jo to ask her to come to tea.*

telescope *noun* **telescopes**
a tube with lenses at each end. People look through telescopes to see things that are far away.

television *noun* **televisions**
a machine that picks up programmes sent through the air and changes them into pictures and sound so that people can watch them.

tell *verb* **tells, telling, told**
to speak in order to pass on news, stories, or instructions.
Dad told me he would be home for tea.
to tell someone off to say you are angry with them because of something they have done.
to tell tales to tell other people when someone has done something wrong.

telly *noun* **tellies**
(*informal*) television.

temper *noun*
the mood someone is in.
He's shouting at everyone because he's in a bad temper.
to lose your temper to get angry.

temperature *noun*
how hot or cold something is.
The temperature today is 22 degrees.

temple *noun* **temples**
a place where people go to pray.

temporary *adjective*
not for ever, for a short time only.
When they dug up the road, they put up temporary traffic lights.

tempt *verb* **tempts, tempting, tempted**
to try to make someone do wrong.

temptation *noun* **temptations**
something that makes you want to do wrong.
Don't leave money around, it's a temptation to thieves.

ten *noun* **tens**
the number 10.
tenth *adjective*

tenant *noun* **tenants**
a person who pays money to live in or use a place.

tend *verb* **tends, tending, tended**
to be likely to do or be something. *Men tend to be taller than women.*

tender *adjective* **tenderer, tenderest**
1 loving. *a tender smile.*
2 soft, easy to eat. *tender meat.*
3 sore, easily hurt. *tender skin.*
tenderly *adverb*

tennis *noun*
a game for two or four players who hit a ball with rackets over a net. Tennis is played on a **tennis court**

tent *noun* **tents**
a shelter made of nylon or canvas stretched over poles. People sleep in tents when they go camping.

tepid *adjective*
only just warm. *tepid water.*

term *noun* **terms**
1 the time between holidays when you go to school.
2 a word or phrase. *We learned some technical terms to do with computers.*

terminal *noun* **terminals**
a place where people begin or end their journeys by aeroplane, bus, train, or ship.

terminus *noun* **termini**
a place where a bus or train stops at the end of its journey.

terrace *noun* **terraces**
a row of houses joined together.

terrapin *noun* **terrapins**
a creature that lives in water and looks like a small tortoise.

terrible *adjective*
very bad.
terribly *adverb*

terrier *noun* **terriers**
a kind of small dog.

terrific *adjective*
1 (*informal*) very good. *I had a terrific idea.*
2 (*informal*) very great. *There was a terrific storm.*

terrify *verb* **terrifies, terrifying, terrified**
to make a person or animal very frightened.
terrified *adjective*
terrifying *adjective*

territory *noun* **territories**
land that belongs to one country or person.

terror *noun*
great fear.

terrorist *noun* **terrorists**
a person who frightens, hurts, or kills people to try to make the government or other people do what he or she wants.

test *noun* **tests**
a set of questions you have to answer or something you have to do to show what you have learned. *a spelling test, a driving test.*

test *verb* **tests, testing, tested**
1 to make someone do a test.
2 to use something in order to find out whether it works. *Sam tested his model aeroplane.*

tether *verb* **tethers, tethering, tethered**
to tie an animal up.

textbook *noun* **textbooks**
a book which gives you the facts about a subject. *a history textbook.*

than *conjunction, preposition*
compared with another person or thing. *You are smaller than me.*

thank *verb* **thanks, thanking, thanked**
to tell someone you are pleased about something they have given you or done for you.

thankful *adjective*
pleased, grateful. *I was thankful it wasn't raining.*

a
b
c
d
e
f
g
h
i
j
k
l
m
n
o
p
q
r
s
t
u
v
w
x
y
z

201

that, those *adjective, pronoun*
the one there. *Those books are yours. That is mine, this is yours.*

thatched *adjective*
with a roof made of reeds or straw. *a thatched cottage.*

thaw *verb* **thaws, thawing, thawed**
to melt, to stop being frozen. *The snow thawed when the sun came out.*

theatre *noun* **theatres**
a place where people go to see plays and shows.

theft *noun*
stealing.

their *adjective*
belonging to them. *their coats.*

them *pronoun* see **they**

then *adverb*
1 after that. *I had breakfast and then I went to school.*
2 at that time. *We didn't know about it then.*

theory *noun* **theories**
an idea someone suggests to explain something.

there *adverb*
in that place or to that place. *You can sit there.*

therefore *adverb*
a word that shows that something is happening. *Sam was ill and therefore he didn't go to school.*

thermometer *noun* **thermometers**
an instrument that measures temperature.

Thermos *noun* **Thermoses**
a container that keeps hot drinks hot or cold things cold. *a Thermos flask.*

thesaurus *noun* **thesauruses**
a book which gives you lists of words that have similar meaning.

these *adjective, pronoun* see **this.**

they, them *pronoun*
the people or things you are talking about. *They were playing tennis. Did you see them?*

thick *adjective* **thicker, thickest**
1 not thin, measuring a lot from one side to the other or from top to bottom. *a thick jumper, a thick slice of bread.*
2 not easy to see through or go through. *thick fog, a thick forest.*
3 not easy to pour, not runny. *thick gravy.*
thickness *noun*

thicken *verb* **thickens, thickening, thickened**
1 to make something thicker. *Add flour to thicken the sauce.*
2 to become thicker. *Tonight the clouds will thicken.*

thief *noun* **thieves**
someone who steals things.

thigh *noun* **thighs**
the top part of the leg down to the knee.

thimble *noun* **thimbles**
a metal or plastic cover for the end of a finger. You wear it when you sew to protect your finger.

thin *adjective* **thinner, thinnest**
1 not fat or thick. *He is tall and thin. Cut the bread into thin slices.*
2 easy to pour, with lots of water in it. *thin gravy.*
thinly *adverb*

thing *noun* **things**
anything that you can see, touch, or think about. *A pen is a thing you use to write with. Have you got your things ready for school?*

think *verb* **thinks, thinking, thought**
1 to use your mind. *Think carefully before you answer the question.*
2 to believe something. *I thought you were older than me.*

third *adjective, adverb*
coming after the second. *I got third prize.*

third *noun* **thirds**
one of the three equal parts something can be divided into. It can also be written as $\frac{1}{3}$.

thirsty *adjective* **thirstier, thirstiest**
wanting a drink.

thirteen *noun*
the number 13.
thirteenth *adjective*

thirty *noun*
the number 30.
thirtieth *adjective*

this, these *adjective, pronoun*
the one here. *These books are mine. This is mine, that is yours.*

thistle *noun* **thistles**
a wild plant with prickly leaves and purple flowers.

thorn *noun* **thorns**
a sharp point that grows on a plant. Roses have thorns.

thorough *adjective*
1 done properly and carefully. *a thorough job.*
2 complete. *a thorough mess.*
thoroughly *adverb*

those *adjective, pronoun* see **that**

though *adverb*
however. *I like Tom. I don't like his brother though.*

though *conjunction*
and yet or although. *It was very cold though it didn't snow.*

thought *verb* see **think**

thought *noun* **thoughts**
something that you think.

thoughtful *adjective*
1 thinking a lot.
2 thinking about others and what they want in a kind way.
thoughtfully *adverb*

thousand *noun* **thousands**
the number 1000.
thousandth *adjective*

thrash *verb* **thrashes, thrashing, thrashed**
to keep hitting someone with a stick.

thread *noun* **threads**
a long, thin piece of cotton, nylon, or wool used for sewing or weaving cloth.

thread *verb* **threads, threading, threaded**
to put a thread through the eye of a needle or the hole in a bead.

threat *noun* **threats**
a promise that you will do something bad if what you want does not happen.

threaten *verb* **threatens, threatening, threatened**
to make threats. *Mum threatened to stop Jo's pocket money if she didn't tidy her room.*

three *noun* **threes**
the number 3.

three-dimensional *adjective*
a three-dimensional object is solid rather than flat.

thrifty *adjective*
careful with money.

thrill *noun* **thrills**
a sudden excited feeling.

thrilling *adjective*
very exciting.

throat *noun* **throats**
the front of your neck and the tube inside it that takes foods, liquid, and air into your body.

a
b
c
d
e
f
g
h
i
j
k
l
m
n
o
p
q
r
s
t
u
v
w
x
y
z

throb *verb* **throbs, throbbing, throbbed**
to keep up a regular beat, like your heart pumping blood round your body.

throne *noun* **thrones**
a special chair for a king or queen.

through *adverb, preposition*
(sounds like *threw*)
from one end or side to the other. *We went through the tunnel. We opened the gate and walked through.*

throughout *adverb, preposition*
all through. *They talked throughout the film.*

throw *verb* **throws, throwing, threw, thrown**
to make something move through the air.

thrush *noun* **thrushes**
a speckled brown bird which sings beautifully.

thrust *verb* **thrusts, thrusting, thrust**
to push hard.

thud *verb* **thuds, thudding, thudded**
to make the low, dull sound something heavy and large makes when it hits the ground.

thumb *noun* **thumbs**
the short, thick finger at the side of each hand.

thump *verb* **thumps, thumping, thumped**
to hit hard.
He thumped on the door.

thunder *noun*
the noise that you hear after a flash of lightning in a storm.

thunder *verb* **thunders, thundering, thundered**
to make the sound that thunder makes.

thunderstorm *noun* **thunderstorms**
a storm with thunder and lightning.

Thursday *noun* **Thursdays**
the fifth day of the week.

tick *noun* **ticks**
a small mark like this ✓ that shows that something is right.

tick *verb* **ticks, ticking, ticked**
1 to put a tick next to something.
2 to make regular sounds like the little clicks some clocks make.

ticket *noun* **tickets**
a piece of paper or card that you buy so that you can travel on a bus or train or get into places like cinemas and theatres.

tickle *verb* **tickles, tickling, tickled**
to touch someone lightly with your fingers to make them laugh.

tide *noun* **tides**
the movement of the sea towards the land and away from the land.

tidy *adjective* **tidier, tidiest**
with everything in the right place. *Is your room tidy?*
tidily *adverb*

tidy *verb* **tidies, tidying, tidied**
to put things away in the right place.

tie *noun* **ties**
1 a long strip of material that you wear round your neck.
2 when two people or players have the same number of points at the end of a game. *The match ended in a tie.*

tie *verb* **ties, tying, tied**
to fasten something with a knot or a bow. *I tied my shoelaces.*

tiger *noun* **tigers**
a big wild cat found in Asia. It has orange fur with black stripes.

tight *adjective* **tighter, tightest**
1 fitting very closely. *tight trousers.*
2 fixed firmly so you cannot move it. *a tight knot.*
tightly *adverb*

tighten *verb* **tightens, tightening, tightened**
to make something tighter, or to get tighter.

tights *noun*
a piece of clothing that fits closely over the feet, legs, and lower part of the body.

tile *noun* **tiles**
a thin piece of baked clay or something else that is stiff, used in covering a roof, wall, or floor.

till *conjunction, preposition*
until. *Wait till I'm ready!*

till *noun* **tills**
a drawer or box for money in a shop.

tilt *verb* **tilts, tilting, tilted**
to make something slope. *Don't tilt the table.*

timber *noun*
wood used for making things.

time *noun* **times**
1 seconds, minutes, hours, days, weeks, months, and years.
2 a certain moment in the day. *'What time is it?' 'It's time for tea.'*
3 the rhythm and speed of a piece of music.

times *preposition*
multiplied by. *Two times four equals eight.*

timetable *noun* **timetables**
a list of times when things such as lessons at school happen, or when buses or trains go.

timid *adjective*
not brave.
timidly *adverb*

tin *noun* **tins**
1 a metal container for food or other things. *a tin of beans.*
2 a silver-coloured metal.

tingle *verb* **tingles, tingling, tingled**
to sting a little bit. *Cold water makes your skin tingle.*

tinkle *verb* **tinkles, tinkling, tinkled**
to make the light, ringing sound a small bell makes.

tin-opener *noun* **tin-openers**
a tool for opening tins.

tinsel *noun*
thin, shiny, silver or coloured material used for decorations.

tiny *adjective* **tinier, tiniest**
very small.

tip *noun* **tips**
1 the part at the end of something. *the tip of a pencil.*
2 a small amount of money given to someone for their help. *a tip for the waiter.*

tip *verb* **tips, tipping, tipped**
1 to move something so that it is not straight. *Don't tip your chair back.*
2 to turn a container over so that something falls out. *I tipped the rubbish into the bin.*

tiptoe *verb* **tiptoes, tiptoeing, tiptoed**
to walk on your toes without making a sound.

tired *adjective*
1 needing to rest or sleep.
2 bored with something.

tissue *noun* **tissues**
1 very thin, soft paper that you use for wrapping things like glass or china.
2 a paper handkerchief.

title *noun* **titles**
1 the name of a book, film, picture, or piece of music.
2 a word like Dr, Mr, and Mrs that is put in front of a person's name.

toad *noun* **toads**
an animal like a big frog. It has rough, dry skin and lives on land.

toadstool *noun* **toadstools**
a plant that looks like a mushroom.

toast *noun*
bread cooked until it is crisp and brown.

tobacco *noun*
a plant with leaves that are dried and smoked in pipes or used to make cigars and cigarettes.

toboggan *noun* **toboggans**
a kind of sledge used for sliding down slopes covered in snow.

today *noun*
this day.

toddler *noun* **toddlers**
a young child just beginning to walk.

toe *noun* **toes**
one of the five separate parts at the end of each foot.

toffee *noun* **toffees**
butter and sugar cooked together and made into sticky sweets.

together *adverb*
1 with another. *I stuck two pieces of paper together.*
2 at the same time as another. *They sang together.*

toil *verb* **toils, toiling, toiled**
to do hard work. *The farmer toiled all day in the fields.*

toilet *noun* **toilets**
1 a large bowl with a seat that you use to empty waste from your body.
2 a room where the toilet is.

token *noun* **tokens**
a piece of plastic, paper, or material that you can use instead of money to pay for something. *a book token.*

told *verb* see **tell**

tomato *noun* **tomatoes**
a soft, round, red fruit with seeds inside it. You can eat tomatoes in a salad.

tomb *noun* **tombs** (rhymes with *room*)
a place where a dead person's body is buried.

tomorrow *noun*
the day after today.

ton *noun* **tons**
a large measure for weight.

tone *noun* **tones**
how something sounds. *He spoke in an angry tone of voice.*

tongs *noun*
a tool that looks like a pair of scissors and is used for getting hold of something and picking it up.

tongue *noun* **tongues** (rhymes with *sung*)
the long, soft, pink part that moves about inside your mouth.

tonight *noun*
this evening or night.

tonne *noun* **tonnes**
a measure for weight.
1 tonne = 1000 kilograms.

tonsils *noun*
part of the throat that sometimes causes an illness called **tonsillitis**

too *adverb*
1 as well.
Can I come too?
2 more than is needed.
too much.

took *verb* see **take**

tool *noun* **tools**
something that you use to help you to do a job. Hammers and saws are tools.

tooth *noun* **teeth**
1 one of the hard, white parts in the mouth which grow in rows and which you use for biting and chewing.
2 one of the sharp parts of a comb or saw.

toothache *noun*
a pain in a tooth.

toothbrush *noun* **toothbrushes**
a small brush with a long handle, for cleaning your teeth.

toothpaste *noun*
a thick paste that you put on a toothbrush and use for cleaning teeth.

top *noun* **tops**
1 the highest part of something.
the top of a hill.
2 a cover that you put on something.
a bottle top.

top *adjective*
highest.
the top shelf.

topic *noun* **topics**
something interesting that you are writing or talking about.

topple *verb* **topples, toppling, toppled**
to fall over because there is too much on top.
The pile of books toppled over.

topsy-turvy *adjective, adverb*
turned upside-down.

torch *noun* **torches**
an electric light that you can carry about with you.

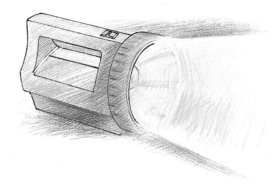

torment *verb* **torments, tormenting, tormented**
to be deliberately cruel to someone or something.

tore, torn *verb* see **tear** *verb*

torpedo *noun* **torpedoes**
a kind of long, round bomb sent under water to destroy ships and submarines.

torrent *noun* **torrents**
a very fast stream of water.

tortoise *noun* **tortoises**
a creature with four legs and a shell over its body, that moves slowly.

torture *verb* **tortures, torturing, tortured**
deliberately to make someone feel great pain.
torturer *noun* **torturers**

a
b
c
d
e
f
g
h
i
j
k
l
m
n
o
p
q
r
s
t
u
v
w
x
y
z

toss *verb* **tosses, tossing, tossed**
1 to throw something. *They tossed the ball to each other.*
2 to move quickly up and down or from side to side. *The boat was tossing around on the waves.*

total *adjective*
complete. *total silence.*
totally *adverb*

total *noun*
the amount when you have added everything up.

touch *verb* **touches, touching, touched**
1 to feel something with part of your body.
2 to be so close to something else that there is no space in between.

tough *adjective* **tougher, toughest**
1 strong. *tough shoes, a tough fighter.*
2 hard to chew. *tough meat.*

tour *noun* **tours**
a journey you make to visit different places.

tour *verb* **tours, touring, toured**
1 to travel about on holiday.
2 to go round a place looking at things. *We toured the castle before we had our picnic.*

tourist *noun* **tourists**
a person on holiday who goes round looking at interesting places.

tow *verb* **tows, towing, towed** (rhymes with low)
to pull along. *The car was towing a boat.*

toward, towards *preposition*
in the direction of something. *He walked towards the school.*

towel *noun* **towels**
a piece of cloth for drying things that are wet.

tower *noun* **towers**
a tall, narrow building, or a tall part of a building. *a church tower.*

town *noun* **towns**
a place with schools, shops, offices, factories, and a lot of houses built near each other.

towpath *noun* **towpaths**
a path beside a canal or river.

toy *noun* **toys**
something you play with.

trace *noun* **traces**
a mark left by something.

trace *verb* **traces, tracing, traced**
to copy a picture using thin paper that you can see through.

track *noun* **tracks**
1 a path.
2 a railway line.

track *verb* **tracks, tracking, tracked**
to follow the marks left by a person or animal.

tractor *noun* **tractors**
a vehicle used to pull farm machines and other heavy things.

trade *noun*
buying and selling. *The shops do a lot of trade at Christmas.*

tradition *noun* **traditions**
something that people have done or believed in for a long time.
traditional *adjective*

traffic *noun*
cars, buses, bicycles, lorries, and other things travelling on the road.
traffic jam a long line of traffic that cannot move.
traffic lights lights that change colour to tell traffic when to stop and go.

tragedy *noun* **tragedies**
1 something very sad that happened.
2 a play with a very sad ending.

trail *noun* **trails**
1 a rough path.
2 smells or marks left behind by something. *The dog was on the trail of a rabbit.*

trail *verb* **trails, trailing, trailed**
1 to follow a trail.
2 to be dragged along the ground. *Jo's scarf is so long that it trails in the mud.*

trailer *noun* **trailers**
something that is pulled along by a car or lorry.

train *noun* **trains**
the vehicle which carries goods or passengers on a railway. It often has several coaches or trucks.

train *verb* **trains, training, trained**
1 to teach a person or animal how to do something.
2 to practise for a competition or game.
trainer *noun* **trainers**

traitor *noun* **traitors**
someone who gives away a secret or gives information to the enemy.

tram *noun* **trams**
a vehicle like a bus which runs along rails in the road.

tramp *noun* **tramps**
someone without a home or job who walks from place to place.

tramp *verb* **tramps, tramping, tramped**
to walk with heavy footsteps.

trample *verb* **tramples, trampling, trampled**
to spoil something by walking heavily on it. *Don't trample on the flowers!*

trampoline *noun* **trampolines**
a large piece of canvas joined to a metal frame for jumping up and down on.

trance *noun* **trances**
a kind of sleep.

transfer *verb* **transfers, transferring, transferred**
to move someone or something to another place. *He was transferred to a different team.*

transform *verb* **transforms, transforming, transformed**
to change someone or something so that they are completely different.

translate *verb* **translates, translating, translated**
to put something into another language.

transparent *adjective*
so clear that you can see through it.

transplant *noun* **transplants**
an operation to move part of the body from one person to another. *a heart transplant.*

transport *noun*
vehicles used to take people, animals, or things from one place to another.

trap *noun* **traps**
a device for catching animals or people.

trap *verb* **traps, trapping, trapped**
to catch a person or animal by using a trap or a clever trick.

trapdoor *noun* **trapdoors**
a door in the floor or ceiling.

trapeze *noun* **trapezes**
a bar hanging from ropes, used by acrobats.

travel *verb* **travels, travelling, travelled**
to go from one place to another.

trawler *noun* **trawlers**
a fishing boat that pulls a large net along the sea bottom.

tray *noun* **trays**
a flat piece of wood, metal, or plastic used for carrying cups, plates, and other things.

treacherous *adjective*
1 if someone is treacherous you cannot trust them.
2 dangerous. *a treacherous sea.*

treacle *noun*
a thick, sweet, sticky liquid made from sugar.

tread *verb* **treads, treading, trod, trodden**
to walk on something.

treason *noun*
giving away your country's secrets to the enemy.

treasure *noun*
gold, silver, jewels, or other valuable things.

treat *noun* **treats**
something special that you enjoy.

treat *verb* **treats, treating, treated**
1 to behave towards someone or something in a certain way. *The horse had been badly treated.*
2 to try to make a sick person well again.
3 to pay for another person's food or drink. *My uncle treated us to lunch in a restaurant.*

tree *noun* **trees**
a tall plant with leaves, branches, and a thick stem of wood. *an oak tree.*

tremble *verb* **trembles, trembling, trembled**
to shake because you are cold or frightened.

tremendous *adjective*
very large or great.

trench *noun* **trenches**
a long, narrow hole dug in the ground.

trespass *verb* **trespasses, trespassing, trespassed**
to go on someone else's land, without asking them if you can.

trial *noun* **trials**
1 trying something out to see how well it works.
2 the time when a prisoner is in court. The people there decide whether or not he has done wrong.

triangle *noun* **triangles**
a flat shape with three straight edges and three corners.
triangular *adjective*

tribe *noun* **tribes**
a group of families who live together and are ruled by a chief.

trick *noun* **tricks**
1 something you do to cheat someone or to make someone look silly.
2 something clever that you have learned to do. *card tricks.*

trick *verb* **tricks, tricking, tricked**
to cheat someone with a trick.

trickle *verb* **trickles, trickling, trickled**
to move like a very small stream.

tricycle *noun* **tricycles**
a cycle with three wheels.

trifle *noun* **trifles**
cake and fruit covered in jelly, custard, and cream.

trigger *noun* **triggers**
the part of a gun that you pull with your finger to fire it.

trim *verb* **trim, trimming, trimmed**
1 to cut something to make it neat and tidy. *She trimmed my hair.*
2 to decorate a piece of clothing. *a collar trimmed with lace.*

trio *noun* **trios**
a set of three people or things.

trip *noun* **trips**
a short journey. *a school trip.*

trip *verb* **trips, tripping, tripped**
to catch your foot on something so that you stumble or fall.

tripod *noun* **tripods**
a stand with three legs. *He put the camera on a tripod to hold it steady.*

triumphant *adjective*
very pleased because you have been successful.

trod *verb* see **tread**

trolley *noun* **trolleys**
a large container on wheels that you carry things in. *a supermarket trolley.*

troops *noun*
soldiers.

tropical *adjective*
belonging to the very hot countries in Africa, Asia, and South America. *tropical rain forests.*

trot *verb* **trots, trotting, trotted**
to move quickly with high short steps.

trouble *noun* **troubles**
something that upsets, worries, or bothers you.
to be in trouble to be in a difficult situation because you have done something wrong or something bad has happened.

trouble *verb* **troubles, troubling, troubled**
to worry, to bother someone.

trough *noun* **troughs**
a long, narrow container that holds food or water for farm animals.

trousers *noun*
a piece of clothing that covers the body from the waist to the ankles and has separate parts for the legs.

trout *noun* **(the plural is the same)**
a fish found in rivers and lakes.

trowel *noun* **trowels**
a tool like a small spade with a short handle.

truant *noun* **truants**
someone who stays away from school without permission.
to play truant to stay away from school without permission.

truck *noun* **trucks**
1 a large vehicle for carrying heavy things on the road.
2 a cart for carrying things on a railway.

true *adjective* **truer, truest**
correct or real. *a true story, a true friend.*
truly *adverb*

trumpet *noun* **trumpets**
a brass musical instrument that you blow into.

a b c d e f g h i j k l m n o p q r s **t** u v w x y z

211

trunk *noun* **trunks**
1 a tree's thick stem.
2 an elephant's long nose.
3 a large box with a lid and handle for carrying things on a journey or storing things.

trust *verb* **trusts, trusting, trusted**
to believe that someone is good and honest and would not hurt you.

truth *noun*
something that is true. *Is he telling the truth?*
truthful *adjective*
truthfully *adverb*

try *verb* **tries, trying, tried**
1 to work hard at something you want to be able to do. *I tried to climb that tree, but I couldn't.*
2 to use or test something to see what it is like. *Try the brakes before you ride your bike.*

T-shirt *noun* **T-shirts**
a piece of clothing like a vest with short sleeves.

tub *noun* **tubs**
a round container. *a tub of ice cream.*

tube *noun* **tubes**
1 a long, thin, round container. *a tube of toothpaste.*
2 a long, thin, hollow piece of plastic, rubber, glass, or metal.

tuck *verb* **tucks, tucking, tucked**
to push the ends of something into or under something else. *Jo tucked her shirt into her jeans.*

Tuesday *noun* **Tuesdays**
the third day of the week.

tuft *noun* **tufts**
a number of feathers, hairs, or blades of grass growing together.

tug *verb* **tugs, tugging, tugged**
to pull hard.

tulip *noun* **tulips**
a spring flower that grows from a bulb and is shaped like a cup.

tumble *verb* **tumbles, tumbling, tumbled**
to fall.

tumbler *noun* **tumblers**
a glass with a flat bottom.

tummy *noun* **tummies**
(*informal*) your stomach.

tuna *noun* **(the plural is the same)**
a large sea fish.

tune *noun* **tunes**
a group of musical notes which make a pleasant sound.

tunnel *noun* **tunnels**
a long hole that has been made under the ground or through a hill.

turban *noun* **turbans**
a long piece of material that you wrap round and round your head.

turf *noun*
short grass and the soil it is growing in.

turkey *noun* **turkeys**
a large bird that is kept on a farm for its meat.

turn *noun* **turns**
the proper time for someone in a group to do something. *your turn next.*

turn *verb* **turns, turning, turned**
1 to move round. *I turned round to see who was behind me.*
2 to move something round. *He turned the key in the lock.*
3 to become. *She turned pale.*
to turn into to change into something different. *Tadpoles turn into frogs.*

turnip *noun* **turnips**
a round, white vegetable.

turret *noun* **turrets**
a small tower in a castle.

turtle *noun* **turtles**
a sea creature that looks like a tortoise.

tusk *noun* **tusks**
one of the two long, pointed teeth an elephant has.

tweezers *noun*
a tool for getting hold of very small things.

twelve *noun*
the number 12.
twelfth *adjective*

twenty *noun*
the number 20.
twentieth *adjective*

twice *adverb*
two times.

twig *noun* **twigs**
a small, thin branch of a tree.

twilight *noun*
the dim light at the end of the day before it gets completely dark.

twin *noun* **twins**
one of two children born to the same mother at the same time.

twinkle *verb* **twinkles, twinkling, twinkled**
to shine with a lot of tiny flashes of bright light. Stars twinkle.

twirl *verb* **twirls, twirling, twirled**
to turn round and round quickly.

twist *verb* **twists, twisting, twisted**
1 to turn or bend. *The path twisted and turned through the wood.*
2 to turn things round each other. *We twisted the wires together.*

twisty *adjective*
bending and turning. *a twisty road.*

twitch *verb* **twitches, twitching, twitched**
to make little, quick movements with part of the body.

twitter *verb* **twitters, twittering, twittered**
to keep making quick, light sounds like a bird.

two *noun* **twos**
the number 2.

two-dimensional *adjective*
a two-dimensional object is flat rather than solid.

type *noun* **types**
a kind or sort.

type *verb* **types, typing, typed**
to write with a typewriter.

typewriter *noun* **typewriters**
a machine with keys that you press in order to print letters and numbers.

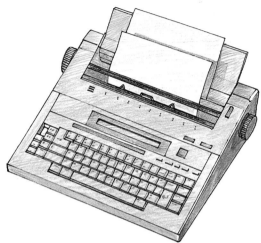

typical *adjective*
normal, usual. **typically** *adverb*

tyre *noun* **tyres**
a circle of rubber round the rim of a wheel.

Uu

ugly *adjective* **uglier, ugliest**
not beautiful to look at.

umbrella *noun* **umbrellas**
a round piece of cloth stretched over a frame that can be opened and shut. You hold an umbrella over your head to keep off the rain.

umpire *noun* **umpires**
someone who makes sure that the rules are kept in games such as cricket and tennis.

unable *adjective*
If you are unable to do something, you cannot do it. *Jo was unable to go to the party.*

unaware *adjective*
If you are unaware of something, you do not know about it. *I was unaware that someone was watching me.*

a b c d e f g h i j k l m n o p q r s **t u** v w x y z

uncertain *adjective*
not sure, not decided. *She was uncertain what to do next.*

uncle *noun* **uncles**
the brother of your mother or father or the husband of your aunt.

uncomfortable *adjective*
not comfortable.

uncommon *adjective*
If something is uncommon, you do not see or hear it often.

unconscious *adjective*
not aware of anything, in a very deep sleep. *Tom hit his head and was unconscious for several minutes.*

under *adverb, preposition*
1 below or lower than something. *The cat is under the table.*
2 less than something. *If you are under 17 you are not allowed to drive a car.*
3 covered by something. *I'm wearing a vest under my shirt.*

underground *adjective, adverb*
under the ground.

underground *noun*
a railway that runs through tunnels under the ground. *the London Underground.*

undergrowth *noun*
bushes and other plants growing under tall trees.

underline *verb* **underlines, underlining, underlined**
to draw a straight line underneath a word.

underneath *adverb, preposition*
in a place under something. *The cat sat underneath the table. She wore a blue jumper with a white T-shirt underneath.*

understand *verb* **understands, understanding, understood**
to know what something means or how it works.

underwear *noun*
clothes such as vests and pants that your wear under your other clothes.

undo *verb* **undoes, undoing, undid, undone**
to open something that has been tied or fixed. *She undid the string and opened the parcel. I can't undo these buttons.*

undress *verb* **undresses, undressing, undressed**
to take clothes off.

unemployed *adjective*
without a job, not working.

uneven *adjective*
not smooth or flat. *an uneven road.*

unexpected *adjective*
surprising because you did not expect it. *an unexpected visit.*
unexpectedly *adverb*

unfair *adjective*
not fair, not right or just.
unfairly *adverb*

unfortunate *adjective*
unlucky, unhappy.
unfortunately *adverb*

ungrateful *adjective*
If you are ungrateful, you do not show thanks when someone helps you or gives you something. *The ungrateful child never thanked them for the present.*

unhappy *adjective*
not happy.
unhappily *adverb*
unhappiness *noun*

unhealthy *adjective*
1 not well or healthy. *an unhealthy diet.*
2 that can make you ill. *unhealthy food.*

unicorn *noun* **unicorns**
in stories, an animal like a horse with a long, straight horn growing from the front of its head.

uniform *noun* **uniforms**
the special clothes that everyone in the same school, job, or club wears. *a school uniform.*

union *noun* **unions**
a group of workers who have joined together to talk to their manager about things like pay and the way they work.

unique *adjective*
not like anyone or anything else. *Every person in the world is unique.*

unit *noun* **units**
1 the number one. *hundreds, tens, and units.*
2 an amount used in measuring or counting. Centimetres are units of length.

unite *verb* **unites, uniting, united**
to join together to make one.

universe *noun*
all the worlds that there are and everyone and everything in them.

university *noun* **universities**
a place where some people go to study when they have left school.

unkind *adjective* **unkinder, unkindest**
not kind, cruel.
unkindly *adverb*

unleaded *adjective*
not containing lead. *unleaded petrol.*

unless *conjunction*
if not. *You'll be late unless you leave now.*

unlike *adjective*
not like, different.

unlikely *adjective*
not likely, not what you expect. *It's unlikely to rain today.*

unload *verb* **unloads, unloading, unloaded**
1 to take off the things that an animal, boat, car, or lorry is carrying.
2 to take the bullets out of a gun.

unlock *verb* **unlocks, unlocking, unlocked**
to open a door or box with a key.

unlucky *adjective* **unluckier, unluckiest**
If you are unlucky, good things do not happen to you.
unluckily *adverb*

unnatural *adjective*
not natural, not normal.
unnaturally *adverb*

unnecessary *adjective*
not necessary, not needed.

unpleasant *adjective*
not nice, not pleasant.

unpopular *adjective*
someone who is unpopular is not liked by many people.

unruly *adjective*
badly behaved and difficult to control.

unsafe *adjective*
not safe; dangerous.

unselfish *adjective*
not selfish, thinking of others.

unsuccessful *adjective*
if you are unsuccessful, you have not done what you tried to do.

unsuitable *adjective*
not suitable.

untidy *adjective* **untidier, untidiest**
not tidy.

untie *verb* **unties, untying, untied**
to undo a knot.

until *conjunction, preposition*
up to a certain time. *I stayed up until midnight.*

untrue *adjective*
not true or correct.

unusual *adjective*
not usual, strange.
unusually *adverb*

unwell *adjective*
ill.

uphill *adverb*
up, towards the top of the hill.

upon *preposition*
on or on top of.

upper *adjective*
higher. *the upper floors of a building.*

upright *adjective*
1 standing straight up. *an upright post.*
2 honest. *an upright person.*

a b c d e f g h i j k l m n o p q r s t **u** v w x y z

215

uproar *noun*
loud noise made by people who are angry or excited.

upset *verb* **upsets, upsetting, upset**
1 to make someone unhappy.
2 to knock over.
He upset a glass of milk all over the table.

upside-down *adjective, adverb*
turned over so that the bottom is at the top. *That picture is upside-down.*

upstairs *adjective, adverb*
the part of a house that you get to by climbing the stairs.

up-to-date *adjective*
modern.

upwards *adverb*
moving to somewhere higher, up.

urge *noun* **urges**
a strong feeling that you want to do something. *I had a sudden urge to laugh.*

urge *verb* **urges, urging, urged**
to try to make someone do something. *I urged him to hurry up.*

urgent *adjective*
so important that you must do it or answer it at once.
an urgent message, an urgent telephone call.
urgently *adverb*

use *verb* **uses, using, used**
to do a job with something. *I used paper and glue to make it. Don't use all the milk!*

useful *adjective*
good and helpful.
a useful bag to put things in, useful information.

useless *adjective*
if something is useless, you cannot use it.
A car is useless without petrol.

user-friendly *adjective*
easy to understand and use. *a user-friendly computer.*

usual *adjective*
normal, happening most often. *Today, I got up earlier than usual.*
usually *adverb*

Vv

vacant *adjective*
with nobody in it. *a vacant room.*

vaccination *noun* **vaccinations**
an injection that stops you getting an illness.

vacuum *noun*
a space with no air or anything inside it.

vacuum cleaner *noun* **vacuum cleaners**
a machine that sucks up dust and dirt from floors and carpets.

vague *adjective* **vaguer, vaguest**
not clear or certain. **vaguely** *adverb*

vain *adjective* **vainer, vainest**
If you are vain, you are too proud of what you can do or how you look.
in vain without success.

valentine *noun* **valentines**
a card you send to someone you love on St Valentine's day, the 14th February.

valley *noun* **valleys**
low land between hills. Valleys often have rivers running through them.

valuable *adjective*
1 worth a lot of money. *a valuable painting.*
2 useful. *valuable advice.*

value *noun*
1 the amount of money something could be sold for.
2 how important or useful something is.

vampire *noun* **vampires**
in stories, a creature that is supposed to suck blood.

van *noun* **vans**
a vehicle with a roof, for carrying goods.

vandal *noun* **vandals**
a person who deliberately breaks things that belong to other people. **vandalism** *noun*

vanilla *noun*
the flavour that white ice cream has.

vanish *verb* **vanishes, vanishing, vanished**
to go away suddenly and not be seen any more.

variety *noun* **varieties**
1 a lot of different kinds of things. *a variety of flavours.*
2 a certain sort. *That shop sells twenty varieties of ice cream.*

various *adjective*
different. *boxes of various shapes and sizes.*

varnish *noun* **varnishes**
a clear liquid painted on to wood or metal to make it shiny.

vary *verb* **varies, varying, varied**
1 to be different, to change. *The date of Easter varies each year.*
2 to make something different.

vase *noun* **vases**
a jar for holding flowers.

vast *adjective*
very big. *Australia is a vast country.*

veal *noun*
meat from a calf.

vegetable *noun* **vegetables**
part of a plant used as food. Potatoes, carrots, and beans are vegetables.

vegetarian *noun* **vegetarians**
a person who does not eat meat.

vegetation *noun*
plants and trees.

vehicle *noun* **vehicles**
anything that takes people or things from one place to another on land. Cars, vans, buses, trains, and lorries are vehicles.

veil *noun* **veils**
a piece of thin material used to cover the face or head.

vein *noun* **veins**
one of the narrow tubes inside the body, that carry blood to the heart.

velvet *noun*
thick material that is smooth and soft on one side. *velvet curtains.*

ventilator *noun* **ventilators**
an opening in the wall of a room for letting in fresh air.

ventriloquist *noun* **ventriloquists**
an entertainer who seems to make a dummy speak.

veranda *noun* **verandas**
a long, open place with a roof built on to the side of a house.

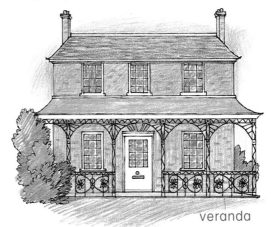

veranda

verb *noun* **verbs**
any of the words that tell you what someone or something is doing. *Come, go, sit,* and *think* are all verbs.

verdict *noun* **verdicts**
what is decided at the end of a trial in a law court.

verge *noun* **verges**
grass growing along the edge of a road or path.

verse *noun* **verses**
part of a poem or song.

version *noun* **versions**
1 a particular way of telling a story. *Jo's version of the accident is different from Sam's.*
2 a particular way of doing or making something. *Jo's bike is a new version of the one Sam has got.*

a b c d e f g h i j k l m n o p q r s t u **v** w x y z

217

vertical *adjective*
standing or pointing straight up, the opposite of horizontal.

very *adverb*
You use 'very' before another word to make it stronger: *I'm very hungry. Australia is a very big country. He is very tall.*

vessel *noun* **vessels**
1 any container for liquid.
2 any kind of ship or boat.

vest *noun* **vests**
a piece of clothing that you wear on the top half of the body under your other clothes.

vet *noun* **vets**
someone whose job is to help animals that are ill or hurt to get better.

viaduct *noun* **viaducts**
a long bridge that is a row of arches with a railway or road on the top of it.

vibrate *verb* **vibrates, vibrating, vibrated**
to move very quickly to and fro. *The whole house vibrates when a lorry goes past.*

vicar *noun* **vicars**
someone who serves God by being in charge of a church.

vicious *adjective*
bad and cruel.

victim *noun* **victims**
someone who has been hurt, robbed, or killed.

victory *noun* **victories**
the winning of a fight or game.

video *noun* **videos**
1 a machine that records and plays back television programmes on videotape.
2 a videotape with a film or television programmes on it.

videotape *noun* **videotapes**
a special tape for recording television programmes.

view *noun* **views**
1 everything that you can see from one place. *a beautiful view of the sea.*
2 what a person thinks about something. *My view is that school holidays are too short.*

view *verb* **views, viewing, viewed**
to look at something, to watch. *We viewed the stars through a telescope.*
viewer *noun* **viewers** television viewers.

vigorous *adjective*
1 active, energetic. *vigorous exercise.*
2 strong and healthy. *vigorous plants.*
vigorously *adverb*

village *noun* **villages**
a group of houses and other buildings in the country. A village is smaller than a town.

villain *noun* **villains**
a bad man.

vine *noun* **vines**
a plant that grapes grow on.

vinegar *noun*
a sour liquid which you can put on some foods.

vinyl *noun*
a kind of plastic.

violent *adjective*
very strong and rough. *a violent man, a violent storm.*
violently *adverb*

violet *noun* **violets**
a tiny purple flower.

violin *noun* **violins**
a musical instrument made of wood with strings across it. You play the violin with a **bow**.

virus *noun* **viruses**
a tiny living thing that can cause diseases. *a flu virus.*

visible *adjective*
that you can see. *Stars are only visible at night.*

vision *noun*
1 the power to see. *Glasses will improve your vision.*
2 a kind of dream.

visit *verb* **visits, visiting, visited**
to go to see a person or a place.
visitor *noun* **visitors**

vitamin *noun* **vitamins**
one of the things in food that you need to keep you healthy. *Oranges are full of vitamin C.*

vivid *adjective*
1 bright.
vivid colours.
2 so clear it seems real.
a vivid dream.
vividly *adverb*

vixen *noun* **vixens**
a female fox.

vocabulary *noun*
1 all the words in a language or that someone knows.
2 a list of words in a book that you must learn.

voice *noun* **voices**
the sound you make with your mouth when you are speaking or singing.

volcano *noun* **volcanoes**
a mountain that contains hot liquid, gases, and ash that sometimes burst out of it.

volume *noun* **volumes**
1 the amount of space filled by something. *We measured the volume of liquid in the bottle.*
2 one of a set of books. *The encyclopedia has ten volumes.*
3 how loud a sound is. *Turn down the volume on your radio.*

voluntary *adjective*
done without being paid and without being forced. **voluntarily** *adverb*

volunteer *noun* **volunteers**
someone who volunteers.

volunteer *verb* **volunteers, volunteering, volunteered**
to offer to do something you do not have to do.

vote *verb* **votes, voting, voted**
to say which person or idea you think should be chosen, by putting up your hand or by making a mark on a piece of paper.

voucher *noun* **vouchers**
a printed paper you can use instead of money.

vow *verb* **vows, vowing, vowed**
to make a serious promise.

vowel *noun* **vowels**
any one of the letters, **a, e, i, o, u,** and sometimes **y.**

voyage *noun* **voyages**
a long journey by boat or in space.

vulgar *adjective*
rude, bad-mannered.

vulture *noun* **vultures**
a large bird that eats dead animals.

Ww

waddle *verb* **waddles, waddling, waddled**
to walk like a duck.

wade *verb* **wades, wading, waded**
to walk through water.

wafer *noun* **wafers**
a very thin biscuit. Ice cream often has wafers with it.

wag *verb* **wags, wagging, wagged**
to move quickly from side to side. *The dog wagged its tail.*

wages *noun*
the money paid to someone for the job they do.

wagon *noun* **wagons**
1 a cart with four wheels that is pulled by horses and used for moving heavy things.
2 an open part of a train where things like coal are carried.

wail *verb* **wails, wailing, wailed**
to make a long, sad cry.

waist *noun* **waists**
the narrow part in the middle of the body.

waistcoat *noun* **waistcoats**
a short jacket without sleeves or a collar.

wait *verb* **waits, waiting, waited**
to stay until someone comes or until something happens.

waiter *noun* **waiters**
a man who brings food to people in cafés, hotels, and restaurants.

waitress *noun* **waitresses**
a woman who brings food to people in cafés, hotels, and restaurants.

wake *verb* **wakes, waking, woke, woken**
1 to stop sleeping.
I woke at six.
2 to make someone stop sleeping.
I asked Mum to wake me early.

walk *verb* **walks, walking, walked**
to move along on your feet.
walker *noun* **walkers**

wall *noun* **walls**
1 a thing made of bricks or stone around a garden or field.
2 one of the sides of a building or room.

wallet *noun* **wallets**
a small, flat case for paper money that you can carry in your pocket.

walnut *noun* **walnuts**
a nut with a hard shell.

waltz *noun* **waltzes**
a kind of dance done with a partner.

wand *noun* **wands**
a thin stick used for casting magic spells.

wander *verb* **wanders, wandering, wandered**
to move about without trying to get anywhere in particular.

want *verb* **wants, wanting, wanted**
1 to feel that you would like to have something.
I want a new coat.
2 to need.
That car wants washing.

war *noun* **wars**
a fight between countries.

ward *noun* **wards**
a bedroom for patients in a hospital.

wardrobe *noun* **wardrobes**
a cupboard where you hang clothes.

warehouse *noun* **warehouses**
a large building where things can be stored.

warm *adjective* **warmer, warmest**
fairly hot.
a warm bath.

warn *verb* **warns, warning, warned**
to tell someone that they are in danger.

warren *noun* **warrens**
an area of ground where a lot of rabbits live in holes called **burrows.**

warrior *noun* **warriors**
someone fighting in a battle.

wart *noun* **warts**
a dry, hard spot on the skin.

wash *verb* **washes, washing, washed**
to clean something with water.
to wash up to clean the plates, knives, and forks.

washing *noun*
clothes that need washing or are being washed.

washing machine *noun* **washing machines**
a machine that washes clothes.

washing-up *noun*
cleaning the plates, knives, and forks after a meal.

wasp *noun* **wasps**
a black and yellow striped insect that flies and can sting.

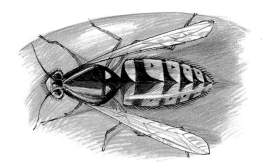

waste *noun*
1 things that you get rid of because you do not need them any more.
2 not using things in a careful way. *It's a waste to throw away all this food.*

waste *verb* **wastes, wasting, wasted**
1 to use more of something than you need to. *Write on both sides so that you don't waste paper.*
2 to throw something away that you could use. *Don't waste this food – we can have it tomorrow.*

watch *noun* **watches**
a small clock that you wear on your wrist.

watch *verb* **watches, watching, watched**
to look at.

watchman *noun* **watchmen**
someone whose job is to guard a building or other place, especially at night.

water *noun*
the clear liquid in rivers and seas.

water *verb* **waters, watering, watered**
1 to put water on the soil to help seeds or plants to grow.
2 to fill with water. *The smoke made my eyes water.*

waterfall *noun* **waterfalls**
a stream of water falling from a high place to a low place.

waterlogged *adjective*
soaked or filled with water.

waterproof *adjective*
made of material that does not let water through. *a waterproof coat.*

watertight *adjective*
closed tightly so that no water can get through. *a watertight lid.*

wave *noun* **waves**
a raised line of water, like those that move across the top of the sea.

wave *verb* **waves, waving, waved**
1 to raise your hand and move it from side to side, as people do when they say goodbye.
2 to move backwards and forwards or from side to side.
The branches were waving in the wind.

wavy *adjective*
with curves in it. *wavy hair.*

wax *noun*
stuff that melts easily, used to make such things as candles and polish.

way *noun* **ways**
1 a road or path that takes you to a place.
This is the way to the station.
2 how you do something.
This is the way to plait hair.

weak *adjective* **weaker, weakest**
not strong.

weaken *verb* **weakens, weakening, weakened**
to get weaker or to make weaker.

wealth *noun*
a lot of money or treasure.

wealthy *adjective* **wealthier, wealthiest**
rich.

weapon *noun* **weapons**
something used to hurt another person in a fight, such as a gun or a knife.

wear *verb* **wears, wearing, wore, worn**
to be dressed in something. *I wore my jeans.*
to wear out to become useless because it has been used so much.
My sweater was wearing out at the elbows.
to wear someone out to make someone very tired.
The children were worn out from their trip to the seaside.

weary *adjective* **wearier, weariest**
very tired.

weasel *noun* **weasels**
a small, furry wild animal with a long body.

weather *noun*
the sun, wind, rain, temperature, and other conditions that you notice when you go out of doors.

weave *verb* **weaves, weaving, wove, woven**
to make cloth by pushing a thread under and over other threads.

web *noun* **webs**
a thin net spun by a spider to trap insects.

web-footed *adjective*
having feet with toes joined together by skin, as ducks have.

web foot

wedding *noun* **weddings**
the time when a man and woman get married.

Wednesday *noun* **Wednesdays**
the fourth day of the week.

weed *noun* **weeds**
a wild plant growing where you don't want it.

week *noun* **weeks**
1 the seven days from Sunday to Saturday.
2 any period of seven days. *My cold will be better in a week.*

weekend *noun* **weekends**
Saturday and Sunday.

weep *verb* **weeps, weeping, wept**
to cry.

weigh *verb* **weighs, weighing, weighed**
1 to find out how heavy something is. *The shop assistant weighed the apples.*
2 to have a certain weight. *How much do you weigh?*

weight *noun* **weights**
1 how heavy something is. *Do you know the weight of the parcel?*
2 a piece of metal that you use on scales to measure how heavy something is.

weird *adjective* **weirder, weirdest**
very strange.

welcome *verb* **welcomes, welcoming, welcomed**
to show someone you are pleased when they arrive.

welfare *noun*
the health and happiness of people.

well *adjective*
healthy, not ill. *I hope you are well.*

well *adverb* **better, best**
1 in a good way.
Jo plays the piano well.
2 very much.
Shake the bottle well before you open it.
as well also. *Can I come as well?*

well *noun* **wells**
a hole dug to get water or oil out of the ground.

wellington *noun* **wellingtons**
a long rubber boot that you wear to keep your feet dry.

well-known *adjective*
known to many people.

went *verb* see **go**

west *noun, adjective*
the direction you face if you look towards the setting sun.

wet *adjective* **wetter, wettest**
1 covered or soaked in water or some other liquid, not dry. *a wet towel, wet paint.*
2 with a lot of rain. *a wet day.*

whack *verb* **whacks, whacking, whacked**
to hit hard. *Sam whacked the ball with the cricket bat.*

whale *noun* **whales**
the largest sea animal there is.

what *adjective, pronoun*
THIS WORD HAS SEVERAL USES. HERE ARE SOME OF THE WAYS YOU CAN USE IT: *What is your name? I don't know what this word means. What a beautiful picture!*

whatever *adjective, pronoun*
1 any or every. *These animals eat whatever food they can find.*
2 no matter what. *Whatever happens, I'll help you.*

wheat *noun*
a plant grown by farmers. It has seeds called **grains** that are used to make flour.

wheel *noun* **wheels**
a circular object that turns on an **axle** through the middle. Cars, bicycles, and buses have wheels.

wheelbarrow *noun* **wheelbarrows**
a small cart with one wheel at the front and handles at the back.

wheelchair *noun* **wheelchairs**
a chair on wheels for a person who can't walk.

when *adverb, conjunction*
THIS WORD HAS SEVERAL USES. HERE ARE SOME OF THE WAYS YOU CAN USE IT: *When are you coming? When I moved, the bird flew away. Since when have you had that coat?*

whenever *conjunction*
at any time. *Come to play whenever you like.*

where *adverb, conjunction*
THIS WORD HAS SEVERAL USES. HERE ARE SOME OF THE WAYS YOU CAN USE IT: *Where are you? Tell me where you are.*

whereabouts *adverb*
in or near what place. *Whereabouts do you live?*

wherever *adverb, conjunction*
no matter where. *I'll find you, wherever you are.*

whether *conjunction*
if. *He asked whether I was ready.*

which *adjective, pronoun*
THIS WORD HAS SEVERAL USES. HERE ARE SOME OF THE WAYS YOU CAN USE IT: *Which way did he go? I like the book which you gave me best. I don't know which to choose.*

whichever *adjective, pronoun*
any person or thing. *You can choose whichever book you want.*

while *conjunction*
during the time that something else is happening. *I'll lay the table while you make the tea.*

whimper *verb* **whimpers, whimpering, whimpered**
to make a weak, crying sound when you are frightened or hurt.

whine *verb* **whines, whining, whined**
to make a long, high sound because you are hurt or unhappy.

whip *noun* **whips**
a piece of rope or strip of leather fixed to a handle.

whip *verb* **whips, whipping, whipped**
1 to hit someone or something with a whip.
2 to stir cream until it goes thick.

a
b
c
d
e
f
g
h
i
j
k
l
m
n
o
p
q
r
s
t
u
v
w
x
y
z

223

whirl *verb* **whirls, whirling, whirled**
to turn round and round very fast.

whisk *verb* **whisks, whisking, whisked**
1 to stir something round and round very fast.
2 to move very quickly. *He whisked the book away before I could look at it.*

whiskers *noun*
hairs or bristles growing on the face of a man or an animal.

whisky *noun*
a strong alcoholic drink.

whisper *verb* **whispers, whispering, whispered**
to speak very quietly.

whistle *noun* **whistles**
something that makes a high sound when you blow it.

whistle *verb* **whistles, whistling, whistled**
to make a high sound by blowing air through a whistle or your lips.

white *adjective* **whiter, whitest**
1 having the colour of snow.
2 very pale.

who *pronoun*
which person. *Who broke my mug?*

whoever *pronoun*
no matter what person. *Whoever did it should own up.*

whole *adjective*
1 with nothing missing or left out. *We ate the whole cake.*
2 in one piece, not broken. *The bird swallowed the fish whole.*

whooping-cough *noun*
an illness that makes you cough and gasp.

whose *adjective, pronoun*
belonging to what person. *Whose coat is this?*

why *adverb*
because of what, for what reason. *Why are you late?*

wick *noun* **wicks**
the string through the middle of a candle, which you light.

wicked *adjective*
very bad, evil.

wicket *noun* **wickets**
the set of three stumps in cricket.

bails
wicket
stumps

wide *adjective* **wider, widest**
measuring a lot from one side to the other.
a wide river.

widow *noun* **widows**
a woman whose husband has died.

widower *noun* **widowers**
a man whose wife has died.

width *noun* **widths**
how wide something is. *We measured the width of the room.*

wife *noun* **wives**
a woman married to someone.

wig *noun* **wigs**
a covering of false hair that you wear on the head.

wigwam *noun* **wigwams**
the kind of tent American Indians used to live in.

wild *adjective* **wilder, wildest**
not looked after by people. *a wild flower, wild animals.*

wilderness *noun* **wildernesses**
wild land where no one lives.

wildlife *noun*
wild animals.

will *noun* **wills**
1 instructions left by a person who has died telling people what they want to be done with their money and things.
2 the power to choose what you want to do.

will *verb*
THIS WORD IS USED IN SENTENCES ABOUT THE FUTURE: *Jo will be ten next birthday.*

willing *adjective*
ready and happy to do what someone wants. *Sam is willing to help in the garden.*

willow *noun* **willows**
a tree that grows near water and has thin branches that bend easily.

wily *adjective* **wilier, wiliest**
crafty. *wily fox.*

win *verb* **wins, winning, won**
to beat all the others in a game, fight, or competition.

wind *noun* **winds** (rhymes with *tinned*)
air moving along quickly. *leaves blowing in the wind.*

wind *verb* **winds, winding, wound**
(rhymes with *find*)
1 to turn a key to make a machine work. *The clock started when she wound it up.*
2 to wrap cloth, thread, tape, or string tightly round something.

windmill *noun* **windmills**
a mill that uses wind to make its machinery work.

window *noun* **windows**
an opening filled with glass to let the light in.

windscreen *noun* **windscreens**
the window at the front of a car.

windy *adjective* **windier, windiest**
with a lot of wind.

wine *noun* **wines**
a strong drink made from grapes.

wing *noun* **wings**
1 one of the parts a bird or insect flaps when it is flying.
2 one of the flat parts which stick out on each side of an aeroplane.

wink *verb* **winks, winking, winked**
to close and open one eye quickly.

winter *noun* **winters**
the coldest part of the year.

wintry *adjective*
cold, like winter. *wintry weather.*

wipe *verb* **wipes, wiping, wiped**
to rub something with a cloth to dry it or clean it.

wire *noun* **wires**
a long, thin strip of metal that can be bent into different shapes. *Electricity passes along wires.*

wise *adjective* **wiser, wisest**
if you are wise you can understand things and make good decisions.

wish *verb* **wishes, wishing, wished**
to say or think what you would like to happen. *I wish I had lots of money.*

wisp *noun* **wisps**
a little bit of straw, hair, or smoke.

witch *noun* **witches**
a woman who uses magic.

with *preposition*
THIS WORD HAS SEVERAL USES. HERE ARE SOME OF THE WAYS YOU CAN USE IT: *I played tennis with Sam. We saw a bird with a red breast. I filled the jug with milk.*

wither *verb* **withers, withering, withered**
to dry up and get paler and smaller. *withered flowers.*

without *preposition*
not having. *without any money.*

a
b
c
d
e
f
g
h
i
j
k
l
m
n
o
p
q
r
s
t
u
v
w
x
y
z

witness *noun* **witnesses**
someone who sees something important happen. *There were two witnesses to the accident.*

witty *adjective* **wittier, wittiest**
clever and funny.

wizard *noun* **wizards**
a man in fairy stories, who can do magic things.

wobble *verb* **wobbles, wobbling, wobbled**
to shake or rock. *Jelly wobbles.*

wolf *noun* **wolves**
a wild animal like a big dog.

woman *noun* **women**
a grown-up female human being.

won *verb* see **win**

wonder *verb* **wonders, wondering, wondered**
to ask yourself about something.

wonderful *adjective*
very good.

wood *noun* **woods**
1 the branches and trunks of trees cut up so that they can be used for making things or burnt on fires.
2 a lot of trees growing together.

wooden *adjective*
made of wood.

woodpecker *noun* **woodpeckers**
a bird that eats insects living in tree trunks. It has a strong beak for making holes in wood.

wool *noun*
the thick, soft hair that covers sheep. It is used for making cloth and for knitting.

woollen *adjective*
made of wool.

woolly *adjective*
made of wool, or like wool.

word *noun* **words**
a sound or group of sounds that means something when you say it, write it, or read it.

word processor *noun* **word processors**
a computer with a keyboard and a screen. It will store and show the words you type into it.

work *noun*
a job or something else that you have to do.

work *verb* **works, working, worked**
1 to do or make something, to be busy. *We worked hard at school today.*
2 to do something as a job and get paid for it. *He works in a shop.*
3 to do or make something do what it is supposed to do. *How does this computer work?*
worker *noun* **workers**
workman *noun* **workmen**

workshop *noun* **workshops**
a place where things are made or mended.

world *noun*
the earth with all its countries and people.

worm *noun* **worms**
a long, thin creature that wriggles about in the soil.

worn *verb* see **wear**

worry *verb* **worries, worrying, worried**
to be upset because you think something bad might happen.

worse *adjective*
less good. *He's a worse swimmer than I am.*

worship *verb* **worships, worshipping, worshipped**
to love and praise.

worst *adjective*
least good. *He's the worst in the class at swimming.*

worth *adjective*
1 with a certain value. *This old stamp is worth £100.*
2 if something is worth doing or having, it is good or useful.

worthless *adjective*
not worth anything.

would *verb*
THIS WORD HAS SEVERAL USES. HERE ARE SOME OF THE WAYS YOU CAN USE IT: *He said he would come. 'Would you pass the salt, please?' I would prefer tea to coffee.*

wound *noun* **wounds**
(rhymes with *spooned*)
a cut or hole in your body, often made by a weapon.

wound *verb* **wounds, wounding, wounded**
to hurt someone with a weapon or by cutting or hitting them.

wound *verb* see **wind** *verb*

woven *verb* see **weave**

wrap *verb* **wraps, wrapping, wrapped**
to put cloth or paper round something. *wrap a birthday present.*

wreath *noun* **wreaths**
(*wr-* in this word sounds like *r-*)
flowers or leaves twisted together into a ring. *a holly wreath.*

wreck *noun* **wrecks**
a wrecked ship or car.

wreck *verb* **wrecks, wrecking, wrecked**
to break or destroy something so that you cannot use it.

wren *noun* **wrens**
a very small, brown bird.

wrestle *verb* **wrestles, wrestling, wrestled**
to fight with someone by trying to throw them on the ground.

wretched *adjective*
unhappy or ill.

wriggle *verb* **wriggles, wriggling, wriggled**
to twist and turn about like a worm.

wring *verb* **wrings, wringing, wrung**
to squeeze and twist something wet to get the water out of it.

wrinkle *noun* **wrinkles**
a small line in the skin that often appears when you get old.
wrinkled *adjective*

wrist *noun* **wrists**
the thin part of the arm where it is joined to the hand.

write *verb* **writes, writing, wrote, written**
to put words or signs on paper so that people can read them. *to write a poem. to write a letter.*
writer *noun* **writers**

writing *noun*
1 something that you have written. *a piece of writing.*
2 the way you write. *neat writing.*

wrong *adjective*
1 not right. *He gave the wrong answer.*
2 bad. *Stealing is wrong.*
wrongly *adverb*

wrote *verb* see **write**

wrung *verb* see **wring**

Xx

X-ray *noun* **X-rays**
a photograph that shows the inside of a body so that doctors can see if there is anything wrong.

xylophone *noun* **xylophones**
a musical instrument with a row of wooden or metal bars that you hit with small hammers.

Yy

yacht *noun* **yachts**
a boat with sails, often used for racing.

yap *verb* **yaps, yapping, yapped**
to make short, barking sounds.

yard *noun* **yards**
1 a measure for length.
2 ground that is next to a building and has a wall round it.

yawn *verb* **yawns, yawning, yawned**
to open your mouth wide because you are tired.

year *noun* **years**
a measure for time. A year is twelve months, or three hundred and sixty-five days.

yell *verb* **yells, yelling, yelled**
to shout.

yellow *noun, adjective*
the colour of a lemon.

yesterday *noun*
the day before today.

yet *adverb, conjunction*
THIS WORD HAS SEVERAL USES. HERE ARE SOME OF THE WAYS YOU CAN USE IT: *Are you ready yet? He hurt his knee, yet he still plays football. Sam is late yet again!*

yew *noun* **yews**
a kind of tree that has dark green leaves it keeps all through the year.

yield *verb* **yields, yielding, yielded**
to give in, to surrender.

yoghurt *noun*
a thick liquid made from milk. You eat it with a spoon.

yolk *noun* **yolks**
the yellow part of an egg.

you *pronoun*
the person or people you are speaking to.

young *adjective* **younger, youngest**
not old, born not long ago. *My brother is younger than me.*

your *adjective*
belonging to you. *Is this your coat?*

yourself, yourselves *pronoun*
you and no one else. *Did you hurt yourself?*
by yourself on your own.

youth *noun* **youths**
1 a boy or young man.
2 the time in your life when you are young.

yule, **yuletide** *noun*
old words for Christmas.

Zz

zebra *noun* **zebras**
an animal like a horse with black and white stripes.
zebra crossing a place marked with black and white stripes where cars must stop for people to cross the road.

zero *noun* **zeros**
nothing, the number 0.

zigzag *noun* **zigzags**
a line with sudden turns in it like this ∧∧∧.

zip, zipper *noun* **zips, zippers**
a fastener for joining two edges of material together. Some dresses, trousers, and bags have zips.

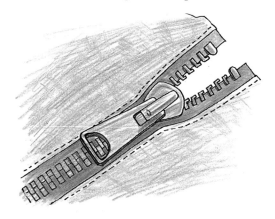

zoo *noun* **zoos**
a place where different kinds of wild animals are kept so that people can go and see them.

zoom *verb* **zooms, zooming, zoomed**
to move very quickly.

228

Word Origins

INTRODUCTION for teachers and parents

The following pages contain word origins for a wide range of words in this dictionary. This supplement aims to provide an accessible introduction to the fascinating subject of, 'where do words come from?'.

The words that we use today come from many different sources. Some have been in the English language since the time of the Angles and Saxons around 1500 years ago. Today we say that these words come from Old English or Anglo Saxon. Many words have been borrowed from other languages, especially from French and Latin. American English, which began to diverge from British English as far back as the 17th century, has become a source for some words in British English (hamburger is a good example). Local English dialects have also contributed some words to the mainstream of the language.

Apart from foreign languages and dialects, words have also come into English from people's names, (sandwich and cardigan) or from an imitation of the sound they describe (buzz and thump). Some words are formed by shortening or combining existing words (these are called abbreviations or blends) or by using the initial letters of several other words (called acronyms). There are also words that have changed their meanings so many times, that the history of these changes is interesting to read for its own sake. There are even words in English whose origin we simply don't know. This variety of sources is mapped out in the diagram below.

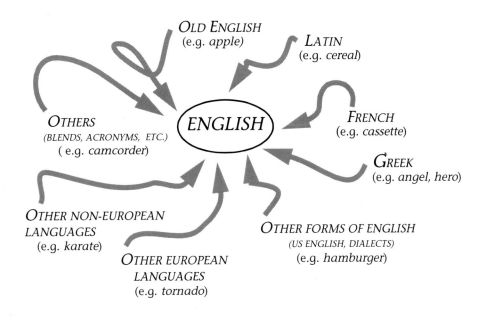

The word origins given here have been chosen for several reasons. First, to interest children in the origins of familiar words. Second, to show the huge range of origins for English words. If the word comes from another language, its form in that language is often given, in italics, and its foreign meaning is also often given. This helps to show how the word has changed (or not) as it came into English. Many different languages are mentioned as sources, including several that are no longer spoken (Old English, Latin, and Ancient Greek).

Days of the week

Monday   Monday is from Old English *Mondaeg* meaning 'day of the moon'.

Tuesday   Tuesday is an Anglo-Saxon name honouring the god of war called *Tiw* (pronounced tue).

Wednesday   Wednesday is an Anglo-Saxon name honouring the god Odin or Woden.

Thursday   Thursday is an Anglo-Saxon name meaning 'day of thunder'.

Friday   Friday is from Old English *Frigedaeg*, and is named after the Norse goddess Frigg, wife of Odin.

Saturday   Saturday is named after the Roman god *Saturn*.

Sunday   Sunday is an Anglo-Saxon name meaning 'day of the sun'.

Months of the year

January   The word January comes from the name of the Roman god *Janus*, who was the patron of doors and beginnings. January is the first month of the year, so it is the gateway into the year.

February   The word February comes from a Latin word *februum* meaning 'purification' because a Roman festival of purification was held about this time.

March   The word March comes from the Roman month *Martius*, named after the god Mars.

April   The word April probably comes from a Latin word *aperio* 'to open' because flowers open in spring.

May   The word May comes from the Roman month *Maius*, named after the goddess Maia.

June   The word June comes from the Roman month *Junius*, named after the goddess Juno.

July   The word July comes from the Roman month *Julius*, named after the Roman Emperor Julius Caesar.

August The word August comes from the name of the Roman Emperor *Augustus*. It became the name of the Roman month in 8 BC because that month was thought to be his lucky month.

September The word September comes from the Latin word *septem* meaning 'seven', because it was the seventh month in the Roman calendar.

October The word October comes from the Latin word *octo* meaning 'eight', because October was the eighth month in the Roman calendar.

November The word November comes from the Latin word *novem* meaning 'nine', because November was the ninth month in the Roman calendar.

December The word December comes from the Latin word *decem* meaning 'ten', because it was the tenth month in the Roman calendar.

month The word month is from an Old English word *monath*, which is related to the word for moon, because time used to be measured by the appearance of the moon.

Words to do with food and drink

breakfast The word breakfast is from two English words put together: *break* meaning 'to put an end to' and *fast* meaning 'a time of going without food or drink'. When you are asleep you do not eat or drink, but when you wake up and have some food or a drink you then 'break your fast' or 'have breakfast'.

cereal The word cereal comes from a Latin word *cerealis*, which is from *Ceres*, the name of the Roman goddess of agriculture.

curry The word curry comes from a Tamil word *kari* meaning hot sauce.

flour The word flour was once just another spelling of *flower*. It meant 'the finest part of something', because flour was food of the finest quality.

hamburger Is named after Hamburg, a town in Germany. This word was first used in American English.

ketchup The word ketchup may come from two Cantonese words, *k'e chap* meaning 'tomato juice'.

liquorice The word liquorice comes from a Greek word *glukurrhiza* meaning 'sweet root'. Liquorice is made from the root of a plant.

lollipop   The word lollipop may come from an English dialect word *lolly* meaning 'tongue' and pop meaning 'to make a sound like a small explosion'.

lunch   The word lunch is short for *luncheon*, which means the same things as lunch, but the word is not used so much now.

macaroni   The word macaroni is from Italian *maccaroni*, which is from Greek *makaria* meaning 'food made from barley'.

muesli   The word muesli comes from a Swiss German word for an oat-based breakfast cereal with fruit and nuts.

nectar   The word nectar comes from a Greek word *nektar* meaning 'the drink of the gods'.

noodle   The word noodle comes from the German word *Nudel*, describing this kind of stringy pasta.

pasta   The word pasta comes from an Italian word *pasta* meaning 'paste'. Pasta is made from a paste of flour, eggs, and water.

pizza   The word pizza comes from an Italian word *pizza* meaning 'pie'.

sherbet   The word sherbet comes from an Arabic word *sharbat* meaning 'a drink'.

Words to do with plants

acorn   The word acorn is from an Old English word *æcern*.

apple   The word apple is from an Old English word *æppel*.

conker   The word conker comes from an English dialect word meaning 'a snail shell' because games like conkers were first played with snail shells.

dandelion   The word dandelion comes from the French words *dent-de-lion* meaning 'lion's tooth' because of the jagged shape of the leaves.

mistletoe   The word mistletoe is from an Old English word *misteltan*, which is from *mistel* meaning 'mistletoe' and *tan* meaning 'twig'.

prickle   The word prickle is from Old English *pricel* meaning 'something that pricks'.

pumpkin   The word pumpkin comes from a Greek word *pepon* meaning 'melon'.

rhododendron   The word rhododendron comes from Greek words *rhodon* meaning 'rose' and *dendron* meaning 'tree'. A rhododendron is a large bush with flowers rather like roses.

Words to do with animals

adder   The word adder is from an Old English word *nædre*, also meaning 'adder'. In Middle English people heard the word wrongly. They thought 'a nædre' was 'an adder', so nædre became 'adder'.

alligator   The word alligator comes from the Spanish words *el lagarto* which mean 'the lizard'.

cobweb   The word cobweb comes from a Middle English word *coppeweb*, which is from an old word *coppe* meaning 'a spider' and the word web.

crocodile   The word crocodile comes from a Greek word *krokodilos* meaning 'worm of the stones'.

cuckoo   The word cuckoo copies the sound made by the cuckoo.

dinosaur   The word dinosaur comes from two Greek words, *deinos* meaning 'terrible' and *sauros* meaning 'lizard'.

fang   The word fang comes from an Old Norse word meaning 'capture, grasp', because fangs can catch and hold things.

hippopotamus   The word hippopotamus comes from two Greek words, *hippos* meaning 'horse' and *potamos* meaning 'river'.

mosquito   The word mosquito comes from Spanish and Portuguese words meaning 'little fly'.

neigh   The word neigh is from Old English *hnaegan* and copies the sound a horse makes.

otter   The word otter is from Old English *otr*. It is related to a Greek word *hudros* meaning 'a water snake'.

rodent   The word rodent comes from a Latin word *rodens* meaning 'gnawing'.

Words to do with buildings

aquarium The word aquarium comes from a Latin word *aquarius* meaning 'of water'.

bazaar The word bazaar comes from a Persian word *bazar* meaning 'a market'.

café The word café comes from a French word *café* meaning 'coffee' or 'a coffee house'.

circus The word circus comes from a Latin word *circus* meaning 'a ring', because a circus is usually held in a ring-shaped area in a tent.

fort The word fort comes from a Latin word *fortis* meaning 'strong'.

gallery The word gallery comes from an Italian word *galleria*.

igloo The word igloo comes from an Inuit word *iglu* meaning 'house'.

kiosk The word kiosk comes from a Turkish word *kiushk* meaning 'pavilion'.

patio The word patio comes from a Spanish word *patio* meaning 'an inner courtyard'.

Words that come from people's names

atlas *Atlas* was the name of a person in Greek mythology who had to hold the universe on his shoulders. A picture of him was often put at the beginning of old books of maps, and this is how they got their name.

braille The word braille is from the name of Louis Braille, a Frenchman who was blind from the age of three and invented this system. He died in 1852.

Biro The word Biro is from the name of Laszló József Biró, a Hungarian man who invented this kind of pen.

cardigan Cardigan is named after the 7th Earl of Cardigan, James Thomas Brudenel. He was a soldier and his men were the first to wear this kind of short jacket with buttons. He died in 1868.

leotard The word leotard is from the name of Jules Léotard, a French trapeze artist who invented this kind of garment. He died in 1870.

mackintosh The word Mackintosh is from the name of Charles Macintosh (spelt without a k) who was the Scottish inventor of the waterproof material that this kind of coat made from. He died in 1843.

Rastafarian The word Rastafarian comes from *Ras Tafari*, the name of a former king of Ethiopia.

shrapnel Shrapnel is named after Henry Shrapnel, a British officer who invented it in about 1806.

tommy-gun A tommy-gun is named after its inventor, J. T. Thompson, an American who died in 1940.

volt Volt is named after an Italian scientist called Alessandro Volta, who invented the electric battery.

watt Watt is named after a Scottish engineer called James Watt, who studied energy. The energy of light bulbs or machines is measured in watts.

Words to do with musical instruments

bugle The word bugle is from Latin *buculus* meaing 'a little ox', because the first kinds of bugle were made from the horn of an ox. A bugle is now made from brass.

harp The word harp is from an Old English word *hearpe*.

piano The word piano comes from Italian, and is short for *pianoforte* meaning 'quiet loud', because a piano can be played quietly or loudly, or in between.

xylophone The word xylophone comes from Greek words *xylon* meaning 'wood' and *phone* meaning 'sound' (the same word as in telephone). A xylophone makes a musical sound when the keys are struck.

Words that come from place names

attic The word attic comes from *Attica*, which is an area of ancient Greece. This area was famous for a special design in the upper part of its buildings.

bayonet The word bayonet comes from a French word *baionnette*, which is from Bayonne, the name of a French town where bayonets were first made.

hamburger   is named after Hamburg, a town in Germany. This word was first used in American English.

jeans   The word jeans comes from *jean*, the name of the cloth first used for trousers like this. Jean is from Janua, the Latin name for Genoa, a town in Italy where this cloth was first made.

marathon   The word marathon comes from the name of a place about 26 miles from Athens in Greece. After a famous battle in 490 BC, which the Greeks won, legend says that someone ran all the way from Marathon to Athens to tell the Greeks the good news. Today a marathon is a 26-mile run.

paradise   The word paradise comes from an old Persian word meaning 'garden'.

rugby   is named after Rugby School in Warwickshire, where this ball game was first played.

tabby   The word tabby originally meant a kind of striped cloth, and was named after a district of Baghdad called *al-Attabiyya*, where the cloth was made.

tangerine   The word tangerine is named after Tangier, a place in Morocco, where the fruit was originally grown.

utopia   *Utopia* is the title of a book about a perfect place written by Sir Thomas More, who lived during the reign of Henry VIII of England.

Words to do with religion

angel   The word angel comes from a Greek word *angelos* meaning 'messenger'.

holiday   The word holiday comes from *holy day*, because holidays used to be religious festivals.

pulpit   The word pulpit comes from a Latin word *pulpitum* meaning 'stage'. A pulpit is like a little stage where you can make a speech.

sabbath   The word sabbath comes from a Hebrew word *shabat*, meaning 'rest'. The sabbath day is meant to be a day of rest.

synagogue   The word synagogue comes from a Greek word *synagoge* meaning 'assembly'.

temple   The word for the kind of temple you worship in comes from a Latin word *templum*, which has the same meaning.

Whit Sunday   The name Whit comes from the Anglo-Saxon word for 'white', because people used to be baptized in white clothes on Whit Sunday.

Words to do with the world around us

earth   The word earth is from an Old English word *eorthe*.

fossil   The word fossil comes from a Latin word *fossilis* meaing 'dug up'.

galaxy   The word galaxy comes from a Greek word *galaxias* meaning 'milky'.

gas   Gas is an invented word based on the Greek word *khaos* meaning 'chaos'.

glacier   The word glacier comes from a French word *glace* meaning 'ice'.

hurricane   The word hurricane comes from a Spanish word *huracán*. In Spanish it probably comes from a word in an old Caribbean language meaning 'god of the storm'.

jungle   The word jungle comes from a Sanskrit word *jangala* meaning 'rough and dry (land)'.

meteor   The word meteor comes from a Greek word *meteoros* meaning 'high in the air'.

ozone   The word ozone comes from a German word *Ozon*, which is from a Greek word *ozein* meaning 'to smell'.

planet   The word planet comes from a Greek word *planetes* meaning 'wanderer', because the planets look as if they are moving among the stars.

solstice   The word solstice comes from Latin words *sol* meaning 'sun' and *sistere* meaning 'stand still'.

tornado   The word tornado comes from a Spanish word *tronada* meaning 'thunder'.

volcano   The word volcano is Italian and comes from *Vulcan*, the name of the Roman god of fire.

Fantasy words

alien   The word alien comes from a Latin word *alienus* meaning 'belonging to another'. An alien is someone who belongs to another country or another world.

demon   The word demon comes from a Greek word *daimon* meaning 'a spirit'.

goblin   The word goblin comes from an Old French word *gobelin*, which may be related to a Greek word *kobalos* meaning 'a mischievous goblin'.

hero   The word hero comes from a Greek word *heros*, meaning 'a brave fighter'.

imp   The word imp is from an Old English word *impa* meaning 'a young shoot or twig'. In Middle English it meant 'a child born into a noble family'. Later it came to mean 'a child of the devil', which is how it got the meaning it has now.

legend   The word legend comes from a Latin word *legenda* meaning 'things to be read'.

nightmare   The word nightmare comes from *night* and Old English *maere* meaning 'an evil spirit thought to cause bad dreams'.

Technical words

camcorder   The word camcorder comes from the first part of the word *camera* put together with the second part of the word *recorder*.

cassette   The word cassette comes from a French word *cassette* meaning 'a small container'.

computer   The word computer comes from a Latin word *computare* meaning 'to reckon together'.

electric, electrical   The words electric and electrical come from a Greek word *elektron* meaning 'amber', because amber gives off a kind of electricity when you rub it.

fax   The word fax is short for *facsimile* meaning 'an exact copy'.

gram   The word gram comes from a Latin word *gramma* meaning 'a weight'.

kaleidoscope   The word kaleidoscope comes from three Greek words, *kalos* meaning 'beautiful', *eidos* meaning 'form' and *skopein* meaning 'to look at'.

laser   The word laser comes from the first letters of five other words which tell us what a laser is: light amplification by stimulated emission of radiation.

lens   The word lens comes from a Latin word *lens* meaning 'lentil', because the lens of the eye was thought to be the same shape as a lentil or small bean.

pendulum   The word pendulum comes from a Latin word *pendulus* meaning 'hanging down'.

steamroller   The first rollers used to flatten the roads were powered by steam.

stethoscope   The word stethoscope comes from the Greek words *stethos* meaning 'breast' and *skopein* meaning 'to look at'.

strobe   The word strobe comes from a Greek word *strobos* meaning 'whirling'.

velocity   The word velocity comes from a Latin word *velox* meaning 'swift'.

Household words

duvet   The word duvet comes from a French word *duvet* meaning 'down', because a duvet is sometimes filled with down or soft feathers.

fire   The word fire is from an Old English word *fyr* (with the same meaning).

marble   The word marble comes from a Greek word *marmaros* meaning 'a shining stone'.

mirror   The word mirror comes from a Latin word *mirare* meaning 'to look at'.

pram   The word pram is short for *perambulator*, which comes from Latin *per* meaning 'all around' and *ambulare* meaning 'to walk'. So a perambulator allows you to take a baby for a walk all around the place.

Other interesting word origins

anorak   The word anorak comes from an Eskimo word *anoraq* meaning waterproof coat.

autograph   The word autograph comes from two Greek words, *autos* meaning 'oneself' and *grapho* meaning 'to write'.

baby   The word baby is probably copied from some of the first sounds babies make when they are trying to talk.

brain   The word brain is from an Old English word *braegen*.

camouflage   The word camouflage comes from an Italian word *camuffare* meaning 'to disguise or deceive'.

enthusiasm   The word enthusiasm comes from a Greek word meaning 'possessed by a god'.

fib   The word fib is related to *fable*, meaning 'story'.

flatter   The word flatter comes from an Old French word *flater* meaning 'to smooth down'. When people are flattered they may feel as if they have been smoothed or stroked like a cat.

groove   The word groove comes from a Dutch word *groeve* meaning 'a furrow or ditch'.

karate   The word karate comes from two Japanese words, *kara* meaning 'empty' and *te* meaning 'hand'. Karate is a way of defending yourself with your bare hands.

nappy   The word nappy is short for *napkin* meaning 'a cloth or paper square to protect your clothes'. Napkin comes from Old French *nappe* meaning 'a tablecloth' plus the ending *-kin* which means 'little'.

nostril   The word nostril is from Old English *nosthyrl*, which is from *nosu* meaning 'nose' and *thyrel* meaning 'a hole'.

o'clock   is short for 'of the clock'.

parachute   The word parachute comes from two French words, *parer* meaning 'to protect' and *chute* meaning 'fall'.

pop *noun*   The word pop (as in pop music) is short for *popular*.

pop *verb*   The word pop (as in 'it will go pop') copies the sound made when something pops.

pyjamas   The word pyjamas comes from Urdu and Persian, from two words, *pay* meaning 'leg' and *jama* meaning 'clothing'.

racket   The word for the type of racket you play ball games with comes from an Arabic word *rahat* meaning the palm of the hand. Before people had rackets to play ball games, they hit the ball with the palm of their hands.

red herring   A red herring was a kipper, used in fox hunting to distract the hounds away from the scent of a fox.

red tape Red tape was once used to tie up bundles of official letters and documents. Now when a decision is delayed or put off, people say that it is tied up in red tape.

regular The word regular comes from a Latin word *regula* meaning 'a rule'.

rival The word rival comes from a Latin word *rivalis* meaning someone sharing the same river (for water) as someone else. This was one of the earliest forms of rivalry in human history.

satchel The word satchel comes from a Latin word *saccellus* meaning 'little sack'.

scale This word scale comes from a Latin word *scala* meaning 'ladder'.

see-saw The word see-saw comes from an old rhyme or chant that people used to say when sawing wood.

slipshod The word slipshod comes from two words *slip shod* and originally meant wearing slippers or badly fitting shoes.

souvenir comes from the French words *se souvenir* meaning 'to remember'.

spell This kind of spell comes from an Old English word meaning a speech or story.

steeplechase One kind of horse race is called a steeplechase because it used to be run towards a church steeple that the riders could see in the distance.

stop press A last-minute addition or late news is sometimes is called stop press because in the newspaper industry, the presses had to be stopped to allow the late news to be put in.

sub- The prefix sub- comes from a Latin word *sub* meaning 'under'.

talent The word talent comes from a Greek word *talanton*, which was a sum of money in ancient times.

tantalize The word tantalize comes from the name of *Tantalus*, who in Greek mythology was punished by having to stand near water and fruit which moved away when he tried to reach out for them.

temple The word for the temple that is part of your head comes from a Latin word *tempora*, which means 'sides of the head'.

thesaurus   The word thesaurus comes from a Greek word meaning 'storehouse' or 'treasure-house'. A thesaurus is a treasure-house of words.

tit for tat   The words were originally tip for tap, meaning a little hit for a little hit.

towpath   It is called a towpath because it was originally a path for horses to walk along while towing barges.

turncoat   The word turncoat is thought to come from a special coat worn by a Duke of Saxony. It had one colour on one side and another on the other side, and he changed it round depending on which side he wanted to support.

upshot   An upshot was originally the last shot in an archery match. Now the upshot of something is the final result.

vandal   The word vandal comes from the name of the Vandals, a German tribe who invaded the Roman Empire in the 5th century, destroying many books and works of art.

vendetta   Vendetta is an Italian word, which comes from a Latin word *vindicta* meaning 'vengeance'. A vendetta is a series of acts of revenge.

vocation   The word vocation comes from a Latin word *vocare* meaning 'to call', because the job or activity is seen as something that calls you. You will find the word calling is also in this dictionary, and has nearly the same meaning.

Picture Section

car

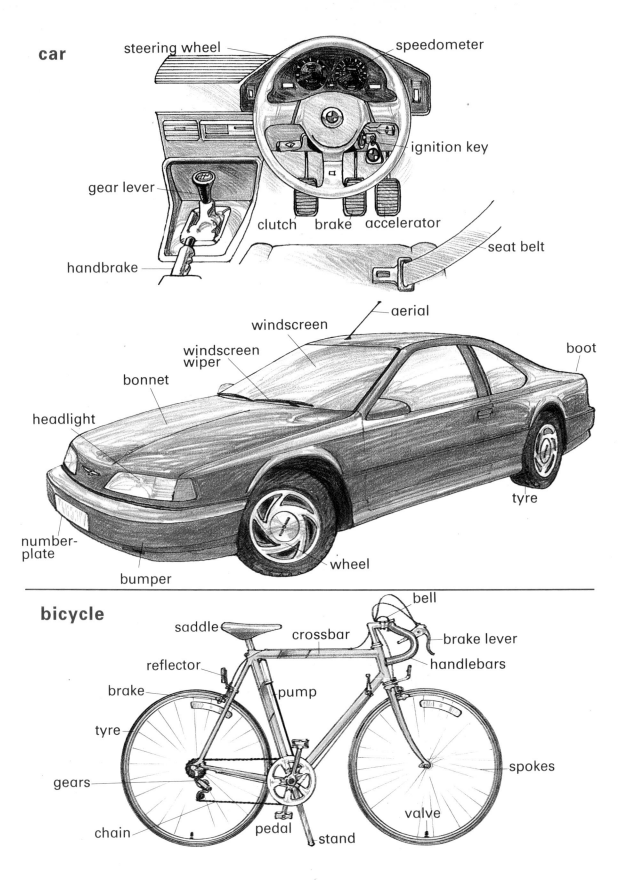

steering wheel

speedometer

ignition key

gear lever

clutch   brake   accelerator

seat belt

handbrake

aerial

windscreen

windscreen wiper

boot

bonnet

headlight

tyre

number-plate

wheel

bumper

bicycle

bell

saddle

crossbar

brake lever

reflector

handlebars

brake

pump

tyre

spokes

gears

valve

chain   pedal   stand

ships and boats

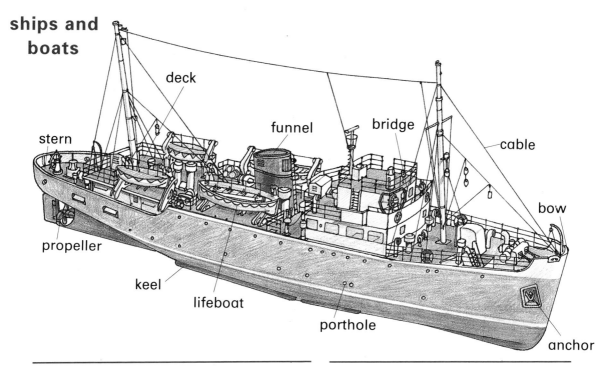

stern

deck

funnel

bridge

cable

propeller

keel

lifeboat

porthole

bow

anchor

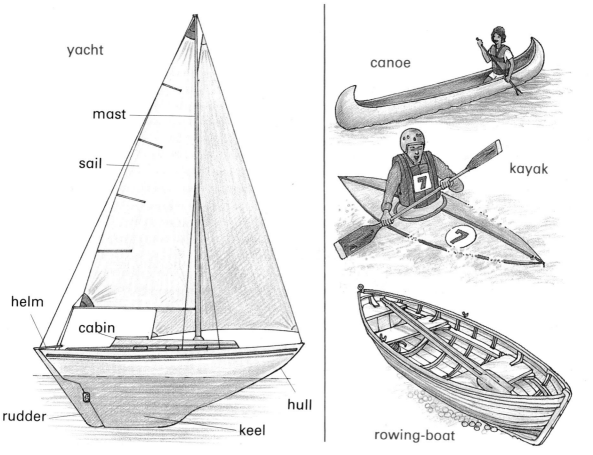

yacht

mast

sail

helm

cabin

rudder

keel

hull

canoe

kayak

rowing-boat

parts of the body

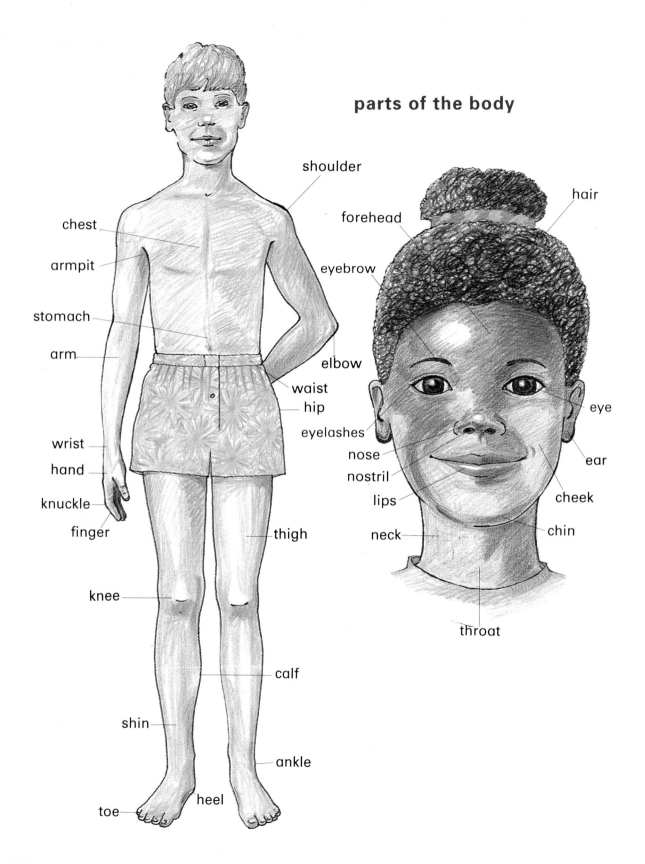

shoulder
chest
armpit
stomach
arm
wrist
hand
knuckle
finger
knee
shin
toe
heel
calf
ankle
thigh
elbow
waist
hip

forehead
eyebrow
hair
eyelashes
nose
nostril
lips
neck
eye
ear
cheek
chin
throat

fruits

vegetables

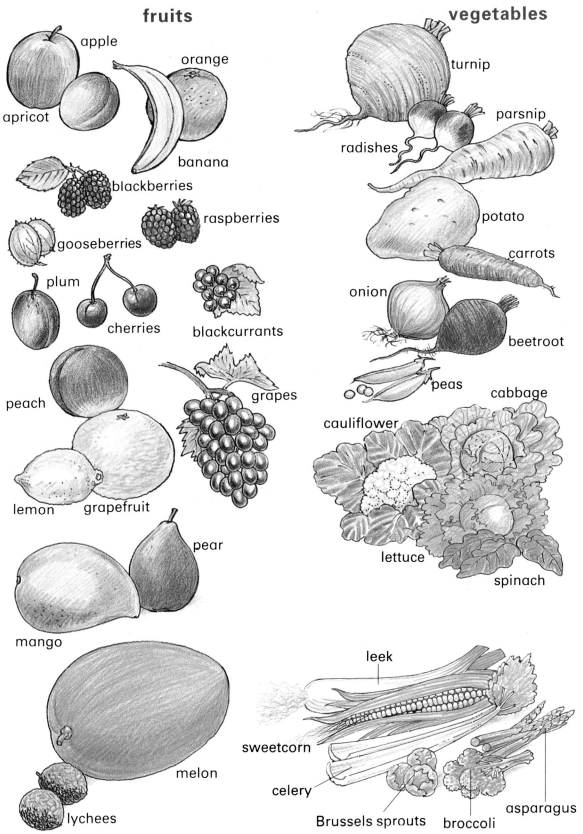

apple

orange

apricot

banana

blackberries

raspberries

gooseberries

plum

cherries

blackcurrants

peach

grapes

lemon

grapefruit

pear

mango

melon

lychees

turnip

radishes

parsnip

potato

carrots

onion

beetroot

peas

cabbage

cauliflower

lettuce

spinach

leek

sweetcorn

celery

Brussels sprouts

broccoli

asparagus

249

flowers and plants

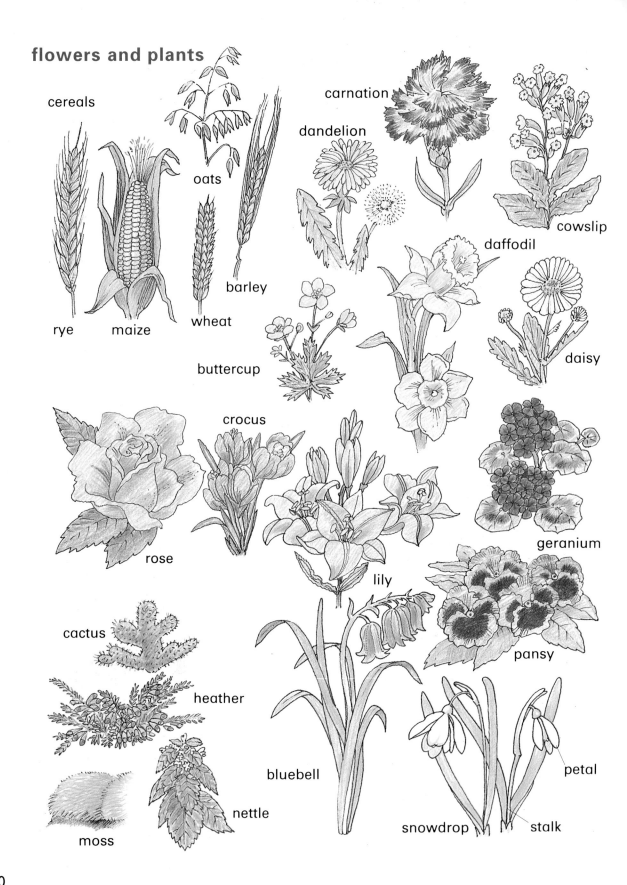

cereals

oats

barley

wheat

rye

maize

buttercup

carnation

dandelion

cowslip

daffodil

daisy

crocus

rose

lily

geranium

pansy

cactus

heather

bluebell

nettle

snowdrop

petal

stalk

moss

trees

leaf

acorn

conker

oak

horse-chestnut

trunk

catkin

willow

beech

poplar

ash

sycamore

cypress

maple

yew

eucalyptus

birch

elm

dogs

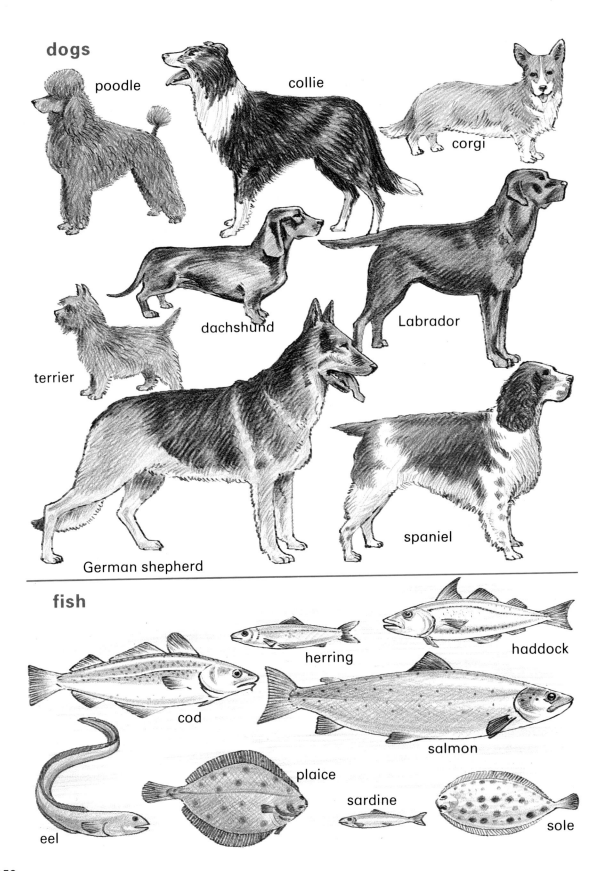

poodle

collie

corgi

dachshund

Labrador

terrier

German shepherd

spaniel

fish

herring

haddock

cod

salmon

plaice

sardine

eel

sole

musical instruments

French horn

violin

cello

double-bass

trumpet

trombone

tuba

piccolo

oboe

flute

clarinet

bassoon

piano

triangle and beater

cymbals

tambourine

scientific equipment

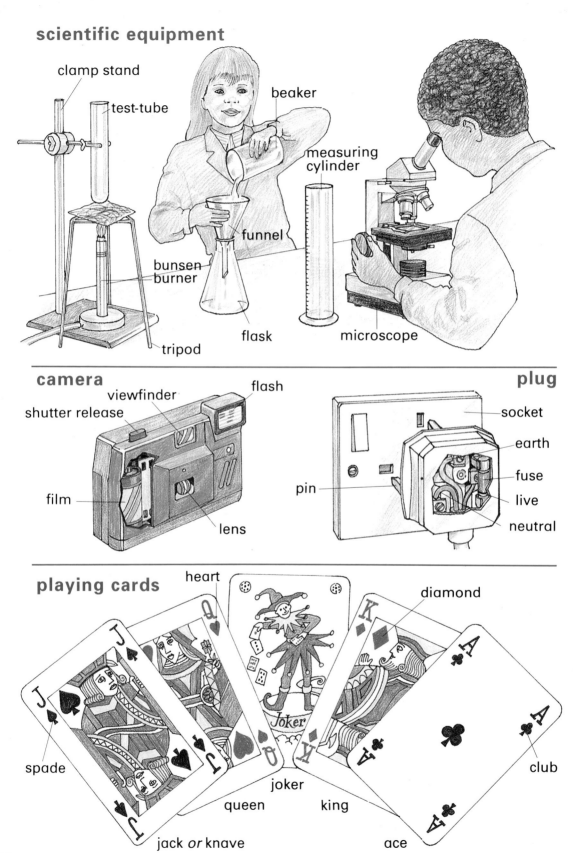

clamp stand

test-tube

beaker

measuring cylinder

funnel

bunsen burner

flask

tripod

microscope

camera

viewfinder

flash

shutter release

film

lens

plug

socket

earth

fuse

pin

live

neutral

playing cards

heart

diamond

spade

joker

club

queen

king

jack *or* knave

ace

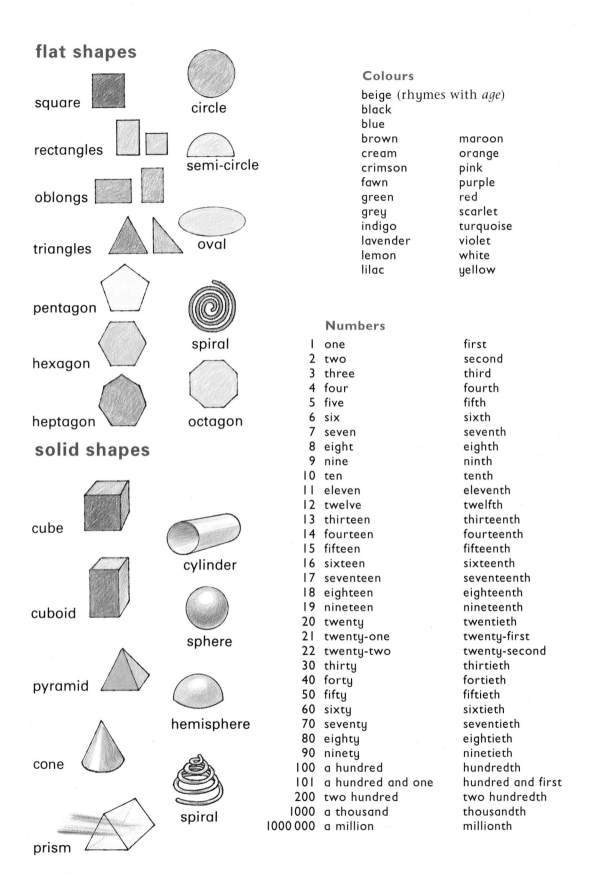

flat shapes

square

circle

rectangles

semi-circle

oblongs

triangles

oval

pentagon

spiral

hexagon

heptagon

octagon

solid shapes

cube

cylinder

cuboid

sphere

pyramid

hemisphere

cone

spiral

prism

Colours

beige (rhymes with *age*)
black
blue
brown   maroon
cream   orange
crimson   pink
fawn   purple
green   red
grey   scarlet
indigo   turquoise
lavender   violet
lemon   white
lilac   yellow

Numbers

1	one	first
2	two	second
3	three	third
4	four	fourth
5	five	fifth
6	six	sixth
7	seven	seventh
8	eight	eighth
9	nine	ninth
10	ten	tenth
11	eleven	eleventh
12	twelve	twelfth
13	thirteen	thirteenth
14	fourteen	fourteenth
15	fifteen	fifteenth
16	sixteen	sixteenth
17	seventeen	seventeenth
18	eighteen	eighteenth
19	nineteen	nineteenth
20	twenty	twentieth
21	twenty-one	twenty-first
22	twenty-two	twenty-second
30	thirty	thirtieth
40	forty	fortieth
50	fifty	fiftieth
60	sixty	sixtieth
70	seventy	seventieth
80	eighty	eightieth
90	ninety	ninetieth
100	a hundred	hundredth
101	a hundred and one	hundred and first
200	two hundred	two hundredth
1000	a thousand	thousandth
1000000	a million	millionth

Days	Sunday	Monday	Tuesday
	Wednesday	Thursday	Friday
	Saturday		

Months	January	February	March
	April	May	June
	July	August	September
	October	November	December

Places	Peoples	Places	Peoples
Afghanistan	Afghans	**Kenya**	Kenyans
Africa	Africans	**Kuwait**	Kuwaitis
Algeria	Algerians	**Lebanon**	the Lebanese
America	Americans	**Libya**	Libyans
Argentina	Argentinians		
Asia	Asians	**Malaysia**	Malaysians
Australia	Australians	**Malta**	the Maltese
Austria	Austrians	**Mexico**	Mexicans
		Morocco	Moroccans
Bangladesh	Bangladeshis		
Barbados	Barbadians	**New Zealand**	New Zealanders
Belgium	Belgians	**Nigeria**	Nigerians
Brazil	Brazilians	**North Korea**	North Koreans
Britain	the British, Britons	**Norway**	Norwegians
Bulgaria	Bulgarians		
		Pakistan	Pakistanis
Canada	Canadians	**Peru**	Peruvians
Chile	Chileans	**Poland**	Poles
China	the Chinese	**Portugal**	the Portuguese
Cuba	Cubans		
Cyprus	Cypriots	**Russia**	Russians
Czech Republic	Czechs		
		Saudi Arabia	Saudi Arabians
Denmark	Danes	**Scandinavia**	Scandinavians
		Scotland	Scots
Egypt	Egyptians	**Singapore**	Singaporeans
England	the English	**Slovakia**	Slovaks
Ethiopia	Ethiopians	**South Africa**	South Africans
Europe	Europeans	**South Korea**	South Koreans
		Spain	Spaniards
Finland	Finns	**Sri Lanka**	Sri Lankans
France	the French	**Sweden**	Swedes
		Switzerland	the Swiss
Germany	Germans	**Syria**	Syrians
Ghana	Ghanaians		
Great Britain see **Britain**		**Tanzania**	Tanzanians
Greece	Greeks	**Thailand**	Thais
		Trinidad	Trinidadians
Holland	the Dutch	**Turkey**	Turks
Hungary	Hungarians		
		Uganda	Ugandans
Iceland	Icelanders	**United States**	Americans
India	Indians	**of America (USA)**	
Indonesia	Indonesians		
Iran	Iranians	**Venezuela**	Venezuelans
Iraq	Iraqis	**Vietnam**	the Vietnamese
Ireland	the Irish		
Israel	Israelis	**Wales**	the Welsh
Italy	Italians	**West Indies**	West Indians
Jamaica	Jamaicans	**Zambia**	Zambians
Japan	the Japanese	**Zimbabwe**	Zimbabweans
Jordan	Jordanians		